T3-BSE-891

Dalits and Christianity

Dalits and Christianity

Subaltern Religion and
Liberation Theology in India

SATHIANATHAN CLARKE

Bob :
With gratitude for your
work on Contextual theology

Sathianathan Clark

Kuala lumpur, Malaysia
27/07/04

OXFORD
UNIVERSITY PRESS

OXFORD
UNIVERSITY PRESS

YMCA Library Building, Jai Singh Road, New Delhi 110001

Oxford University Press is a department of the University of Oxford. It furthers the
University's objective of excellence in research, scholarship, and education
by publishing worldwide in

Oxford   New York
Auckland   Bangkok   Buenos Aires   Cape Town   Chennai
Dar es Salaam   Delhi   Hong Kong   Istanbul   Karachi   Kolkata
Kuala Lumpur   Madrid   Melbourne   Mexico City   Mumbai   Nairobi
Sao Paolo   Shanghai   Singapore   Taipei   Tokyo   Toronto

and an associated company in Berlin

Oxford is a registered trade mark of Oxford University Press
in the UK and in certain other countries

Published in India
By Oxford University Press, New Delhi

© Oxford University Press 1998

The moral rights of the author have been asserted
Database right Oxford University Press (maker)

Oxford India Paperbacks 1999
Second impression 2002

All rights reserved. No part of this publication may be reproduced,
stored in a retrieval system, or transmitted, in any form or by any means,
without the prior permission in writing of Oxford University Press,
or as expressly permitted by law, or under terms agreed with the appropriate
reprographics rights organization. Enquiries concerning reproduction
outside the scope of the above should be sent to the Rights Department,
Oxford University Press, at the address above

You must not circulate this book in any other binding or cover and you must
impose this same condition on any acquirer

ISBN 019 565 130 8

Typeset by Print Line, New Delhi 110 048
Printed in India at Wadhwa International, New Delhi 110 020
Published by Manzar Khan, Oxford University Press
YMCA Library Building, Jai Singh Road, New Delhi 110001

Acknowledgements

Many communities sustained and nourished me through the writing of this book. Professors Gordon D. Kaufman, John B. Carman, and Lawrence E. Sullivan of Harvard University Divinity School were instrumental in helping me work through the initial stages of this manuscript in its dissertation form. My encounter with Professor Kaufman's thought began in 1980 at United Theological College, Bangalore, India. At that time I never imagined that I would work with him and interact, critically and constructively, with his theology in such depth. I am most grateful to Professor Kaufman for his mentorship.

The reviewers of Oxford University Press and State University of New York (SUNY) press gave me invaluable suggestions to make this book more comprehensive, systematic and accessible. Anita Roy (editor, OUP) and Shalini Sinha (Asst. editor, OUP) have been gracefully prodding and professionally prompt in their dealings with a lingering author.

The community of friends and helpers at Karunguzhi, Tamilnadu, South India, taught me immensely through my time among them. I would specially like to thank Prince and Roza Singh. When I returned to live in the field during the Summer of 1992 they offered me their home as a work site and a reflective arena. My colleagues at the Social Action Center (Karunguzhi) were also a great resource; I thank Paul Duraikannu, Gunadayalan, Gunaseelan, Kalyana Sundaram, Prem Kumar and John Vellankani. I also thank the communities of the colonies of Malaipallayam and Thottanavoor for opening their lives and their religion to me as a researcher and friend.

Friends play an invaluable role in the process of writing. Michael Fonner has been a great source of encouragement, fun and camaraderie from the first day of my writing. Suresh and Shoba Reginald, Nick and Anne Read, Jackie Kraus, Ian and Kristen Douglas, Phil and Victoria Jackson, Aju and Mary John, Ninni and James Jacob, Patrick Michael, and Nancy MacArdle were friends who drummed up love and support through my journey in a far away country.

My parents provoked and promoted my theological inquiry. Clara

Theophilus and Sundar Clarke gave us the privilege of inhabiting an abode of intellectual freedom and religious devotion. Dorothy Stairs has been an adopted parent of the Clarke children for the last 35 years. Her enduring affection and gracious financial commitment made possible much of my evolvement as an academician. T.P. Chandy (my father-in-law) was there to encourage me both in the US and in Bangalore.

Our children, Avinash and Ashwin, just grew up while this book was being written. My wife, Prema Chandy Clarke, has contributed in a way that cannot be recorded. Most of all she has made this journey great fun.

Contents

Introduction

The Pariah

Years ago
you and I went our separate ways
without regret.
Only one thing I never quite understood
when you and I said goodbye
and the house was sold.

Some empty vessels lay outside
in the courtyard
staring at us.
Others lay overturned,
hiding their faces.
A wilted creeper
climbed down the door,
perhaps complaining to us
or to the water tap
about the lack of water.
All these are now memories.

I only remember
that Pariah
who entered our empty room
for some unknown reason.
And the door was locked outside.

Three days later
when the deal was clinched
our house was sold.
We exchanged the keys for money.
The new owner
was shown each room.
And in one of the rooms we found
the corpse of that dog.

I have never heard that dog bark.
I only remember the smell of its corpse.
That smell still haunts me:
it returns from everything I touch.
Amrita Pritam[1]

This book wilfully and obstinately sets out to recollect and remember.
It involves a process of re-collection and re-membering with a view
to enrich the inclusive, dialogical and liberative objectives of theology.
In the Indian context, it attempts to tune into the subjugated knowledge
of subaltern communities by studying the Paraiyar of South India, a
major and specific community of Dalits (The Untouchables or outcastes
of India).[2] In contrast to the poem by Amrita Pritam, which reflects
upon a 'Pariah' who is caged in a room and left to die, this work
aspires, at a community level, to release the shut-in, unloose the shut-up,
and integrate the shut-out: to unlock the doors of the rooms that have
been locked from the outside so that the immured 'outcastes' may be
free to hear the soundings of the Paraiyar, whose voices have not been
heard, and reach out to embrace the materiality of the Dalits that was
shunned as untouchable and unapproachable.

Chapter one begins with a substantial discussion on theology in
the Indian context. I propose that theology is the critical and constructive
reflection on the dialogical symbolic interaction of the community in
its effort to make sense of, find meaning in, and determine order for
living collectively under the Divine. I then undertake the diagnostic
exercise of criticizing Indian-Christian theology from the implications
of my proposed definition of theology.[3] This is done consciously from
the Dalit perspective. Two conclusions can be drawn from this diagnosis.
First, Indian-Christian theology tends to be exclusionary and non-
dialogical by turning a deaf ear to the collective religious resources of
the Dalits. Second, and in collaboration with the first aspect just alluded
to, Indian-Christian theology fosters the hegemonic objectives of the
caste communities. Thus, in order to capture the dialogical, inclusive
and liberative dimensions of theology, it is determined that the religious
world of the Dalits must be re-collected and re-membered.

Chapter two and three are the result of an analysis of the communal
religious life of one representative subaltern Dalit community, i.e. the
Paraiyar of Tamil Nadu in South India. The second chapter is introductory: a descriptive arrangement of the historical and religious life
of the Paraiyar prevails over an analytical approach. Three themes
emerge from the historical reconstruction of the origins of the Paraiyar.

First, they are an ancient people claiming to be the original inhabitants of the land. Second, the Paraiyar are a culturally distinct community with the drum as a key symbol of this particularity. And, third, they are an economically oppressed and religiously and culturally marginalized community, mainly because their distinctive heritage is not in conformity with the traditions of the Hindu caste communities. A comprehensive view of the religion of the Paraiyar is proffered through a study of their deities, rituals and religious functionaries.

Chapter three moves from descriptive enumeration to interpretive analyses. The leitmotif of the dialectic between the resistive and the constructive dynamics of the Paraiyar's religion is explicated through a creative interpretation of goddess Ellaiyamman and the drum. In an analysis of Ellaiyamman, on the one hand, the focus is on the positioning of her stone image at the border of Dalit habitations and on her unwillingness to be co-opted into a subservient position within the Hindu hierarchy of deities. Ellaiyamman symbolizes the distinctiveness and particularity of the Paraiyar's religion in its resistance against the invading and co-opting tendencies of caste Hinduism. On the other hand, the mythology surrounding the origins of Ellaiyamman is also examined. An artful and conscious reweaving of mythography to reimagine and reinterpret the Paraiyar's own communal identity, both as a contestation of the hegemonic mythology circulated by the caste community and as an affirmation of their own rationale for communal existence, is uncovered.

The analysis of the drum provides an important key to understand the particularity of the religion of the Paraiyar: the drum is their unique, creative and constructive text of resistive and emancipatory theography. Through a synchronic (the multiplex functioning of the drum in the life of a Paraiyar individual and community) and diachronic (the functioning of the drum through the history of the Paraiyar) study, the creatively resistive and emancipatory characteristics of the drum as a 'dominant symbol' of the Paraiyar are established. Two contextual significances of the drum are underscored. First, the drum is a fitting counter-image to the caste Hindu conception of the Word in a historical setting in which the Paraiyar were severed from the sacred word. Second, the drum represents the functional power of the Divine that operates on behalf of the Paraiyar: it functions as the agent of Divine power both to resist the co-optive tendencies of dominant caste Hinduism and to empower the collective subjectivity of this subaltern community. In concluding my analysis of Dalit religion, as represented by the

Paraiyar, I offer a general interpretation of the significant features of subaltern religion. Three characteristics emerge from the findings of Dalit religion and culture. 1) Subaltern religion is not mere 'false consciousness' that is manufactured by the vested devices of the dominant classes. Rather, it is a locus for the reconfiguration of subaltern subjectivity. 2) Subaltern religion is a complex interweaving of at least the following factors: profuse, though cautious, borrowing from dominant religion; resourceful, though piecemeal, patching together of all available symbolic capital; and creative use of alternate forms to express collective experience. 3) And finally, subaltern religion incorporates realistic elements of the tacit and the subtle in its manifestation.

Chapter four explores the relevance of the religious expressions of the Paraiyar for Indian theology. This chapter begins with the interpretation of the drum in its relatedness to other South Indian religious traditions. Three themes surface: the drum is related to the mediation of Divine power; it is 'the word of wisdom' that is prior and complementary to the spoken and written sacred Word; and the drum conjoins both material and spiritual aspects of the mediation of divine blessedness. In studying the importance of the drum in local South Indian traditions I underscore two further features: on the one hand, the drum gathers together the strivings of subaltern communities and, on the other hand, it symbolizes the centripetal dimensions of orality in a dominantly literacy-based context. After reinterpreting, through a process of qualification and modification, two modes of thought and representation (orality and literacy), I propose that the drum can be considered as an 'organizing symbol' for subaltern-based orality just as the word can exemplify aspects of the dominant-situated literacy. The drum as an organizing symbol represents the various features of the mode of thought and representation that are engendered by subaltern-based communities of orality: it unites communities by connecting interiority with interiority; it situates human beings in context-dependent 'present actuality', which is participatory; and it nurtures collaborative and eclectic patterns of community behaviour.

This leads to a further theological stretching of the symbol of the drum, in which it is interrogated to provide experiential markings/soundings of the Divine. The drum in this section is more than just an organizing symbol; it is projected as a 'theological interpretant' through which the Divine is both experienced and explicated. With respect to Indian-Christian theology, subaltern-based orality as symbolized by the drum has specific ramifications. On the one hand, theology is beckoned to include various modes of expression in its reflective conversation, i.e. music, art, architecture, etc. Orality as epitomized by the drum, thus, represents an array of discursive and non-discursive theophonic voices within the theological conversation. On the other hand, the drum engenders religious themes that are advocated by the religion of orality. On a formal level, three aspects of orality are found to be suitable complements to the exclusionary and hegemonic patterns of Indian theological discourse as regulated by literacy: incorporativeness, immediacy (as in 'present actuality' rather than non-mediated) and eclecticism. On a material level, the emergent themes from the symbol of the drum in the Paraiyar's religious tradition put into circulation resources that are ignored by theology done from within the dictates of the culture of literacy. Again three themes materialize: the drum as a medium of divine-human communication that invokes, contains and dispenses divine power; the drum as an instrument of linking the subalternity of communities for resistive and emancipatory communal affirmation, which exemplifies the solidarity of the human and divine in their resistance of human and demonic forces; and the drum as a symbol of manifesting and managing corporate suffering.

In the final chapter I venture to work out a provisional christology by drawing upon my theological explications of the symbol of the drum in subaltern religion, specifically as seen in the religion of the Paraiyar. After establishing the methodological significance of Christ to the programme of Indian-Christian theology, I argue for a modified version of the correlational model of doing christology: Dalit christology is construed as harmonizing its expansive and constrictive poles. The expansive pole of christology renders a creative interpretation of the Christ dynamic in consonance with themes of the drum which were presented in the earlier chapters. Accordingly, Christ as interpreted in relation with and in reference to the drum is envisaged as the immanental presence of God that directs and draws humanity toward the human and the humane through the dynamics of emancipatory resistance and emancipatory reconciliation.

The constrictive pole of christology is influenced by the expansive pole in that it posits a Dalit Jesus. On a formal plane, interpreting Jesus through the christic presence as represented by the drum involves both a shift from concerns about the ontology of Jesus to his functionality; and a move from a correspondance notion of determining Jesus's validity to an acceptance of living with a sense of ambiguity. On a material plane, Jesus is interpreted through the model of deviance.

Jesus as deviant, firstly, depicts a human being who is immanent among the people that lived within the space labelled 'polluted'. Jesus's praxis thus is one of immanental solidarity with the 'outcaste'. Secondly, Jesus as deviant sets into motion the resistive forces which challenge the social, cultural, economic and religious structures that maintain the unjust division between the prominents (dominant) and the deviants (subaltern). On the one hand, Jesus affirms the human identity of deviants by affirmatively gathering it up and constraining it towards emancipatory collective action in the face of societal tendencies to demonize it. On the other hand, Jesus empowers the deviants to subvert, in their own subaltern way, the hierarchies, distinctions and discriminations of such an inhuman and inhumane system. And, finally, Jesus as deviant postures his praxis at the borderline of emancipatory resistance and emancipatory reconciliation despite the suffering that this inbetweenness entails. Thus, while being a liberator for the deviants he does not cease to be saviour for the prominents too.

The term 'subaltern' requires brief explanation, especially in its relatedness with religion. The term was popularized by Antonio Gramsci, an Italian Marxist writing to counter Fascism in the 1920s and 1930s, who substituted it for the much-in-use 'proletarian class'. In India, this term has been brought to the centre of critical scholarship by a group of thinkers referred to as the Subaltern Studies Collective. From 1982 to 1996, the Subaltern Collective has published nine substantial volumes on South Asian history and society from a 'subaltern perspective'. In the Preface to *Subaltern Studies*, Volume I, Ranajit Guha proposes the following definition:

> The word 'subaltern' ... stands for the meaning as given in the *Concise Oxford Dictionary*, that is, 'of inferior rank'. It will be used...as a name for the general attitude of subordination in South Asian society whether this is expressed in terms of class, caste, age, gender and office or in any other way.[4]

In a clarificatory note, at the end of this same Preface, he further states,

> The terms 'people' and 'subaltern classes' have been used synonymous throughout this note. The social groups and elements included in this category represent the *demographic difference between the total Indian population and all those whom we have described as the elite.*[5]

While I have no objections to the general trend pioneered by Guha *et al.* to rewrite history and write about society (inclusive of religion) from a people's viewpoint, my own use of the term is somewhat more circumspect.

First, I move away from a homogenization of the subaltern by clubbing together all categories of differentiation ('Class, caste, age, gender and office and any other way'). At one level many groups share in a multiplicity of handicaps and oppressions. However, to unify collectives that persevere and struggle to maintain their own particularity is to fall prey to the fallacy of hasty and unwarranted generalization. Spivak appropriately warns those involved in the Subaltern Studies project in India not to essentialize the multiple identities of the subaltern as if it is 'a single underlying consciousness'.[6] In keeping with this, I have tried to concentrate on fleshing out the caste dimension of subalternity. The subordination and subjection that marks the life of Dalits in India bring them into the contours of a particularly contextual assembly of subalternity.

> Untouchables [Dalits] have retained their identity as a subordinated people within Indian society, and by this we mean to identify a condition that is far more severe than merely being bottom of an inevitable hierarchy.[7]

This is not to deny that collectives held together by commonalities of age, gender, class and office do share in the state of subalternity. Rather, this study takes seriously the specific manner by which the institution and ideology of caste engenders a contextual manifestation of subalternity, which is intrinsically tied up to religion in India. The subaltern, thus, are the communities (the Dalits) that are cumulatively and comprehensively disadvantaged and subordinated through the caste system, which operates to benefit the dominant groups (caste communities). The words of Partha Chatterjee are relevant here:

> no matter how we choose to characterize it, subaltern consciousness in the specific cultural context of India cannot but contain caste as a central element in its constitution.[8]

Second, I am careful not to construct subaltern as a unitary 'negative consciousness' which is either mainly passive or merely oppositional. Rather, by a careful analysis of the religion of the Paraiyar, I garner the active and creatively constructive aspects of subalternity. Subalternity is a collective consciousness that actualizes its subjectivity through a process of creative and calculating engagement with the material and symbolic order of the dominant communities within the restrictions of severe subjection.[9] In this book subaltern symbolic order (rather than its material domain) is located and interpreted with due respect to collective agency. Thus, the convergence of the oppositional in the rendering of the subjectivity of the subaltern is construed in terms of a tendency and a loose arrangement. This is in keeping with the definition of the word, subalternate in the *Random Unabridged Dictionary* (IInd edition): 'placed singly along an axis, but *tending to become* grouped oppositionally.'[10] Within the context of the above two comments I propose that subaltern religion is an emerging symbolic order, which obstinately expresses the collective subjectivity of outcast communities, and which purports to emanate at the locus of Divine-Human encounters, within the overall dynamics of subjection by and subordination to the mechanisms of the caste system.

Throughout this work I have tried to be as precise as possible with regard to the semantics surrounding the notion of 'symbol'. Without getting into a needlessly complex semiotic discussion let me clarify the general framework within which I employ the term symbol and the specific nuances with which I utilize it in particular contexts through this book. Like Charles S. Peirce I take the sign to be the basic building block of semiotics: 'A sign, or representamen, is something which stands to somebody for something in some respect or capacity.'[11] The above definition makes us aware of a triadic dynamic. The sign (representamen) is something that represents for somebody (interpretant) something (object) with respect to certain aspects.

In a Peircian sense, signs can be classified according to the relation of the sign to its object. Accordingly, signs can be icons, indices or symbols. Peirce succinctly spells out the difference between the three:

> The Icon has no dynamical connection with the object it represents; it simply happens that its qualities resemble those of that object, and excite analogous sensations in the mind for which it is a likeness. But it really stands unconnected with them. The Index is physically connected with its object; they make an organic pair, but the interpreting mind has nothing to do with this connection, except remarking it, after it is established. The Symbol is connected with its object by virtue of the idea of a symbol-using mind, without which no connection would exist.[12]

I use the term symbol mainly because of the 'arbitrary' and 'conventional' relationality between the sign and the object. Specifically, when I take the drum to be a symbol I am well aware that what the drum as a symbol stands for stems from the interpretive relationship that is dependent on the mind of the interpreter (either an individual or a group). Thus, there is neither obvious resemblance nor 'physical connection' between the symbol of the drum and the object for which it stands, be it the divine or human significations that are being talked about. The connection arises from either conventionally forged or arbitrarily contextual association. I also use the term symbol to include concrete entities. Here I may be veering away from the way in which Peirce makes use of the term. However, this is not unlike the use of the word in the field of history of religion. Mircea Eliade, for example, recognizes such concrete entities as 'trees, labyrinths, ladders, and mountains as symbols insofar as they...point beyond themselves to something wholly other, which manifests itself in them.'[13] These two characteristics of the symbol, arbitrariness and concreteness, are attested to by the Oxford dictionary in its definition of this term: Symbol is 'something that stands for, represents, or denotes something else (not by exact resemblance, but by vague suggestion, or by some accidental or conventional relationship); especially a material object representing something immaterial or abstract.'[14]

In the explication of the drum through this lengthy reflection, three expressions are used to further qualify the notion of symbol. First, I refer to the drum as a 'dominant symbol'.[15] This phrase suggests two things. On the one hand, it points to the predominance of the drum in the ritual life of the Paraiyar. In a sense the drum condenses and unifies diverse and disparate elements of the religiosity of the Paraiyar. On the other hand, it refers to the 'axiomatic value' ascribed to this symbol. Thus, the drum symbolizes more than just values that are ends in themselves. For example, the drum refers to the Divine and the Community as a whole. Second, I utilize the term 'organizing symbol'. In this context the drum is used as a symbol that organizes and interprets the sets of premises that underlie a culture and religion. Thus, the drum is introduced as a symbol that gathers up, represents, circulates and interprets the various dimensions of subaltern-based orality. Third, I also utilize the term 'theological interpretant'.[16] By introducing the drum as an 'interpretant' I am distancing myself further from a notion of a diadic relationship between the sign and the object. Thus, the interpretant is one step removed from the symbol in that it is 'a sign that interprets another sign as standing for an object in a certain respect.'[17]

Two further traits of the symbol, in relation to the general notion of signs, must also be explicitly stated in order to appreciate the manner in which this concept is utilized in this book. At one level, '[s]igns, including symbols, are polysemic'.[18] In other words, symbols are multivocal; they possess the faculty of accommodating manifold meaning.

Like Bynum, I, too, adopt 'Turner's term 'polysemic symbol' to signify an emphasis, first, on the multivalent quality of images and, second, on symbol using as an active process of appropriation.'[19] At another level, signs are multimodal. This means that symbolic, iconic and indexical aspects may coexist in a particular sign. This multimodality or polychromy is assumed in an extended discussion of two major symbols of the religion of the Paraiyars: the goddess Ellaiyamman and the drum. In accordance with the multimodal postulate of signs, I have referred to Ellaiyamman as a 'dominant iconic symbol' and the drum as a 'dominant aniconic symbol'.

Throughout this book I have simplified the process of transliteration by avoiding diacritical marks. In general, I have doubled vowels to represent the long vowel sound in Tamil and capitalized consonants to represent the hard or stressed sound of Tamil letters. To help the cause of consistency I have followed the orthography that is worked out by Michael Moffatt.[20]

Much against the methodological injunction of liberation theology in general, which advocates starting theology from human situatedness, I commence from my theoretical reflections.[21] There are two reasons for this conscious decision. On the one hand, the 'liberation theology' worked out in these pages is the outcome of a complex personal journey in which the relationship between theory and practice is dialectical.

On the other hand, this structure compels me to honestly admit my own locatedness as the author. I am doing theology from the distance and immunity built into living within the academy. Realistically, I am writing, as it were, from the other side of the fence. I thus start with no pretensions of being one among the subaltern Dalits that I am in solidarity with; rather I begin from the world with which I am more familiar: the advocacy-affirming and solidarity-seeking discourse of reflective and committed academics, mainly consisting of theologians, religionists and anthropologists. I thus first seek to introduce the reader to an overview of the many dimensions in Indian theological discourse. Having done this, I then set out to do 'feet-on-the-ground' theology by staking a place for the inclusion of subaltern communities.

While on the issue of methodology, another concern involves both the legitimacy and prudence of drawing so heavily on western theory in doing Indian liberation theology. As one anonymous reviewer of this manuscript put it, 'the advocacy turns out to be a mixed bag of advocacy both for Paraiyar of Tamil Nadu and for the theology and methodology of the west'. Though this study is inspired and influenced by western theologians (particularly from the Constructivist School), anthropologists, social historians and religionists, three justifications counter any suggestions that may imply a tendency towards 'western methodolatry' (worship of or complete devotion to western method). First, although I use many western theoreticians I do so from a critical perspective, which comes through the filter of subalternity, i.e. both western and caste community theories are dealt with critically; and, even if used constructively, they are put to work on behalf of the Dalits. Second, I also make a concerted attempt to incorporate much of the writing of Indian scholars in fields that are relevant to the analysis and interpretation of subaltern culture, religion and theology. Third, and most importantly, the process of utilizing all possible resources, irrespective of where they originate from and who they belong to, for the weaving together of liberative symbolic frameworks is a characteristic of Dalit and subaltern religions. I am thus working in harmony with the principles of subaltern religion as I have explicated them in chapter three. From the subaltern viewpoint, the issue is not so much whether the material or symbolic resources are western in descent or caste community in pedigree; rather the potency and efficacy of these resources for the enhancement of Dalit subjectivity and corporate self-actualization becomes the key. In the final analysis, a continuous attempt has been made to contract all methods and theories for the supreme purpose of advocating for the liberation of the Dalits. Substantively, all theory advanced at various junctures of this study is for the overriding purpose of advocacy for the subaltern Dalit communities, particularly as encountered in the Paraiyar of South India. The semantic difference between advancement and advocacy is important here.

The usefulness of this work is at multiple levels. At the most basic level, it is my hope that this project would benefit the Paraiyar and other subaltern Dalit communities. It starts the process of justifying a search for subjugated knowledge among marginalized communities. It also provides Dalit communities with conceptual resources and direction for exploring their own religious resources with the assurance that it is rich, resourceful and liberative. In a sense, it provides a subaltern perspective through which subjugated knowledge can be located, retrieved and interpreted. The norm of what constitutes acceptable or appropriate knowledge is reinscribed. And, in so doing, the distinctive characteristics of persistent attainment of collective subjectivity, through the process of religion-making among the subaltern, is ascertained.

At a second level, this book is addressed to the Indian-Christian community. Drawing on the symbolism of the positioning of the christic presence, as epitomized by the drum, at the inbetweenness of emancipatory resistance and emancipatory reconciliation, it promises to be liberative to the Dalits and non-Dalits in the Christian community. But mostly this effort of systematically recalling and creatively remembering the silenced voices within the contours of social discourse enriches both the process and the content of theology as I define it.

The theological summons served here open a new way for Christians to deal with Dalit religious experience, which manifests the birth of the Divine in the womb of suffering ('pathos'). There was a time when Dalits in South India, who wished to convert to Christianity, were required to break the drum in public before entering the Church for baptism. This was necessary to demonstrate the Dalits' complete rejection of the non-Christian Divine as experienced in their local context.[22] This was in keeping with the general fear among some Christian leaders in the early part of this century that the drum (which symbolizes Dalit supernatural communication) was to be eradicated from the life of Christian Dalit communities. Christian Dalits were thus forbidden the use of 'the tappeta [parai drum] for any purpose and even to possess it.'[23] The theological reconstruction that is undertaken here, through imaginative subaltern reclamation and reinterpretation, calls for the restoration of the drum for the liberation of the Dalits. The drum becomes the source of subaltern theological knowledge and symbolizes the unfailing presence of God in the midst of human beings. It represents the yearning and the working of God in the heart of the subaltern communities of South India. Thus, that which was defiled becomes the means of wholeness; that which was shameful becomes the instrument of veneration; and that which was rejected by the so-called 'pure' becomes the primary symbol of God's faithful presence among the so-called 'polluted'. On the one hand, the dalitness of the Christian community is affirmed and incorporated into the discussion of theology by drawing on their particular experience of God. On the other hand, Indian-Christian theology is expanded as it continues to discern the consequences of what has been known to be the direction of the Christ dynamic:

> Consider your call, brothers and sisters: not many of you were wise by human standards, not many were powerful, not many were of noble birth. But God chose what is foolish in the world to shame the wise; God chose what is weak in the world to shame the strong; God chose what is low

and despised in the world, things that are not, to reduce to nothing things that are, so that no one might boast in the presence of God.[24]

Relatedly, this book can benefit the Christian community as a whole. On the one hand, it provides a critique to Christian theology's 'biblicism' and 'culture of literacy', which appear to aid the colonizing and the demonizing of the working of God within the religions of orality. On the other hand, it offers Christian theology a whole array of resources (truths) concerning aspects of God and human beings that have not come from its own literary sources.

And finally, this work opens up avenues for religionists by reclaiming and reinterpreting the religious reflexivity of communities around the world that identify themselves with the orientation of orality. The drum could provide a key to explore and expound the collective religious themes of the indigenous communities for whom drumming is prior to and complementary to the 'sacred Word'. It no doubt may be in a posture of resistance to the co-opting or ejecting power of the dominant forms of the orientations of literacy that one locates the function of the drum. This intimate relationship between drumming and the voicing of the Divine can be noticed in certain Native American tribes and African communities. Further, the coupling of subaltern representation with alternate-mode expression is pointed to in local South Indian communities.

I conclude with a plea to allow the drum to do its own theological voicing. Lalrinawmi Ralte, writing about the oral tradition of the Mizo's of North-East India, captures this aspect of the drum in the following poem entitled *Don't Bury Me Yet*:

Don't bury me, don't kill me
you bury music, you bury songs
I don't want to die now
I have more songs for you
Chief, you order my death
but my name will live
Elders, who supported the chief
your children will remember me
Boys, who dug my grave
will sing my song
My drum, that you gave me
you will hear until I die
My body will die

my song and my music will survive
The clothes you gave me
give me strength to beat my drum
Don't go away as long as
you hear my drum "vawng, vawng"...
...My song, my music
your song, your music
Our song, our music
our drum, our dance.[25]

Notes

1. A.K. Ramanujan and Vinay Dharwadker, 'Sixteen Modern Indian Poems', *Daedalus*, vol. 118, no. 4 (Fall 1989), 325–6. By the term 'Pariah' this poem could be referring either to a stray dog *per se* or a community of Dalits. In South India there is a somewhat dexterously malicious conjoining of these two references. Thus, the Dalits and dogs could be spoken of as being part of the same reference. This has its roots in the notion that Dalits are less-than-human and ought to be kept outside the contours of the societal household, just as dogs (as is the general custom in rural India) are to be kept outside the living space of the human household. In using this I draw upon the latter interpretation of the term 'pariah'.
2. I will offer a more elaborate definition of the Dalits in chapter one.
3. I use the hyphenated term 'Indian-Christian' in accordance with the suggestion of Christopher Duraisingh that our 'Indian hyphenated Christian' identity lies in the fact that our corporate consciousness is 'doubly determined and co-constituted' by the synchronous functioning of both elements of our Judeo-Christian and pan-Indian heritage. In this chapter, I shall argue that the pan-Indian aspect of this heritage is highly vulnerable to being co-opted by caste Hinduism. Thus I propose a Dalit expression to facets of this strand of Indian tradition. See Christopher Duraisingh, 'Indian Hyphenated Christians and Theological Reflections: A New Expression of Identity', in *Religion and Society*, vol. XXVI, no. 4 (December, 1979): 95–101.
4. Ranajit Guha, 'Preface', in *Subaltern Studies I: Writings on South Asian History and Society*, ed. Ranajit Guha (New Delhi: Oxford University Press, 1982), p. vii.
5. Ibid., p. 8. Emphasis in text.
6. For an extended critique of the notion of subaltern advanced by Guha et al. see Gayatri Chakravorty Spivak 'Subaltern Studies: Deconstructing Historiography', in *Subaltern Studies IV: Writings on South Asian History and Society* (New Delhi: Oxford University Press, 1985), pp. 330–63.

7. Oliver Mendelsohn and Marika Vicziany, 'The Untouchables' in *The Rights of Subordinated Peoples*, eds. Oliver Mendelsohn and Upendra Baxi (New Delhi: Oxford University Press, 1994), p. 115.

8. Partha Chatterjee 'Caste and Subaltern Consciousness', in *Subaltern Studies VI: Writings on South Asian History and Society*, ed. Ranajit Guha (New Delhi: Oxford University Press, 1989), p. 169.

9. Within the Subaltern collective this dimension is highlighted in a splendid article on 'low caste' religion by Dube: 'The new symbolic order was marked by interrogation and critique of the relationship of power with the region. The resistance, which was conducted in a religious idiom, engaged with as well as subverted — but was also contained by — hegemonic limits.' Saurabh Dube, 'Myths, Symbols and Community: Satnampanth of Chhattisgarh', in *Subaltern Studies VII: Writings on South Asian History and Society*, eds. Partha Chatterjee and Gyanendra Pandey (New Delhi: Oxford University Press, 1993), pp. 121–58.

10. *Random House Unabridged Dictionary*, 2nd edition (New York: Random House, 1993), p. 1891. Emphasis mine.

11. Justus Buchler, ed., *Philosophical Writings of Peirce* (New York: Dover Publications, 1955), p. 99. Also see Philip P. Wiener, ed. *Charles S. Peirce: Selected Writings* (New York: Dover Publications, 1958), pp. 391 ff.

12. Justus Buchler, *Philosophical Writings* of Peirce, p. 114.

13. Paul Ricoeur, *Interpretation Theory: Discourse and the Surplus of Meaning* (Fort Worth, Texas: The Texas Christian University Press, 1976), p. 53. For Eliade's argument, see Mircea Eliade, *Patterns in Comparative Religion,* trans. Rosemary Sheed (Cleveland: The Word Publishing Company, 1963), pp. 437–58.

14. *The Compact Edition of the Oxford English Dictionary*, vol. II (P-Z) (Oxford, UK: Oxford University Press, 1971), p. 3206.

15. I am drawing on the term developed by Turner. For a thorough discussion of 'senior' or 'dominant' symbols see Victor Turner, *The Forest of Symbols: Aspects of Ndembu Rituals* (Ithaca: Cornell University Press, 1967), pp. 1–47.

16. I am adopting the terminology that is suggested by Neville; see Robert C. Neville, *Behind the Masks of God: An Essay in Comparative Theology* (Albany, NY: State University of New York Press, 1991), pp. 1-50.

17. ibid., p. 47.

18. E. Valentine Daniel, *Fluid Signs: Being a Person the Tamil Way* (Berkeley: University of California Press, 1984), p. 39.

19. Caroline Walker Bynum 'The Complexity of Symbols', in *Experience of the Sacred: Readings in the Phenomenology of Religion*, eds Summer B. Twiss and Walter H. Conser, Jr. (Hanover: Brown University Press, 1992), p. 270.

20. Michael Moffatt, *An Untouchable Community in South India: Structure and Consensus* (Princeton: Princeton University Press, 1979), p. xxi. I have chosen to use Moffatt's scheme mainly because I am dealing with the same Tamil region (Chingelput district) and Dalit community (Paraiyars) that he studied.

Thus, he has already transliterated most of the Tamil words that I use in this book.

21. It must be stated, however, that I do start from the Dalit situation when I am experimentally involved in doing christology in the last chapter. There I am closer to the dictates of liberation methodology.

22. This came from discussions with John B. Carman on Dalits in the Telugu region for whom the drum symbolized intimate connection with the 'idols' of their old religion. For his early work on Dalit religion, see P.Y. Luke and John B. Carman, *Village Christians and Hindu Culture: Study of Rural Churches in Andhra Pradesh, South India* (London: Lutterworth Press, 1968).

23. A.T. Fishman, *Culture Change and the Underprivileged* (Madras: The Christian Literature Society, 1941), p. 184. Also see, A.T. Fishman, *For This Purpose* (Madras: American Foreign Mission Society in India, 1958). 'Requiring converts to change their conduct was an integral part of the message. This emphasized moral and ethical living and specially forbade...participation in the worship of temple idols in any form including the beating of the temple drums...', p. 14.

24. I Corinthians 1: 26–9. *The Holy Bible: Containing the Old and New Testament*, New Revised Standard Version (Nashville: Holman Bible Publishers, 1989), p. 985.

25. Lalrinawmi Ralte, 'Don't Bury Me Yet', *Saplings 96–97* (April, 1997): 36.

1

Indian-Christian Theology and the Dalits

This is the man whom we once held in derision
And made a byword of reproach – we Fools!
We thought that his life was madness
and that his end was without honour.
Why has he been numbered among the sons of God?
And why is his lot among the saints?
So it was we who strayed from the way of truth,
and the light of righteousness did not shine on us,
and the sun did not rise upon us.
(Wisdom of Solomon 5: 4-6).
Behold, my servant shall prosper,
he shall be exalted and lifted up,
and shall be very high.
As many were astonished at him-
his appearance was so marred,
beyond human semblance,
and his form beyond that of the sons of men-
so shall he startle many nations;
kings shall shut their mouths because of him;
for that which has not been told them they shall see,
and that which they have not heard they shall
understand. (Isaiah 52: 13-15)

Indian-Christian theology has predominantly been fuelled by the momentum resulting from the coalescence of at least two streams: a dynamic understanding of the Christian message and a deliberate remembering of its rich indigenous religious heritage. For at least the last two hundred years, Indian-Christian theology occupied itself with the challenging process of recollecting, reinterpreting and reappropriating its religious and cultural legacy mainly in terms of the Hindu tradition. Correspondingly, theology in India continually sought to translate, adapt and correlate the 'good news' of Christian proclamation by taking into consideration its Hindu philosophical and cultural framework. Doing contextual Indian-Christian theology was, thus, overwhelmingly conceived of as baptizing the gospel of Christ into the holy waters of Hindu philosophy and culture.

This chapter seeks to problematize the assumptions behind such a lopsided theological venture. It puts forth the argument that Indian-Christian theology cannot elude its responsibility of dealing with the culture and religion of a significant portion of its subaltern members who are not part of the Hindu community: the Dalits represent a large percentage of Indian society that did not come within the confines of the Hindu human community.[1] They have been called by various terms: *Dasu, Raksasa, Avarna* (the no-caste), Untouchables, Harijans, Protestant Hindus, Scheduled castes, Outcasts, Depressed classes, Exterior castes, *Chandaalas, Panchamas* (the fifth caste), and Dalits. I use the term Dalits in this presentation for three reasons: it 'has become an expression of hope', which Dalit writers and activists have chosen both in recovering their past identity and in representing themselves as a group;[2] the word means 'oppressed', 'broken', and 'crushed', which most realistically describes the lives of almost all those who are part of this cluster of communities;[3] and it forces caste people to reckon with the reality of a surviving human community that has been wronged by them for centuries.[4]

In this chapter, first, I lay out a general conception of theology. After suggesting a definition of theology, I go on to explicate its main features. Second, keeping my exposition of theology in the background, I analyse specific drawbacks that have contributed to the theological dismissal of the world of Dalits. Third, I point to formal ways in which Indian-Christian theology will be enriched through the inclusion of the historical context of the Dalits. Correspondingly, I also suggest how such an enterprise will be fruitful to the Dalit community.

I. A Working Definition of Theology: Constructive Proposals

Theology is the critical and constructive reflection on human dialogical symbolic interaction in its attempt to make sense of, find meaning in, and determine order for living collectively under the Divine.[5] There are myriad theological assumptions and assertions packed into such an apparently innocuous and seemingly temperate statement. I want to focus primarily upon three aspects that I think need clarification and interpretation in an attempt to decipher the above definition. In defining theology, however, I am not steered by a desire to legislate, encapsulate, and complete the ongoing creative aspects of theological activity. As Smith says,

> to define need not be imagined as to finalize. To define is not to finish, but to start. To define is not to confine but to create something, to refine – and eventually to redefine. To define, finally, is not to destroy but to construct for the purpose of useful reflection.[6]

This section presents an ongoing dialogue between the emerging school of 'constructive theology' in the west and the legitimate voice of subaltern communities in India. My proposition is that constructive theology can be contextualized in India to be a productive and enriching model for doing Christian liberation theology.

Theology as critical reflection on dialogical communal symbolic intercourse

Theology is an enterprise which reflects critically on the shared dialogue of a particular community. Two elements of this dimension of theology require further explication. From one angle, this particular view of theology expresses its communal basis. The starting point of theology is the ongoing collective dialogical interaction of the community. Theology is not the exposition of a brilliant religious thinker who has an illuminating disclosure. Neither is it merely a codification of the majority opinion with regards to the relationship between the divine, the world and human beings. Both of these could and do influence the agenda and the directionality of discourse. However, theology expands its parameters to reflect on the dialogical voices of the community in its entirety. Dialogue here is not an abstract and conceptual activity. Along with Paulo Freire dialogue is taken to mean the 'encounter in which the united reflection and action of the dialoguers are addressed to the world which is to be transformed and humanized'.[7] Theology undertakes to reflect on the dialogical activity of an inclusive religious community that continually 'names' and 'transforms' human life in the world under God. And because dialogical symbolic interaction takes place in varied contexts, theology is attentive to all kinds of voices within the community — the complying and resisting, the constructive and disruptive, the resonant and hushed.

Any community involves multiple sub-communities. In the Indian theological context three communities can be delineated: the Indian-Christian community, the Dalit community, and the Dalit-Christian community. In this study I take the Indian-Christian community to be the locus of dialogical social intercourse. This is mainly because there is a shared core of beliefs and practices, however loosely defined, which ground and fund theological discourse concerning what is sensible, meaningful, and orderly living under God. However, in seeking to reclaim the voices of a major segment of the Indian-Christian community, i.e. the Dalit-Christians, I go to one Dalit community (the Paraiyar) that is not Christian. There is primarily one reason for harvesting the religious resources of the Dalit community rather than the Dalit-Christian community. As we shall see later in this chapter, Dalit-Christians (Paraiyars, in this case) either officially disassociated from or completely disowned much of their own native symbolic religious world.[8] Thus, in order to recollect Dalit religious resources I am forced to turn to Dalits outside the Christian community.

From another angle, this notion of theology recognizes and affirms the specialized function of theology as critical reflection on this ongoing community dialogue. Theology is not a mere verbatim report of the community's reflection. It involves a conscious attempt to critically ponder upon the dialogue that emerges within the community. The theologian then is an instrument in facilitating this critical reflection. The term critical highlights the following two connotations. First, theology reflects on what is crucial, decisive and significantly important to the collective life of the community. This may be referred to as the crucial dimension of theology. Second, the term critical also embraces the analytical, discriminating and skeptical dimensions of theology. This, which may be called the critique dimension of theology, is directed both to the content that is circulated as the community's dialogical discourse and to the ideational material and practices that are missing from this corpus.

My drawing attention to and lifting up the religious practices of a specific Dalit community in next chapter arises out of certain convictions concerning the necessity to animate and intensify the critical function of theologizing in India. First, because the religious arena is an important instrument of hegemonic control we must critically analyse the many elements that dominate its contents. Indian theology has tended to serve the interest of the dominant caste community. Its symbolic forms, themes and media are not attuned to the religious sensibilities of the subaltern communities. Second, as just stated, the critical role of theology moves beyond mere astute diagnosis of the content; it also ascertains what is missing from theological discourse. It is thus crucial to locate, recover and validate critique-based voices that are contesting the content and the process of the dominant and dominating religious discourse. My concern in an analysis of Dalit religion has to do with searching out the forms by which these marginalized, oppositional and disruptive voices remain operative. The role of theology involves taking on the task of advocating for the marginalized so that they will be seen and heard within the reflective and dialogical process of theologizing. Theology thus puts into circulation oppositional, discordant and anomalous voices that are generally suppressed or evicted. In so doing, theology is ambitious: it strives to overcome its identity as an overseer of the reproductive knowledge that is generated by a certain section or class in society; instead, it functions to precipitate the voicing of various crucial counter-hegemonic forces. Within the Indian context, the critical focus of this reflection will comprise in sifting out and lifting up the collective expression of one such marginalized community. This work embarks on a process to discover how their voice transfigures theological discourse in India.

The advocacy function of theology in this context is committed to making room in the theological arena for the symbolic reflections of Dalits. In a sense it is committed to the forging of a level field for dialogical symbolic interaction. This does not undercut the notion of inclusive plurality for the theological community. Two questions, pertinent to the Dalits, still require answers: (1) Do communities that have been continuously and deliberately excluded and marginalized from theological interaction for decades require a preferential status in this dialogical intercouse? (2) Are marginalized communities the special source of theological knowledge because God is revealed in a unique manner in their pain and suffering? Both these questions will have to be taken up as part of the agenda of theological discourse and can only be answered through a difficult process of negotiation within the same mechanisms of dialogue. It must be stated though that the advocacy function of theology that I propose does not imply a silencing of other voices. Thus, in Indian-Christian theology the caste communities' voices are in constructive and critical dialogue with the voices of Dalit communtiues.[9]

This leads to another characteristic that is implicit in this particular understanding of theology and which must be addressed: symbolic interaction that is dialogical implies both a plurality of voices and a plurality of forms. Theology, if it must be inclusive of all the goings-on of the community, must be concerned with the multiplex manner by which people express their deepest and most significant feelings and thoughts. Western configurations of theology have on the whole taken for granted the equivocal relationship between reflection and language. This may not do justice to the varied ways in which people express themselves and their constructive imaginations. In general, in India, anyone familiar with the complexity of symbolic interaction will know that along with what is said one must also be as attentive to what is communicated through actions (gestures and postures) and what is communicated through deliberate non-action and silence. More specifically, among subaltern communities, one must be sensitive to the manner in which unconventional modes (in the sense of not being part of what is dictated as normative by the status quo-maintaining majority) are preferred to express their deepest thoughts and feelings. Jyoti Sahi reminds theologians to move beyond the realm of words in locating and interpreting common people's religious reflection: we need 'to liberate the symbol from its secondary position to the word, as part of a much bigger programme of finding the sources of insight in the common people.'[10]

To be truly inclusive of the multiform character of the discourse of the entire community, theology requires a modal recalibration. Specifically, it is not simply enough for Indian-Christian theology to champion the inclusion of the subaltern communities; it must also create space for their particular mode of expressing and communicating their reflections. Through a history of representation in which Dalits have been prevented from using the 'sacred' mode of the written word, their rich communal religious reflectivity is expressed in non-textual/non-scriptive forms, i.e. music, painting, dance, weaving, song, architecture, etc. Dalit communal symbolic interaction is thus a multimedia configuration. If Indian-Christian theology wants to critically reflect on the dialogical symbolic intercourse that is all-inclusive, it must go beyond the text and language in its traditional sense. Theo-logia (literally, words or language about God) in India, thus, ought to become inclusive of theo-graphia and theo-phonia.[11]

Theology as constructive reflection on human symbolic interaction

A second factor that is evident in this definition of theology is its constructive nature. In this proposal I want to strive for a certain symmetry between the many uses of the term 'constructive', particularly as used in relation to theology. There are two levels at which this constructive character of theology must be accepted. At one level, from the point of view of the community, this underscores the communal process of ongoing symbolic creation. On the one hand, this results from a general epistemological presupposition: it is not possible to know reality as it is or to know reality in its comprehensiveness. Kaufman has made theologians aware of the inevitability of the constructive dimension of theology based on epistemological grounds. In his view, since theology cannot adequately know God in an objective manner, as one would know any object in the world, it cannot claim to be a descriptive enterprise. Also, since all revelation is itself a kind of theological construction of what is imaginatively construed as being the experience of God, theology ought not to assert that it is a pronouncement of how things really are. Rather the 'proper business' of theology lies solely in the realm of imaginative constructive activity:[12]

> analysis, interpretation, criticism and reconstruction of the concept and images of God as found in the common language and traditions of the West.[13]

On the other hand, the constructive character of theology stems from an anthropological presupposition: Anthropos completes itself by the symbolic worlds that it weaves in order to frame its collective living both systematically and meaningfully. In this sense all communities testify to an ongoing process of what it means to be human. Human beings are 'plastic', 'incomplete', and 'unfinished'. They complete and fulfill themselves through their culture, which they create and inhabit.[14] Because theology involves human beings within specific social, cultural, economic, political and religious historical settings, it will tend to be continually constructive, in as much as it constantly construes what it means for that particular community to live collectively under the

Divine. Theology at this dynamic, everyday-level becomes, as Kaufman points out,

> an activity of adjusting certain of our ideas about human life and the world to those of others, of thinking together on matters of ultimate importance.[15]

A kind of dialectic dynamic is involved in theological activity: a movement towards creating contextual grids for collectively living sensibly, meaningfully and fruitfully under the Divine and an ongoing process of adapting to the dialogically emerging version of what this vision may propound.

The constructive character of theological reflection when viewed from this angle constrains us to unmask the disinterested pretences of theology. It invites human beings to take on culpability for the potential directionality of theological work and be aware of its general ramification. Human beings are the only species capable of destroying each other and decimating the entire planet. We are obliged to take responsibility for the central position we occupy among all of creation. The summons, thus, to acknowledge this pivotal posture is simultaneously a call to accept our creative and constructive responsibility in its totality — technological and theological.[16] This means that theology must become conscious of its constructive nature and deliberate in its constructions.

At another level too, from the point of view of the working theologian, one must be conscious of the constructive nature of theology. Theologians are creatively constructing both the dialogical discourse that is represented as what constitutes the content of reflection and the substance of what materializes as critical reflection about this content. In the first instance, they select, edit, valorize, configure, order and contribute to the raw material which represents the discourse of the dialogical community. But secondly, and equally importantly, they document and record their own theological reflections about what crystallizes as dialogical social intercourse.

Liberation theology has been consciously criticizing this gap between the expressed reflective voice of the people and the professional theologians' imaginative construal of the same. Gutierrez suggests that 'a whole new theological perspective' cannot be reached 'until the oppressed themselves theologize, until the "others" themselves personally reflect on their hope of a total liberation in Christ.'[17] While this may well be true as a projection of the ideal situation, it obscures the actual practice of much that is written in the name of theology, in some cases, even if promoted as 'liberation theology'. Every theological exercise, thus, is a mediated and interpreted version of how the theologian sees the perspective of the community being represented. Schreiter maintains a critical balance between the roles of the community and the theologian:

> The Community is a key source for theology's development and expression, but to call it a theologian in a narrow sense of authorship is inaccurate. Significant members within the community, often working together as a group, give voice to the theology of the community.[18]

It must be admitted, thus, that this representation of the Dalits is not devoid of my own creative rendition of their situation, which includes my own resourceful skills of selection, editing, categorization, and configuration.

Nonetheless, theologians are not the primary constructors: they live off the innovative constructions that emerge from the dialogical discourse of the community. Therefore, while I do agree with Constructivists that human beings take more responsibility for their own theological work, I am not willing to see theology distanced from the lived community. In my view the critical and constructive elements of theology are inextricably intertwined with the dialogical discourse of the community.[19]

The key, I think, is the relationship of the theologian to the experience of the community. I differ from Constructive theologians with regards to the role that human experience plays in theological construction. I do not object to their silence with respect to their individualized life-journeys and its influence on their particular theological symbolizations. Also, I do not repudiate their claim that there is no way of getting to pre-linguistic forms and modes of experience and that experience, even if taken under the rubric of religious experience, is excessively diverse and cornucopian. I do not, however, agree with the Constructivist's decision to simply accept experience as an integral part of life that merely must be acknowledged. By treating human experience as an ever-present universal, intrinsic to every kind of human activity, covertly one runs the risk of devaluing the effects that different collectives of human experience have in fabricating what is projected as normative human experience. There are competing groupings of human experiences. In this context, the theologian is called upon to commit herself to the valorization of particular collectives of human beings that exhibit a somewhat homogeneous symbolic expression of their experience. As stated earlier, since theology is critical and constructive reflection on the dialogical interaction of a community there is a pressing need to validate and advocate for the experience of marginalized sub-communities so as to have them included in the normative-formulating discourse. Segundo states this advocacy function of theology succinctly:

> theology always presupposes a profound human commitment, a *partiality* that is consciously accepted — not on the basis of theological criteria, of course, but on the basis of human criteria.[20]

Without this commitment to privileging the experience of marginalized communities, theology as critical construction is prone to be elitist — reinforcing the construals of the dominant discourse-producing and discourse-orchestrating coterie. Considering that there is nearly always a control on the procedures that produce, construct and sustain discourse, it is quite probable that human experience will-be constructed to be definitive of a certain kind of humanity that serves the interest of the dominant type, race, class, caste or gender. Theology, then, without being conscious of it, may contribute to a discriminatory tendency whereby most of humanity is assessed according to the norms of 'humanity' and 'collective living' fabricated from the human experience of some. One way to circumvent this tendency is through a deliberate commitment of the theologian to privilege and to valorize the collective experience of a human community that has been consistently and calculatingly excluded from the process of critical and constructive reflection.[21] I intentionally stress the term 'experience of the marginalized' even though I am well aware that what I am dealing with and focussing on is the thematized symbolic expression of this experience. I do this mainly to underscore the fact that what gives it validity is not the acceptability or the coherence of the culture and the discourse of marginalized communities but rather their experience, which, more often than not, gets jettisoned from the overall cultural-linguistic framework.

Let me situate this criticism of western Constructive theology by viewing the shortcomings of the 'cultural-linguistic' school. From the Dalit point of view there are two primary problems with this overall framework. First, the cultural-linguistic school does not take seriously the hegemonic nature of culture and discourse. This leads to a kind of entrapment whereby the theologian works within the confines of what is taken to be the general world of culture and language. One way out of this entanglement is a deliberate attempt at eliciting and empowering the experience of those who have been subordinated and overpowered by this cultural-linguistic framework. This will provide a clue to the gaps, cracks and fractures that are regnant within the generally accepted cultural-linguistic framework. By drawing upon the thematized experience of the Dalits, Indian-Christian theology can hope to uncover the hegemonic tendency of theology that has primarily stuck to working from within the framework of 'classical' Hindu culture and language. This general framework, in turn, is unable to account for the experience of the marginalized Dalits whose alienation is accentuated by the discourse of Indian theologizing.

Second, and relatedly, the cultural-linguistic approach seems to reinforce and enhance forms of the status quo. Again, from the Dalit viewpoint, the reliance on language and culture tends to easily slip into a confidence of textuality. For the Dalits, and many other such oral and non-literate cultures, textuality in itself is alienating and exclusionary. George Lindbeck's 'cultural-linguistic' method of doing theology from a post-liberal perspective, although quite different from Kaufman's Constructivist proposal, may be cited as an example of text-centredness. He states in support of his version of the 'cultural-linguistic' approach:

> It is the religion instantiated in Scripture which defines being, truth, goodness, and beauty, and the nonscriptural exemplifications of these realities need to be transformed into figures (or types or antitypes) of the scriptural ones. Intratextual theology redescribes reality within the scriptural framework rather than translating Scripture into extrascriptural categories. It is the text, so to speak, which absorbs the world, rather than the world the text.[22]

Not only does Lindbeck's call for 'intratextuality' place meaning within the texts of the Christian scripture but it, furthermore, seeks to fit all other worlds into this textual world. Here, because 'intratextuality' is homologous with a literary framework 'talk about "text" stands in the place of talk about "God".'[23] Much can, no doubt, be said to defend Lindbeck's proposal by reminding ourselves that the 'cultural' and the 'linguistic' are not collapsible but point to two dialectical and different symbolic modes. Nonetheless, 'Truth is defined intratextually – not as a relationship between text and some "world out there" or some "common human experience".'[24] Thus, in the end, the crucial question put by Stephen L. Stell remains: 'when Lindbeck speaks of 'God' in the Christian cultural-linguistic reality, is he speaking of the intratextually identified God or the identification of God in the text?'[25] In the Indian context, where the experience of the Dalits has been discounted and disparaged by the knowledge-producing and knowledge-preserving theorists, theologians need to commit themselves to empowering the various forms and modes that house the experience of these marginalized peoples, which will function as a corrective component in the formulation of discursive procedures and practices. Two specific areas will need to be pursued in any such endeavour. First, the multimodal nature of God-reflection, exhibited by Dalit communities, needs to be incorporated into the current text-dependent reflection of Indian-Christian theology. This is the task with which much of this book is engaged. Second, the hermeneutics of oral traditions (which is the dominant strand of Dalit reflective representation), along with the principles of its interaction with Christian written scripture, must be studied.

I also want to retain the notion that theology is a constructive response to the community's affirmation that it is being impinged upon by the active presence of the Divine.[26] If theology seeks to reflect on discourse about what it means to live collectively under the Divine, all the constructing must at the same time be some kind of interaction with the Divine. In this sense theology is acting on its being acted upon. This affirmation that theology arises out of a desire to explicate and order the sometimes nebulous, but consistently ongoing, encounter with the Divine lies at the root of most religious traditions. It merely grounds the claim of faith that there is something rather than nothing which authenticates all theological reflection. Let me state this within the terminology of this proposal of theology: It is definitely assumed that the primary dialogue involves the relationality between the Divine and human beings; thus, all human dialogical symbolic interaction is based on our response to the significance of the dialogue between the 'heavens' and 'the earth'.[27]

This leads to another inevitable and important consequence for theology. The fact that theology is continuously constructed by the affirmation that human beings are being impinged upon by the Divine means that scripture and tradition cannot be undervalued. They represent the cumulative expression of the ways by which our ancestors made sense of, found meaning in, and structured order for living collectively under this Divine that was continually encountered. Tradition, thus, is a configurative web of histories, habits and hopes of what was construed as living faithfully and wholesomely under the Divine. And scripture is its integrating and interpreting core, which consensually functions to both normativize and relativize all tradition.

In a pragmatic sense, theology is being constructed by scripture and tradition even as it constructs. Contemporaneous construction is influenced by the reflections of its ancestors. The story that it seeks to construe thus does not profess to be a totally new story. This is particularly true of Christian theology which is constructed from and constricted by the story of Jesus Christ as remembered by scripture and recovered by tradition. It is true that this story is always a constructed version of the story as it is handed down to the community. Nonetheless, it is, at the same time, not a different story.[28] This indeed instils modesty into the theological task. The humility to accept that the stories of our forbears, which gave past generations meaning and fulfillment in life, may have clues to our own dysfunctional version of how to live collectively under the Divine. Theology, as argued above, is critical and constructive reflection on human dialogical symbolic interaction in its attempt to make sense of, find meaning in, and determine order for living collectively under the Divine. Scripture and tradition in this context represent the various configurations of the general pattern or sets of patterns that made sense, gave meaning, and determined order for a given community; thus it was transmitted with devotion and hope by its ancestors to their descendants.

It is important to comment further on three of its connected and interdependent features: scripture and tradition are local, plural, and dynamic. The insights of post-modernism are, no doubt, in vogue within the academic world. One dimension is pertinent here. Post-modernism has instigated a general attitude of suspicion towards any unitary, totalizing, and grandiose theoretical conception. This includes a static, generalized and universal notion of tradition. This is quite true even within a relatively manageable geographical area of Tamil Nadu where one can distil at least three configurates of tradition: the tradition and religious resources of the Brahmins, of the other caste Hindus, and of the Dalits.[29]

More specifically, it can be argued that the Christian tradition is local, plural and dynamic within the context of South India. There is really no common or unitary manner in which Christian tradition operates in the life of the community. The sources and processes of compiling such a tradition itself is varied. On the one hand, it involves selective though diverse elements such as the myths, religious symbols and worldviews that have been handed down within one local community. On the other hand, what is conserved is only reconstructed versions of that which is meaningfully and contextually appropriated as the story of Christianity. Thus, while the educated and literate caste Christians may evolve traditions based on the written scripture, the uneducated and illiterate Dalit Christians may have handed down traditions that are based more on oral versions of scriptural stories that made sense to their world.

Thus, scripture too is local, plural, and dynamic. Even though Christians have one fixed book — the Bible, which in its two parts (Old and New testaments) comprises of sixty-six books — it is the local and dynamic versions of oral scriptures that function in the life of the not-so-literate Dalit communities. Much needs to be done to identify the nature and function of oral scriptures in the life of Dalit Christians and the ways in which it is both dependent on and free from the written scripture. However, my own reflections merely problematize the notion that the Bible in its fixed, unitary written form operates as scripture and tradition in the lives of the Paraiyar. For example, in a Dalit village near Karunguzhi, South India, I became aware of the manner in which Dalit Christians carved out a meta-narrative of a Dalit Jesus by weaving together certain oral gospel stories in an ingenuous way. Two biblical narratives helped propagate this image of Jesus – a meta-story that is representative of the Dalit community's oral tradition and scripture. The first involved the story of Nicodemus, emphasizing the fact that Nicodemus came to Jesus by night (John 3: 1-21). An important implication of this narrative for the Dalit community stems from the fact that Nicodemus did not want to be seen interacting with Jesus; and yet he needed Jesus. Jesus was a kind of Dalit like them. Just as a Dalit could not be approached in public by respectable people of society, so also Jesus could not be associated with in public by people that mattered. They believed that Jesus was a Dalit in his time. The second gospel narrative they drew heavily upon was Jesus's encounter with the Samaritan women at the well (John 4: 1-45). Here importance is given to Jesus's request for a drink of water from the Samaritan well and from the vessel of a Samaritan. This took place within the historical context of first century Palestine where Jews were severely restricted in their social interaction with the Samaritans because of the latter's low social position. For this subaltern community of South India, Jesus thus becomes dalitized. He is deliberately baptized into the realm of the Dalit through his partaking of water from the common well and the common vessel of the Samaritan.

Focussing on the nature of the subaltern community's contextual Christian meta-story permits us to notice the local, plural, and dynamic functioning of scripture and tradition as they operate in the Christian context. The refiguring of the key symbol of Jesus through the collective experience of a Dalit community brings to the fore the process in which oral tradition and oral scripture nurture and nourish the religious life of living people. That which is remembered as scripture and tradition is influenced by what makes sense to the world of the Dalits. Oral scripture thus functions as normative for the community — it becomes the scripture of the Paraiyar in South India. Further, it also suggests that Christian scripture and tradition evolve in a manner that entails plurality. In modern Biblical scholarship, the accepted western tendency is to construct the historical Jesus from what are taken to be authentic textual sources. Thus, the corpus of the synoptic gospels (Matthew, Mark and Luke) are utilized as the most reliable textual sources. However, in the Dalits' reconstruction of Jesus from oral scriptures the Synoptic texts are ignored, and the somewhat suspect fourth gospel of John becomes the main source. What is historically suspect as written scripture in one Christian tradition is refurbished as the cornerstone of another oral tradition.

This notion of scripture and tradition informs my view of the contextual character of all theology. All theological projects are initiated and swayed by the historical context of the particular community involved in the dialogical discourse. One must, thus, question the categorization and the differentiation that is generally made between 'classical theology' and 'contextual theology'. If we take seriously the dominant proposition of one influential contemporary school of history, literature and philosophy, which advances the notion that all knowledge is intimately coupled with power and affected by the interests of the producers of scholarship, then, one can be instructed by the conditionality and contextually determined character of so-called 'classical theology'.

Finally, and briefly, I want to invoke the term constructive to label theological activity in order to highlight the beneficial and emancipatory character of doing theology. It is here that theology must move beyond the 'sterility', 'passive fatalism', 'anti-humanism' and 'anti-normativism' that some of the post-modern schools represent. Rather it can be instructed by the words of Cornel West when he says, 'The goal of reflection is amelioration, and its chief consequence is the transformation of existing realities.'[30]

Let me conclude this section on the 'constructive' character of theology by summing up the three themes that I have expounded. i) Human beings are continually constructing their conceptual and symbolic world. This happens even when they symbolize on the Divine; so human beings are required to take responsibility for this work. ii) While emphasizing this active dimension of the theological enterprise, there is also the need to retain the responsive element: human beings are being acted upon by 'The Divine' and by the traditions of the elders. iii) The term constructive also reminds us that theology aims towards something beneficial and fruitful in terms of collective and inclusive human living.

Theology as facilitating collective living under the Divine

Religion involves far more than what is proffered as other-worldly concerns. One need only take note of the intricate and continuous manner in which economic, political and social dynamics appear rooted in and solicit legitimation from religion. Theology acknowledges this relationship between religion and mundane human life. Thus, theology cannot but continually grapple with the question of how to order and organize human social life under the Divine.

Let me offer an example for my claim that religion inspires and authorizes human collective living. In India, the substantive and ontological difference between the caste community and the Dalits is grounded in an influential Hindu creation story. The norms of what constitutes human life and who is part of the human collective emerges from the theological implications of this myth. According to the *Vedas* (literally meaning knowledge), which is the revealed Scripture of the Hindus, 'God created the four *varnas* [human classes or castes] thus: The *Brahmin* from His head, the *Kshatriya* from His arms, the *Vaishya* from His thighs, and the *Shudra* from His feet.'[31] Two principles derived from this religious myth have governed human worldly affairs for centuries in India. On the one hand, knowledge that was produced and interpreted was legitimated when it originated from those who symbolized the head or the mouth, i.e. the Brahmins. The Brahmins produce and interpret religious knowledge with a view to maintaining overall order and harmony within society. Here discourse is defined and delimited according to the view of the Brahmins. On the other hand, this myth promulgated the theory that God's being only encompassed the members of the caste community. It suggests that there is no ground on which to warrant the anthropological claims of large section of the Indian population that lived outside the caste syste.

These are the outcasts or the Untouchables or the Dalits — the oppressed, the broken and crushed of Hindu society. The myth suggests that Dalits are ontologically separate from all other human beings. This means that their religious perspectives and their discursive and symbolic practices were easily jettisoned from the sphere of dialogical interaction.

It is within this historical and socio-religious context that Indian-Christian theology must concern itself with alternate forms of living collectively under the Divine. From the point of view of the Dalits, it is crucial that Indian-Christian theology facilitate a framework for collective living that includes and celebrates their humanity. Indian-Christian theology, thus, cannot but be intrinsically intertwined with human life and with how this can be lived collectively under God.

The Constructivist's methodology addresses this issue. Theologians are invited to start out with a metaphysical task which 'move[s] beyond the items and objects of experience itself to construct a notion of the context within which all experience falls'.[32] This idea of constructing a general conception of the world helps us work out a broad inter-relationship pattern within the framework of the cosmological system.[33] Human life is viewed in its relatedness to all else: collective living in relation to all created reality under the Divine involves both inter-relationship among all of creation and intrarelationship among human beings. The usefulness and the relevance of a cosmological and metaphysical conception of the world may be called into question from a Dalit standpoint. It hardly seems to do justice to the socio-political and economic factors that form the immediate and mundane network of forces that order and imprison the lives of a majority of Indian people. Who indeed from one of the oppressed communities is bestowed with the leisure for speculating about the cosmos and its metaphysical import for all of creation? Rather, is not the real world for subaltern communities the societal and economic environs that de-humanize them? And must not the materiality of the world, which impinges upon human beings in direct and commonplace ways, be the basis on which the concept of the 'world' is founded?

In my view theological method ought to start with an affirmation and exposition of the mundane and expressed world of the Dalits. Therefore, an effort is made towards sympathetically comprehending the 'real' world of the Dalits. However, my overall conception of theology incorporates the cosmological dimensions of the discourse of the Dalits. Theology, as stated is concerned with the task of 'collective living under the Divine'. This has to do with a broad cosmological notion of living in creaturely harmony under the Divine and a more confined anthropocentric view of living in human consonance under the Divine. I contend that both elements are present in this communal discourse: the aspects of living in cosmological relatedness and living in humane collectivity under the Divine.

One of the reasons for the lack of success of the liberational movements in India stems from the fact that social analysis has been divorced from the already internalized religious world-picture of the marginalized peoples. Conceivably, human beings need to ground their aspirations of freedom, liberation, and humanization upon their existing overall conception of living under the Divine. In this book I attempt to uncover the religious dimension of the Dalit worldview without slighting the materiality of its everyday social, economic and political functioning. This aspect of the theological enterprise, no doubt, has to do with its creaturely and humane character. Theology in any community is, in a sense, connected to the well being of all its practitioners. It critically and constructively configures ways by which the community attempts to live humanely and collectively under the Divine.

The term living collectively 'under the Divine' implies that whatever is taken to be the conception of the Divine/God is supreme with regard to both normativizing and relativizing everything else in this attempt to live collectively within a sensible, meaningful and orderly framework. In Christian theology this notion of the Divine/God is tied up with the conception of Jesus Christ, since it is through Jesus Christ that we claim to know who God is and what it means to live collectively in consonance with God. Thus the key to any Christian theology involves the category of Jesus Christ. This will be discussed in detail as a methodological issue in the final chapter. Furthermore, in chapter five I seek to retell this paradigmatic story of Jesus Christ through the experiences of the Dalits. It is funded by the same conviction that Indian-Christian theology will be enriched and empowered by employing the ears, eyes and minds of subaltern communities in reconstructing Jesus as the Christ. Suffice to say, at this point, that we can explain Christian theology's particularity by adding a supplementary clause to our general definition of theology. Christian theology, thus, is critical and constructive reflection on human dialogical symbolic interaction in its attempt to make sense of, find meanings in, and determine order for living collectively under God through the paradigm of Jesus Christ.

II. A Working Denouncement of Indian-Christian Theology: Deconstructive Propositions

Using the preceding discussion of theology I intend to evaluate the ways in which Indian-Christian theology has unfolded. Primarily, I shall constrict my discussion to the positively non-representative and possibly vested-interest character of Indian theology. While I want to maintain that the implications of the overall discussion involving Indian-Christian theology and the Dalits are applicable to the entire Christian community in India, in this section I shall deal only with Protestant Indian-Christian theology. Also, I deal only with that which is accepted as mainstream Protestant theology, which is almost entirely written and circulated in English.[34]

Indian-Christian theology as non-dialogical and non-representative of the symbolic interaction of the whole community

In general there are many classifications to understand and analyse Indian society — class, caste, gender, language and race; this study utilizes the caste paradigm. Traditionally, Indian social reality has been analysed in terms of the four-fold caste system and the fifth group of outcasts. Thus, while Hindu society embraced the four hierarchical castes (the Brahmins; the Kshatriya; the Vaisyas; and the Sudra), it was well established that there was a large proportion of people who lived outside this societal configuration. This outcast group is referred to as 'the outcaste' and claim the name Dalit. In South India, and in Tamil Nadu in particular, there is a characteristic absence of the Kshatriyas and the Vaisyas. South Indian society can thus be classified into a three-fold caste hierarchy — the Brahmins, who were the preservers and promoters of Sanskritic or Classical Hindu religious values and culture; the Sudras (non-Brahmin caste Hindus), who mostly lived in collaboration and assimilation with the Brahmins (this group can be further sub-divided into the pure-Sudras and the not-so-pure Sudras); and the Dalits, who were by and large cut-off from the everyday ritual and cultural life of the caste communities.[35] From the viewpoint of the Dalits, this tripartite division of South Indian society is more adequate and fruitful than its dualistic variants. I like to borrow Tyler's categorization to refer to the distinction between the Brahmin, the other caste Hindu and the Dalit streams of religious tradition: "the dominant, the dependent and the degraded".[36] Binary models (such as pure and polluted castes, right-hand and left-hand divisions, Brahminical and non-Brahminical communities, and Sanskritic and non-Sanskritic traditions) tend to obscure the radical fissure between the non-Brahmin caste communities and the Dalit communities by projecting the main split as existing between Brahmin and the non-Brahmin communities.[37]

Among these three major sections of Indian society, the Dalits seemed more ready than the Hindu communities to embrace Christianity. Thus historians argue that 'the modern Dalit movement began with what Christian missionaries called mass movement.'[38] The identity of the Dalits was to some extent shaped by the spread of Christianity among the rural Dalit populations. But this is not so much the focus of this reflection. Rather, it is concerned more with the fact that Christianity in India was transformed by the dalitization of the Christian church. Even if this impact was largely ignored, it must no longer be thought of as being irrelevant. The words of Webster are fitting here:

> The most important social fact about Christian congregations which I have confronted and which I find recent theologians have tended to ignore is that, while estimates vary, between 50% and 80% of all Christians in India today are from schedule caste origin. It is this social fact and its psychological consequence which I think we need to take as the most appropriate commonality for our theological constructions.[39]

Though Dalits account for a major proportion of Christians in India, Indian theology has largely ignored the factuality and fecundity of this socio-historical reality. This means that theology was constructed by the caste converts to Christianity with a passion to wed together their particular heritage with the Christian story, while traditions of the majority of the Dalit converts were considered inconsequential. Arvind P. Nirmal, a prominent Dalit theologian, draws our attention to this trend:

> Most of the contributions to Indian Christian theology in the past came from high caste converts to Christianity. The result has been that Indian Christian theology has perpetuated within itself what I prefer to call '*Brahmanic* tradition'.[40]

Reflecting upon this from the standpoint of subaltern communities, he concludes with a rhetorical question: 'One wonders whether this kind of Indian Christian theology will ever have a mass appeal.'[41] There is little doubt that it will neither have mass appeal nor mass relevance. But this does not alter the fact that in the past the voice of the Dalits has not been strengthened or considered as consequential to the theological task.

As stated, the focus of this review is limited to theology as expounded by Indian nationals from the Protestant Christian tradition. Indian-Christian Theology arose in the nineteenth century in response to neo-Hinduism or, 'neo-vedantism'. Traditionally, Hindu thought had been disinterested in foreign cultures and religions.[42] But the beginnings of a dialogue between Christianity and Hinduism was initiated by Ram Mohan Roy (1772-1833), a Hindu reformer and intellectual, who 'called for an openness towards and a willing to learn from Western science and Christian ethics.'[43] The Brahmo Samaj, which was founded by Roy, became one of the vibrant intellectual centres of the cultural renaissance and the Hindu philosophical and ethical reformation through the nineteenth century. It not only testified to a long and rich tradition of 'neo-vedantists', which extended the prospects of wedding together the principles of the vedanta with the teachings of Christianity, but it also encouraged the first attempts at contextual Christian theology. As Kaj Baago suggests, 'The first persons to attempt an indigenous interpretation of Christ in India were neither missionaries nor Indian Christians, but Brahmo Samajist.'[44] Some of the Brahmo Samaj's reputed leaders were Debendranath Tagore (1817-1905), Keshab Chandra Sen (1838-1884) and Pratap Chander Mozoomdar (1840-1905). It is important to note that the origins of Indian-Christian theology can be located in the context of the intense popularity and the extensive influence of the Brahmo movement. Thus, the agenda for Indian-Christian theology was set by caste Hindu (mainly Brahmin) intellectuals.

For their part, Indian-Christian theologians 'sought not only to establish the Christian truth against Brahmoism, but also showed a positive response to the Brahmo demand for a National Christianity.'[45] Along with this response-character of Indian-Christian theology to Brahmoism there was also a burning desire to express their own caste Hindu-Christian constitutedness. M.M. Thomas, referring to the pioneering work of Indian theologians in the nineteenth century, states:[46]

> They [Indian Christian theologies] were in the beginning mainly the reflections of converts or children of converts from Brahmanism to Christianity, who carried the dialogue between Christianity and Brahmanism within themselves and sought to express their faith in God, Christ and the Church in relation to their own past Hindu tradition in the setting of the Indian National self-awakening.

Krishna Mohan Banerjee (1813-1885), Brahmabandhav Uppadyay (1861-1907), and Lal Behari Dey (1824-1894) in Bengal; Nehemiah Gore (1825-1895), Narayan Vaman Tilak (1862–1919), and Pandita Ramabai (1858-1922) in Maharashtra; and A.S. Appasamy Pillai (1848-1926) in Madras exemplified this nineteenth century defence against Brahmoism and dialogue with caste Hinduism as Indian-Christian theology commenced in earnest. The theological implications of this inaugural era of Indian-Christian theology are clear. On the one hand, it revealed a posture of apologetics in response to the substantial theorizing of the burgeoning neo-vedantism of caste Hindus. In this regard, it is pertinent to add that M.M. Thomas's book, which is one of the main texts of Indian-Christian Theology, reflects this in its structure and content: the thoughts of Indian-Christian theologians are presented in the context of and in response to pre-eminent Hindu philosophers.[47] The respondent character of Indian-Christian theology to the principal agenda of caste Hinduism is evident. On the other hand, Indian-Christian theology in the nineteenth century made a concerted effort to prove itself as an integral part of an emerging national community by incorporating 'Indian' concepts and symbols from the 'Brahminic' tradition. Even a cursory reading of the works of the above mentioned Indian-Christian theologians points to the emphasis placed on reconciling the meaning of the Hindu scriptures (the Vedas) with the Christian scriptures (the Bible) and on reinterpreting the incarnation and atonement of Christ through the symbolism of Vedanta. The result was a vision of a national Christian church which would be a haven for Hindu-Christians, with the Hindu component seen primarily along Brahmanic lines.

The twentieth century saw the strengthening of these directions within Indian-Christian theology in response to specific historical challenges. First, in order to oppose the western Christian current of theological triumphalism and expansionism, Indian-Christian theology attacked the projected gap between Christianity and Indian religious traditions. There was a concentrated effort to denounce the claim of Christian exclusivism by explicating the harmonious relationship between Christian and Hindu religious themes. The neo-orthodox missionary theology, justifying the dialectic, even adversarial, relationship of Christianity to Hinduism, was rigorously and systematically challenged by Indian-Christian theologians. The most notable theological exchange took place around the International Missionary Conference at Tambaram (Madras) in 1938. A group of theologians active in this discourse came

to be called the 'Madras Re-thinking Group'. P. Chenchiah (1886–
1959), V. Chakkarai (1880–1958), Bishop V.S. Azariah (1874–1945),
S. Jesudason (1882–1969), and A.J. Appasamy (1891–1975) were some
of the pre-eminent theologians in this re-thinking Christianity group.
They continued to harmonize Hindu and Christian theologies as the
authentic expression of a truly indigenous Church community. This
involved a process which was directed towards

> an alliance between Christian theology, and different types of non-Christian
> philosophical thought, in order that the Hindu tradition may be transformed
> — not into a new syncretistic religion but into a Christianity which is
> simultaneously faithful to the *sruti* and yet culturally 'at home' in India.[48]

Second, the incorporation of the spirit of national independence led
to a theology of Indian renaissance. Referring to people like S.K. Rudra
(1861–1925), S.K. Datta (1878–1948), K.T. Paul (1876–1931) and
V.S. Azariah (1874–1945), Thomas comments, 'They were Christians
responding positively to the national renaissance, in their lay and spiritual
vocations, for avowedly Christian reasons.'[49]

Both these themes still remain alive in two of the most noted post-
independence thinkers: Paul D. Devanandan (1901–1962)[50] and M.M.
Thomas (1916–1996).[51] 'Devanandan's is primarily a theology of Christian participation in nation-building and of dialogue with religious
and secular faiths.'[52] Thomas, through his prolific theological writing,
represents a genuine attempt to present the Christian gospel within
the framework of India's quest for 'fuller humanity'. His theological
contribution emerged from the dialectic and dynamic interrelation between salvation, which is based on the life, death and resurrection of
Jesus Christ, and the continuing process of humanization, which finds
expression in the religious and political movements in India. Both
these theologians shifted the focus of dialogue. The Brahmanic traditions
of Hinduism was no longer the only dialogical partner for Christian
theology; rather, the political ideologies and secular movements that
strived toward humanization within the ethos of nationalism and national integration became a pre-eminent element in doing theology.
A major contribution of both these theologians is their capacity to
discern the collaboration between counter-ideological movements and
the process of liberation. The humanization current in popular anti-
Brahmin movements (in the case of Devanandan) and Marxist inspired
anti-capitalist movements (in the case of Thomas) were correlated with
the process of salvation in the movement the Christian community

founded on the Jesus event of 'cruciform humanity'. Despite their tremendous theological insight, these theological stalwarts of Independent India were unable to represent and articulate the voice of the Dalits. The caste Hindu agenda was not unveiled and confronted; instead a more secular and class-based discourse was propagated for a just nation.

These trends in Indian-Christian theology discussed above lead to three specific difficulties for the Christian Dalit communities. First, the foundation of Indian-Christian theology was laid by and for the elite minority of caste Hindus and caste Christians. Theology, thus, was done from the perspective and for the welfare of the caste Christians by drawing from their religious and cultural brahminic traditions. Second, it prevented theology from being interactive with the dialogical symbolic intercourse of the whole community. The reflective and critical construals of the vast majority of its constituents were not brought into the discursive arena. In so doing, it invalidates and repudiates the culture and religion of the Dalits. The latter constitutes a serious problem for the Dalits since Christian theology has failed to provide a framework within which it can interpret and integrate its particular communal experience. Third, the conscious forging of a unitary national movement and ideology tended to encourage hegemonic propensities. In the name of nationalism, the experiences and yearnings of the subaltern communities were sacrificed for the universal concerns of the nation as envisioned by caste communities. It may be relevant to end this discussion on Indian-Christian theology by quoting exhaustively from a recent appraisal by a renowned Dalit theologian. James Massey cogently summarizes the non-dialogical and non-representative features of Indian Christian theology over the last couple of centuries:

> The roots of the current Indian Christian theology lie in the experience of mostly upper caste/class christian converts of this century and the last. Well known examples are: Upadhaya, from a Bengali Brahmin family; Sadhu Sundar Singh, from a high caste, wealthy Punjabi Sikh family; Nehemiah Goreh, a Marathi Brahmin; H.A. Krishna Pillai, a high caste Vaishnavite non-Brahmin; Narayan Vaman Tilak, from a Brahmin family; A.J. Appasamy, from a high caste Saivite family; P. Chenchiah, from a Chetty, non-Brahmin upper caste in Tamilnadu; and so on.
>
> Now if these names are deleted from Indian Christian theology, nothing will be left. We must remember that these thinkers and their experiences and search were very different from those of an average Christian in India... These high caste converts' immediate concern was how they should relate or

interpret their new faith or experiences in Indian thought form, i.e. based on the Brahmanic religion and culture in which they had grown up...

Thus their theology did not address itself to or reflect the issues which the majority of the Christians faced either before or after they became Christians specially the Dalits.[53]

Indian-Christian theology as an instrument of ideological co-option rather than human liberation

Indian-Christian theology by excluding and ignoring the voice of the majority, who testify to centuries of oppression and marginalization, has been an ideological vehicle in the hands of the status quo. It could be said that theology sustained a process of hegemony by which the interests of the caste communities were espoused, strengthened and furthered in India.

An exegesis of the notion of hegemony is important here. There are various, sometimes conflicting, uses of the term hegemony. In this reflection I draw upon the work of Antonio Gramsci, particularly as expounded by Henry A. Giroux and Cornel West.[54] Gramsci (1891-1937) was an Italian socialist who founded the Communist Party in Italy in 1921. He became a theoretician and writer after his arrest by the Fascists in 1926. Although loyal to socialist ideas, Gramsci was radically uneasy with the economism and scientism of much of Marxist thinking. He devoted much time and effort into exploring and explicating both the non-economic means of exploitation and control of the masses and the role that the subaltern people themselves play in the perpetuation of such ideological mechanisms. Gramsci's expanded framework finds a much needed place for critically examining the role of culture and religion:

> Class struggle is not simply the battle between capitalists and the proletariat, owners and producers in the work situation. It also takes the form of cultural and religious conflict over which attitudes, values and beliefs will dominate the thought and behavior of people.[55]

Hegemony, in accordance with Gramsci, has the following two connotations. On the one hand, 'It refers to a process ... whereby a fundamental class exercises control through its moral and intellectual leadership over allied classes.'[56] There is no doubt that this is generally tied up with the already existing social and economic hierarchy within any given society; thus, this hegemonic process reinforces the legitimate authority of a certain class.[57] However, what is striking about this process is that this 'moral and intellectual leadership' is maintained through a superficial, though convincing, incorporation of the interests and belief-systems of the dominated class. On the other hand, hegemony 'points to the relationship between the dominant and the dominated classes'.[58] Interestingly, this relationship is seldom maintained by imposing the ideology of the dominant class upon the subaltern; rather the 'class exercises control' through the discriminating and artful use of existing institutional forms (in our case, this includes the sphere of religion) so as to float a symbolic pattern that appears inclusive, universal and normative for all. This in some ways disguises the exploitation and domination that the ideational structure consistently funds. In any case, this suggests that the dominated participate, most of the time unconsciously, in their own domination. However, I do not accept the fact that hegemony can be complete. The next section highlights subtle ways in which Christian Dalits are able to minimally actualize their own subjectivity through a process of sharing in some forms of hegemonic practice, while chapter three details the processes by which the subaltern communities creatively construe counter-hegemonic procedures.

The weaving of a meta-narrative, which combines together the Christian story with the tradition of the caste Hindus, has tended to serve hegemonic purposes. The cultural and religious traditions of one dominant group of Christians were gradually elevated to serve as the framework within which to do Christian theology. Within the sphere of Indian-Christian theology this may have served both the hegemonic interests of the caste people and the short-term benefits of the Christian Dalits. From the caste communities' point of view, they were given an opportunity to configure a normative master-narrative that combined together the heritage of their Hindu ancestors and the Christian story. From the point of view of the Dalits, they were given an opening to mask their real identity and live with illusory conviction that they were truly part of the overall Hindu society and heritage. As noted, on the one hand, the overall context of countering western force brought together caste Hindu and caste Christian theological efforts to produce a Brahmanic based Hindu-Christian theology. This was, on the other hand, combined with the spirit of nationalism, which evoked a unitary theological vision that ignored the particularly of the Dalits. Both these tendencies contributed to an ingenuous form of theological hegemony whereby the caste people within the community gradually established their tradition as the common and neutral heritage of all Christian people. This is again tied up with the a general process of establishing hegemonic control. The powerful group, in this case the caste people, elevate and valorize their tradition as the common, public and national tradition. This has a corresponding effect on subaltern communities. In this case the Dalits tend to denigrate and eject their own traditions, which are not commensurate with the common narrative. Raymond Williams points to this process of elevating 'selective tradition':

> At a philosophical level, at the true level of theory and at the level of the history of various practices, there is a process that I call the *selective tradition*: that which, within the terms of an effective dominant culture, is always passed off as 'the Tradition', *the* significant past. But always the selectivity is the point; the way in which from a whole possible area of past and present, certain meanings and practices are chosen for emphasis, certain other meanings and practices are neglected and excluded.[59]

III. Towards a Dialogical and Inclusive Theological Project: Recollection and Remembering of Dalit Voices

In the case of the Dalits there have been two ways in which they have responded to this process of theologizing, which transpired to interpret the Christian story through the caste Hindu tradition. The first, is analogous to 'sanskritization'. According to M.N. Srinivas,

> Sanskritization is the process by which a 'low' Hindu caste, or tribe or other group, changes its customs, ritual, ideology or way of life in the direction of a high, and frequently 'twice-born', caste.[60]

The chief aim for such collective refigurations is to acquire a better social location within the hierarchy. Therefore, it is not surprising that 'generally such changes are followed by a claim to a higher position in the caste hierarchy than that traditionally conceded to the claimant caste by the local community.'[61]

Srinivas is describing a sociological phenomenon. Nonetheless, this is not irrelevant to the Dalit communities and the dynamics of Indian-Christian theology. In South India mass conversion to Christianity was a social movement. Many of the communities that embraced Christianity came from Dalit and the not-so-pure Sudra communities. They were fleeing their past and risking a new and liberated future away from centuries of caste and class oppression. But this flight from the past also gave them an option to enter into a new and transformed symbolic framework. This framework of Indian-Christian theology facilitated the blossoming of an appropriate symbolic nexus whereby the caste people could reclaim their history and their new found faith. But it also gave Dalit Christians the occasion to be housed by a ready-made caste Hindu symbolic world that was more esteemed and venerated than their own tradition.

This dimension of theology has been underplayed by both the caste and Dalit Christians. The caste Christians assumed that what they circulated under the label 'Indian-Christian Theology' is genuinely a pan-Indian theological expression. The Dalits generally failed to admit to their tacit compliance with certain forms of Indian theology. Instead of interpreting this as an act of subaltern agency to forge a kind of transformed subjectivity, the usual rationale points to the helpless and marginalized situation of the Dalits. This is no doubt true. However, one cannot ignore the copious and well-thought out critical responses of other non-Christian Dalit thinkers, as early as in the 1920s. One need only point to the intensely critical and popular writing of B.R. Ambedkar.[62]

But what happened to the voice of the Dalit Christians? For many decades they cherished the hope that Christianity would liberate them from caste oppression. This aspiration may not have had much to do with reality. Ambedkar bemoans the fact that even though 'caste is no doubt primarily the breath of Hindus... everybody is infected, Sikh, Muslim and Christian.'[63] Nonetheless, Dalit Christians lived with this somewhat unrealistic assumption that their conversion would bring them a new status in society as a whole and within the Christian community in particular.[64] But their overall silence also may have resulted from their desire to uplift themselves from their Dalit status by donning the religious identity of the caste people as expressed in Indian-Christian theology. A caste Hindu based theology served the purposes of sanskritization. By inhabiting the representations of the caste peoples the Dalits could claim to have a 'higher position' in the community. Indian-Christian theology, thus, in its caste Hindu guise provided Dalits with the illusive feeling that Christianity is liberative since it incorporated them within the one complete and undivided pan-Indian theological framework. It also served as an ideology for their own social mobility by giving them access to the claim that they too live out of the caste Hindu traditions.

A second way in which Dalits have responded to the course of Indian-Christian theology can be termed 'liberationism'. The beginning of this movement can be traced to a radical and innovative address entitled 'Towards a Sudra Theology', delivered by Arvind P. Nirmal at the United Theological College in Bangalore in March 1981. This was a watershed event, in that it called upon Dalits to shun theological passivity and sociological camouflage in order to embrace the more demanding task of reclaiming the liberative ends of theology. The tacit inclination towards theological sanskritization was confronted and a new way that put the motif of liberation at the centre was opened.[65] This model, I believe, continues to influence the direction of Dalit-based theological reflection. Liberation is central to theology. In my reflections concerning theology, I have stated that theology has to do with facilitating humane and collective living under the Divine. This includes a sense of what it means to live with justice and freedom in the economic, social, political and religious realms. The term 'liberationalism', however, is deliberately adopted in order to draw attention to some of the shortcomings that prevent the flourishing of a comprehensive liberational thrust in Indian-Christian theology.

Like many 'isms', 'liberationism' is simultaneously too narrow and too broad. It is too narrow because its focus is limited to the economic and the social realms of life. On the one hand, it utilizes the economic based analysis that is expounded by Latin American theology which is the inspiration behind much of Indian liberation theology. On the other hand, it expands the focus of a merely economic analysis to encompass the particularity of the social phenomenon of caste. What is hardly dealt with within this process of analysis are the elements of religion and culture.[66] In a sense this plays into the hands of the forces that want to obscure Dalit culture and religious forms as if they are either defiled and unworthy because they represent the collective symbolic expression of the Dalits or because they merely reflect the clever and cunning creations of the caste communities that are passively adopted by the Dalits.[67]

The term 'liberationism' is too broad because it easily glosses over provincial and contextual complexities in its desire to project universal scope. The breadth of 'liberationism' tends to construct liberation in terms that find commonality with all oppressed communities throughout the world. At times this neglects to do justice to the particularity and complexity of the nature of local emancipation. For example, in the case of the Dalits, liberation from the dominant and coercive powers of caste religion is definitely needed. However, turning their backs completely on their own religion and culture which has sustained them through centuries, may in fact be a collective act of avoidance: an attempt to evade and dodge their own identity and selfhood. In a way it is a caving in to the enticement of sanskritization.

Thorough emancipation for Dalits cannot be achieved without a direct encounter and reconciliation with their history, which is inclusive of religion and culture. Of course, liberation may involve a conscious rejection of Dalit religion. But this rejection must come through a process of looking squarely into the face of Dalit religion and culture. Thus liberation for the Dalits involves taking a journey into their religion and culture. Liberation in a holistic sense includes finding the Dalit identity through encountering the various forms manifested in its particular cultural and religious collective representations. In the words of Minz, 'The self-understanding of the Dalits and the Tribals cannot be completed without discussing their problems along with the God/Gods they worship.'[68]

Another encumbrance of 'liberationism' is its enigmatic epistemological premise. On the one hand, it wants to maintain that Dalit epistemology is founded in the experience of pathos. In the words of Nirmal:

> For a Dalit theology Pain or Pathos is the beginning of knowledge. For the sufferer, more certain than any principle, more certain than any proposition, more certain than any thought and more certain than any action is his/her pain.[69]

He goes on to conclude that 'it is in this pain-pathos that the sufferer knows God.'[70] However, on the other hand, 'liberationism' fails to utilize traditional Dalit representations of the knowledge of God that have emerged through centuries of unparalleled community pain and pathos. Instead, Dalit liberationism's explication of pathos is worked out mainly within the Christian symbolic world. In Nirmal's own theologizing there is a wedding together of the pathos that comes out of the alienation and oppression which has shaped the historical consciousness of the Dalit people with the dalitness of Jesus Christ. This theological effort under the banner 'Dalit theology' must be lauded as a genuine contextual application of the correlation method. But, it is strange that the Dalits' religious and cultural world, which represents their knowledge of God through the centuries of experiencing pain-pathos, does not become a site for locating knowledge about the Divine. The particularized manner in which the Dalits experienced the Divine presence and power at the threshold of suffering ('pathos') is completely slighted. My criticism of the epistemology of 'liberationism' can be restated in the following way: while it affirms that the experience of pain-pathos is the source of knowledge about God, it fails to take seriously the symbolization of this experience of pain-pathos that is manifested by Dalit religion. Therefore, there is an unwillingness to work under the directives of its own epistemological presuppositions.

Keeping the limitations of both the 'sanskritization' and the 'liberationism' approach in mind, my own theological exercise attempts to present a third option. In continuity with my critical reworking of A.P. Nirmal, I want to affirm that the constructive approach that has been laid out in this chapter can be fruitfully employed for doing liberation theology within the Indian situation.[71] It incorporates the communal, critical, constructive, contextual and liberational needs of Indian-Christian theology. Furthermore, this particular constructive model is most suited to Dalits, even as it leads to the expansion of the scope of theology itself. First, it deliberately and substantively includes the collective religious world of the Dalits. This is necessary in order for theology to be faithful to its ambition of being critical and constructive reflection on the social interaction of the whole community. Also, by circulating these resources into the dialogical discourse, theology sets into motion a process that may counter the hegemonic forces of ideology. Second, it constructively refigures a framework that would lead to a humane and collective way of living under God for the community, particularly inclusive of the people struggling against the multidimensional forces of hegemony. It does this by resurrecting the religion of Dalits which we presume sustained and nourished them through centuries of oppression.

The liberational aspect of what I propose to do is two-fold. On the one hand, theology is liberated. Indian-Christian theology accepts its critical and constructive task to reflect on the symbolic interaction of its entire community. It is funded by the dialogical voices of an inclusive community.[72] In this sense theology is praxis. Inclusivity, dialogical interaction and empowerment form the theological means and substance for reflection and practice. On the other hand, theology becomes the locus of Dalit liberation. This is so because liberation in a comprehensive sense for the Dalits must confront their identity. Not merely the identity that is forced upon them by the dominant caste communities but also the identity as they experienced and comprehended it among themselves and before the Divine.[73]

The most pressing need that could initiate this process of theologizing within the Indian context has to do with an enquiry into the Dalit people, in particular their cultural and religious expressions that may provide us with clues of their notions of God and themselves. 'Remembrance recalls past misery as well as past hope.'[74] The religious world of Dalits must have been a sanctuary built from both of these: without misery it would not have been sincere and without hope it would not have preserved them as human beings. Sharon Welch succinctly states the relationship between theology that is liberational and forms of knowledge that are suppressed:

> To state that liberation theology is an insurrection of subjugated knowledge means that the discourse of liberation theology represents the resurrection of knowledge suppressed by a dominant theology and a dominant culture. Further analysis involves three elements of genealogy: (1) the preservation and communication of memories of conflict and exclusion; (2) the discovery and exposition of excluded contents and meanings; and (3) the strategic struggle between the subjugated and dominant knowledges.[75]

In the following chapter I shall attempt 'an insurrection of subjugated knowledge'. As argued in the course of this chapter, I believe that this is in the overall interest of liberation theology. It liberates both Indian-Christian theology, by making it more inclusive and representative of the symbolic interaction of the whole community, and the Dalits, by unveiling and countering their sanskritizing tendency and valorizing their own symbolic world so as to facilitate an authentic and contextual quest toward humane and collective living under God. In the next chapter, in order to avert the sanskritization lure, an attempt has been made to unearth the central religious elements of one of the Dalit communities living in Tamil Nadu. Furthermore, to avoid the drawbacks of 'liberationism', I shall keep the study of the religion and culture of Dalits as local as possible by analysing one particular Dalit community, the Paraiyar.

Notes

1. The relationship of the Dalits to the Hindu community is complex and volatile. My own analyses stress the discontinuities between Dalit communities and Hindu communities, which, as I shall demonstrate through this book, does not mean that there are no continuities and congruences. For a recent scholarly, though polemic, contribution to flesh out this disjunction between Dalits and caste Hinduism see, Kancha Ilaiah, *Why I am Not a Hindu: A*

Sudra Critique of Hindutva Philosophy, Culture and Political Economy (Calcutta: Samya, 1996).

2. James Massey, *Towards Dalit Hermeneutics: Re-reading the Text, the History and the Literature* (New Delhi: ISPCK, 1994), p. 31.

3. See James Massey, *Roots: A Concise History of the Dalits* (New Delhi: ISPCK, 1994), p. 7.

4. The Dalits have long resisted the term that M.K. Gandhi used to refer to them: Harijan, which literally means 'the children of God'. This nomenclature was, no doubt, adopted in good faith by Gandhi in order to represent those communities, which were reckoned to be polluted and polluting to the conscientious Hindu, as favored human beings. However, the use of this word to refer to these oppressed and marginalized communities did have negative consequences from the Dalits' point of view: it led to a condescending attitude among the caste people; it veiled the actual social, economic, and political plight of the Dalits; and it gave the caste Hindus an illusion that they had transformed their relationship to the Dalits.

5. This definition is influenced by the Constructive Theology perspective. Because of my long association with Gordon D. Kaufman, I shall use his writings as representative of this school. There is no doubt that Kaufman has greatly influenced my thinking on theological method. I do, however, deliberately utilize the term 'The Divine' rather than Kaufman's symbol 'God' for the following reasons. (1) The concept of The Divine is much more generic to the varied religious traditions that are represented in India. This is particularly relevant since the different languages in India use different words to refer to the idea of the Divine. (2) The term God still retains a gender-specific connotation, which does not incorporate the important and influential goddess traditions of India. (3) There is much value in the traditional distinction made between two uses of the term God, one that denotes the referent and the other the symbol: *Gott* and *Gottheit* (Eckhart), *Nirguna Brahman* and *Saguna Brahman* (Hinduism's distinction between God without and with attributes), 'The God beyond God' and God (Paul Tillich), and 'the Real God' and 'the available God' (Kaufman). I believe that one must make a distinction between the referent (what the symbol wants to symbolize) and the symbol in theologizing, mostly in order to preserve the universal and open-ended character of the referent. Thus, as suggested by Organ, I utilize 'God' as the symbol and 'The Divine' as the referent. See Troy Wilson Organ, *Third Eye Philosophy: Essays in East-West Thought* (Athens, Ohio: Ohio University Press, 1987), p. 1–14. Also for source material on Constructive Theology, see Rebecca S. Chopp and Mark Lewis Taylor, eds., *Reconstructing Christian Theology* (Minneapolis: Fortress Press, 1994) and Denise L. Carmody, *Christian Feminist Theology: A Constructive Interpretation* (Oxford, UK: Blackwell Publishers, 1995).

6. Brian K. Smith, *Reflections on Resemblance, Ritual, and Religion* (New York: Oxford University Press, 1989), p.4.

7. Paulo Freire, *Pedagogy of the Oppressed*, (New York, Continuum, 1990), p. 77.
8. See my discussion of 'sanskritization' and 'liberationism' in the last section of this chapter.
9. I am thankful to my colleague David C. Scott for his perceptive criticisms on my own ambiviance with regard to this issue of conflating the advocacy function of theology with the objectives of an inclusive and plural theological community. See David C. Scott, 'Theological Reflection in Multiform Comminity: A Response to the Contextual Indian Proposal for Constructive Christian Theology', in *Bangalore Theological Forum*, vol. XXIX, nos. 1 and 2 (March & June, 1997): 112–17.
10. Jyoti Sahi, 'Dance in the Wilderness', in *Doing Theology with Asian Resources*, volume II, ed. Yeow Choo Lak (Singapore: ATESEA, 1995), p. 113.
11. My professor at Harvard Divinity School, Richard R. Niebuhr, first introduced me to the enormous possibilities of doing 'theographia'. The many twists that I give to this concept though are my own. It must be admitted, however, that this critical and constructive reflective undertaking, as one can well notice, is very much unimodal. Nonetheless, it will linguistically reflect upon forms of symbolic intercourse that are not transacted in language as understood by spoken and written communication.
12. 'Imaginative construction is the proper — indeed, the *only mode* — through which one can become aware of God in his [sic] full autonomy and self-integrity.' *Gordon D. Kaufman, An Essay on Theological Method*, Revised Edition, (Missoula: Scholars Press, 1979), p. 34. Emphasis mine.
13. Ibid., p. 43.
14. I am aware that these interrelated ideas of (1) the open-ended nature of human beings and (2) the plasticity of reality as construed by human beings have a long and influential history. William James is a notable advocate of the latter. For example he states:

> we *add*, both to the subject and to the predicate part of reality. The world stands really malleable, waiting to receive its final touches at our hands. Like the kingdom of heaven, it suffers human violence willingly. Man [sic] *engenders* truths upon it.

William James, *Pragmatism and The Meaning of Truth* (Cambridge, MA.: Harvard University Press, 1978), p. 123. Emphasis in text. Clifford Geertz is the most renowned proponent of the former. Talking about human beings he says:

> We are, in sum, incomplete or unfinished animals who complete or finish ourselves through culture — and not through culture in general but through highly particular forms of it: Dobuan and Javanese, Hopi and Italian, upper-class and lower-class, academic and commercial.

Clifford Geertz, *The Interpretation of Culture* (New York: Basic Books, 1973), p. 49. In quoting Geertz it must be kept in mind that he presents religion as a cultural system. For an example of how these ideas take on theological expression, see Gordon Kaufman, *In Face of Mystery: A Constructive Theology* (Cambridge, MA.: Harvard University Press, 1993), pp. 112–24.

15. Ibid., p. 64.

16. Michel Foucault has been a powerful and systematic thinker in our century to explore and explicate the non-economic dimensionalities of power. His particular interest and ingenuity for our purposes lies in the capturing and expounding of the constructive and productive nature of the ideational. In his words,

> We must cease once and for all to describe the effects of power in negative terms: it 'excludes', it 'censures', it 'abstracts', it 'masks', it 'conceals'. In fact, power produces; it produces reality; it produces domains of objects and rituals of truth.

Michel Foucault, *Discipline and Punish: The Birth of The Prison,* trans. Alan Sheridan (New York: Vintage Books, 1979), p. 194.

Furthermore, in Foucault's view, power is integrally linked to knowledge: 'power/knowledge'. The process of human interaction thus 'cannot but evolve, organize, and put into circulation a knowledge, or rather an apparatus of knowledge.' Michel Foucault, *Power/Knowledge: Selected Interview and Other Writings, 1972–1977,* ed. Colin Gordon, (New York: Pantheon Books, 1980), p. 102. A Foucauldian analysis helps us comprehend the productive and constructive nature of knowledge. More specifically it directs the theologian to take note of the overall ramifications of her work.

17. Gustavo Gutierrez, *The Power of the Poor in History* (New York: Orbis Books, 1983), p. 65.

18. Robert J. Schreiter, *Constructing Local Theologies* (Maryknoll, NY: Orbis Books, 1986), p. 17.

19. Paolo Freire suggests a notion of 'cultural synthesis' for revolutionary action, which involves the dialogical coordination of leaders and the local people:

> The oppressor elaborates his theory of action without the people, for he stands against them. Nor can the people — as long as they are crushed and oppressed, internalizing the image of the oppressor — construct for themselves the theory of their liberating action. Only in the encounter of the people with the revolutionary leaders — in their communion, in their praxis — can this theory be built.

Pedagogy of the Oppressed, p. 185–6.

20. Juan Luis Segundo, *The Liberation of Theology* (Maryknoll, NY: Orbis Books, 1976), p. 13. James Cone's work also exemplifies an endeavour of doing theology from a prior commitment to a particular historical community. Cone consciously commits himself to lift up the representations of God as experienced and appropriated by the Black community in the United States of America. In his words, 'Black theology must take seriously the reality of black people ...This must be the point of departure of all God-talk which

seeks to be black-talk.' James H. Cone *Black Theology and Black Power* (San Francisco: Harper and Row, 1989), p. 117. More pertinent to the relationship between particularized experience and theological conceptualization, he writes:

> There is no truth for and about black people that does not emerge out of the context of their experience... This means that there can be no Black Theology which does not take the black experience as a source for its starting point.

James H Cone, *God of the Oppressed* (San Francisco: Harper and Row, 1975), p. 17 f.

21. This advocacy posture has been developed in Christian Feminist Theology, through an explication of the conceptual relevance of the 'Women-Church', primarily by Elizabeth Schussler Fiorenza and Rosemary Radford Ruether. See Elizabeth Schussler Fiorenza, *In Memory of Her: A Feminist Reconstruction of Christian Origins* (New York: Crossroads, 1983), pp. 1–95 and *Bread Not Stone: The Challenge of Feminist Biblical Interpretation* (Boston: Beacon Press, 1984), pp. 1–42. See Rosemary Radford Ruether, *Sexism and God-Talk* (Boston: Beacon Press, 1983). Also see Rebecca S. Chopp, *The Power to Speak: Feminism, Language, God* (New York: Crossroads, 1991).

22. *The Nature of Doctrine: Religion and Theology in a Postliberal Age* (Philadelphia: The Westminster Press, 1984), p. 118.

23. Ronald F. Thiemann, 'Response to George Lindbeck', *Theology Today*, no. 43 (1986): 378.

24. Richard Lints, 'The Postpositive choice', *Journal of the American Academy of Religion*, vol. LXI/no. 4 (Winter, 1993): 659.

25. Stephen L. Stell, 'Hermeneutics in Theology and the Theology of Hermeneutics: Beyond Lindbeck and Tracy', *Journal of the American Academy of Religion*, vol. LXI/no. 4 (Winter, 1993): 694.

26. Even though this is not accented in his work, Kaufman's overall approach has consistently affirmed a relationship between the *'presence'* of the real (God) and the imaginative constructive activity of theology. In his most recent work he writes:

> It is sometimes supposed that a constructivist approach to theology implies that our religious symbols consist in *nothing more* than our fanciful imaginings. That is, however, a seriously misleading over-simplification. Theological reflection and construction are human responses to what is believed to be *really there* in the world, what has brought us into being as human and sustains us in being; responses, thus...to God's own activity.

Gordon Kaufman, *In Face of Mystery*, p. 486. Also see his book *The Theological Imagination: Constructing the Concept of God* (Philadelphia: The Westminster Press, 1981) p. 48–51.

27. I am deliberately putting the Divine first sequentially when talking about the dialogue between God and Human beings.

28. Lash puts it well.

We can and must tell the story differently. But we do so under constraint: what we may *not* do, if it is *this* text which we are to continue to perform, is to tell a different story.

Nicholas Lash, *Theology on the Way to Emmaus* (London: SCM Press, 1986), p. 44. I shall deal with the implications of this in the final chapter that is an experiment in christology.

29. In general the classification of Indian religious tradition in India is influenced by Robert Redfield's distinction between the 'great' and the 'little' traditions. In India this is contextually developed by Milton Singer (Great tradition of Sanskritic Hinduism and the Little tradition of non-Sanskritic Hinduism) and M.N. Srinivas (All-India Hinduism and Local Hinduisms). See Milton Singer, *When a Great Tradition Modernizes* (New York: Praeger Publishers, 1972); M.N. Srinivas, *Religion and Society Among the Coorgs of South India*, (London: Oxford University Press, 1952) and *The Village Remembered* (Berkeley: University of California Press, 1976). My own three fold classification stems from taking the Dalit historical and socio-religious context seriously. I maintain that a two-fold schema undercuts the necessity to study Dalit religion as a semi-autonomous social, religious, and cultural sphere.

30. Cornel West, *Prophesy Deliverance! An Afro-American Revolutionary Christianity* (Philadelphia: The Westminster Press, 1982), p. 21.

31. This is a colloquial version of the following translation:

When they divided primal Man, Into how many parts did they divide him? What was his mouth? What his arms? What are his thighs called? What his feet? The Brahman was his mouth, The arms were made the Prince, His thighs the common people, And from his feet the serf was born.

(*Rig-Veda*, X, xc. 11 & 12); R.C. Zaehner, *Hindu Scriptures* (London: J.M. Dent & Sons, 1966), pp. 9–10. Also see, James Massey, *Towards Dalit Hermeneutics*, p. 90–1.

32. Kaufman, *An Essay on Theological Method*, p. 47.

33. Ibid., pp. 59–65. See also Kaufman, *Theology for a Nuclear Age*, (Philadelphia: The Westminster Press, 1985), pp. 16–46.

34. I am thankful to my colleague, O.V. Jathanna, for bringing this to my notice. The implications of this is that interaction between Dalits and the Christian gospel could have taken place at a local level in the vernacular. However, a study of Tamil hymns and lyrics do not give us any indication that the worldview of the Dalits in Tamil Nadu were incorporated into the theological expressions of the same.

35. The tripartite schema is suggested by Andre Beteille, *Caste, Class and Power: Changing Patterns of Stratification in a Tanjore Village* (Berkeley: University of California Press, 1965). Also see Pauline Kolenda 'Caste in South India', in *Studies of South India: An Anthology of Recent Scholarship*, eds, Robert E. Frykenberg and Pauline Kolanda (Madras: New Era Publications, 1985), pp.

239–63 and Burton Stein, *Peasant State and Society in Medieval South India* (Oxford: Oxford University Press, 1980), pp. 30–62.

36. As quoted in Gail Omvedt, *Dalits and the Democratic Revolution: Dr. Ambedkar and the Dalit Movement in Colonial India* (New Delhi: Sage publishers, 1994), p. 36. For further reading see, Stephen Tyler, *India on Anthropological Perspective* (San Francisco: Good Year Publishing House, 1983).

37. It must be noted that there is an exception to this when it comes to certain overt symbolic functions performed by the Dalits in order to reiterate their low status. This is particularly true of village festivals in which the Dalits are expected to perform certain roles that submit to the hierarchy maintained by the caste community.

38. John C.B. Webster, *The Dalit Christians: A History* (Delhi: ISPCK, 1992), p. 33. He goes on to add that 'while in some parts of India there were Dalits who chose to become Muslims or Sikhs, the vast majority of Dalit converts throughout the country became Christians.' This further strengthens the point that Christianity certainly impacted the Dalit community in India in a profound manner.

39. John C.B. Webster 'From Indian Church to Indian Theology: An Attempt at Theological Construction', in *A Reader in Dalit Theology*, ed. Arvind P. Nirmal (Madras: Gurukul, 1992), p. 95.

40. Arvind P. Nirmal, *Heuristic Explorations* (Madras: The Christian Literature Society, 1990), p. 27.

41. Ibid.

42. Wilhelm Halbfass, *India and Europe: An Essay in Understanding* (Albany: SUNY, 1988), p. 172.

43. Ibid., p. 215.

44. Kaj Baago, *Pioneers of Indigenous Christianity* (Madras: CLS, 1969), p. 10.

45. M.M. Thomas, *The Acknowledged Christ of the Indian Renaissance* (Madras: CLS, 1970), p. 38–9.

46. M.M. Thomas and P.T. Thomas, *Towards an Indian Christian Theology: Life and Thought of Some Pioneers* (Tiruvalla: New Day Publications, 1992), p. 4.

47. M.M. Thomas, *The Acknowledged Christ.*

48. Robin Boyd, *An Introduction to Indian Christian Theology* (Madras: CLS, 1969), p. 263.

49. M.M. Thomas, *The Acknowledged Christ.* p. 242.

50. For a thorough understanding of Devanandan's thought see, *Paul D. Devanandan: Selected Writing with Introduction*, vol. I and II, ed. Joachim Wietzke (Madras: CLS, 1983 and 1986).

51. Among M.M. Thomas's work, the following are relevant: *Salvation and Humanization* (Madras: CLS, 1971); *Man and the Universe of Faiths* (Madras: CLS, 1975); *The Secular Ideologies of India and the Secular Meaning of Christ* (Madras: CLS, 1976), *Religion and the Revolt of the Oppressed* (Delhi: ISPCK, 1981); and *Risking Christ for Christ's Sake* (Geneva: WCC, 1987).

52. M.M. Thomas and P.T. Thomas, *Towards an Indian Christian Theology*, p. 188.

53. James Massey, 'Ingredients for a Dalit Theology', in *Indigenous People: Dalits, Dalit Issues in Today's Theological Debate* (New Delhi: ISPCK, 1994), p. 339.

54. Henry A. Giroux, *Ideology, Culture, and the Process of Schooling* (Philadelphia: Temple University Press, 1981) and Cornel West, *Prophecy Deliverance!*, pp. 118–27. Also see Carl Boggs, Gramsci's Marxism (London: Pluto Press, 1976), pp. 36–84 and Walter L. Adamson, *Hegemony and Revolution: A Study of Antonio Gramsci's Political and Cultural Theory* (Berkeley: University of California Press, 1980), pp. 104–246.

55. West, *Prophecy Deliverance!*, p. 118–19.

56. Giroux, *Ideology, Culture, and the Process of Schooling*, p. 23.

57. This must be emphasized because there may be a tendency to delink the cultural and religious aspects of hegemonic control from the economic aspects. This is clearly not how Gramsci interpreted hegemony. He sees a connection between both these dimensions of human activity. A quote from David Forgacs, ed., *An Antonio Gramsci Reader* (New York: Schocken Books, 1988) expresses Gramsci's views succinctly. In Gramsci's words

> Undoubtedly the fact of hegemony presupposes that account be taken of the interests and tendencies of the groups over which hegemony is to be exercised, and that a certain compromise equilibrium should be formed – in other words that the leading group should make sacrifices of an economic-corporate kind. But there is also no doubt that such sacrifices and such a compromise cannot touch the essential: for though hegemony is ethico-political it also must be economic, must necessarily be based on the decisive function exercised by the leading group in the decisive nucleus of economic activity (pp. 211–12).

For a brief commentary on the term hegemony as found in Gramsci's writings see ibid., pp. 422–4.

58. Ibid.

59. Raymond Williams, 'Base and Superstructure in Marxist Cultural Theory', in *Schooling and Capitalism: A Sociological Reader*, ed. Roger Dale et al. (London: Routledge & Kegan Paul, 1976), p. 205.

60. M.N. Srinivas, *Social Change in Modern India* (Hyderabad: Orient Longman, 1972), p. 6.

61. Ibid.

62. It is noteworthy to observe the reclamation and celebration of Ambedkar's work by the Dalit Christian movement. There was a National Seminar to commemorate Ambedkar's birth centenary put together by the Department of Dalit Theology of Gurukul Lutheran Theological College in Madras from April 11–13, 1991. See Arvind P. Nirmal and V. Devasahayam, eds, *Dr. B.K. Ambedkar: A Centenary Tribute*, (Madras: Gurukul, 1991).

63. B.R. Ambedkar, *Annihilation of Caste*, (Bangalore: Dalit Sahitya Akademi, 1987), p. 78. This book was first published in 1936.
64. I say unrealistic because in actual fact Christian Dalits became doubly oppressed and alienated. Chatterji states this clearly. He says:

> The Christian dalits are 'twice-alienated'. They are regarded by the society's non-dalits, whether rich or poor, in the same way as are the dalits and tribals and they suffer from the same economic, social, and educational disparities as the other dalits. In addition, the hope of the dalit converts for a better life, free from stigma and humiliation, appears not to have been fulfilled for the bulk of them within the churches.

Saral K. Chatterji 'Why Dalit Theology?', in *A Reader in Dalit Theology*, p. 29. Also see K. Wilson, *The Twice Alienated* (Hyderabad: Booklinks Corporation, 1982) and Antony Raj, 'The Dalit Christian Reality in Tamilnadu', in *Jeevadhara*, xxii/128 (March, 1992).
65. For an excellent review of Nirmal's contribution to Dalit theology, see J. Russell Chandran, 'A.P. Nirmal: A Tribute', in *Bangalore Theological Forum*, vol. XXIX, nos. 1 & 2 (March & June, 1997): 19–35.
66. A.M. Abraham Ayrookuzhiel is an exception to this trend in that he has consistently studied the religion and culture of the Dalits in parts of South India. However, in my judgement he remained only a social scientist and was unable to reflect theologically on his finding that Dalits' exhibited a 'counter-culture'. See next note for relevant publications.
67. The first attitude stems from an internalization of the caste mind-set, which presumes an oppositional relationship between the religion and culture of the caste Hindus and that of the Dalits: the former is pure, holy and good while the latter is polluted, profane and evil. The second attitude is influenced by Dumont's work on Indian religion and society. Ayrookuzhiel is a good contemporary example of this view. He seems to project Dalit religion primarily either as a passive product of 'vedic and puranic myths...serving the interests of the dominant castes and classes' or as a form of 'counter culture' that expresses itself in a form of anti-brahminism. See A.M. Abraham Ayrookuzhiel, 'Dalits Move Toward the Ideology of Nationality', in *A Reader in Dalit Theology*, p. 175–8. Also see his book *Swami Anand Thirth-Untouchability: Gandhian Solution on Trial* (Delhi: ISPCK, 1987), pp. 43–50 and 'Dalit Theology: A Movement of Counter-Culture', in M.E. Prabhakar, ed., *Towards a Common Dalit Theology* (New Delhi: ISPCK, 1988), pp. 83–103.
68. Nirmal Minz, 'Dalit-Tribal: A Search for a Common Ideology', in *Toward A Common Dalit Ideology*, p. 106.
69. Arvind P. Nirmal, 'Doing Theology from A Dalit Perspective', in *A Reader in Dalit Theology*, p. 141.
70. Ibid.
71. I want to reiterate that this third option really builds upon the work of the Dalit theologians working within what I have termed the 'liberationist'

collective. Although it modifies and qualifies their theologies, it is, nonetheless, quite influenced by and very much in line with the general direction of the following three pioneers of Dalit theology: A.P. Nirmal, James Massey and M.E. Prabhakar.

72. Kaufman in his explication of theology as conversation underscores this inclusivity:

> In this interchange among many diverse voices, each with its own concerns, academic theology would also have its own particular 'advocacy': namely, the maintenance of a free and open ongoing conversation, as inclusive as possible, on theological issues.

Kaufman, *In Face of Mystery*, p. 68. I have already argued that I think that it takes more than agreeing on the principle of maintaining such ground rules (freedom, openness, and inclusivity) if theology actually wants to benefit and be enriched by the discourse of the whole community.

73. For a detailed discussion of the relationship between memory and present emancipatory praxis see Johann Baptist Metz, *Faith in History and Society: Toward a Practical Fundamental Theology* (New York: The Seabury Press, 1980), pp. 10–35 and Sharon D. Welch, *A Feminist Ethic or Risk* (Minneapolis: Fortress Press, 1990), pp. 49–64. Metz's words are relevant here:

> There is another form of memory: there are dangerous memories, memories which make demands on us. There are memories in which earlier experiences break through to the centre-point of our lives and reveal new and dangerous insights for the present. (p. 109)

Also for an excellent account on the nature and role of social memory see James Fentress and Chris Wickham, *Social Memory: New Perspectives on the Past* (Oxford, UK: Blackwell Publishers, 1992).

74. This quote is attributed to Herbert Marcuse. He has influenced the thinking of Johann Baptist Metz, particularly in his exposition of the 'Memoria-thesis'. Quoted in Roger Dick Johns, *Man in The World: The Theology of Johannes Baptist Metz* (Missoula, Montana: Scholars Press, 1976), p. 108.

75. Sharon D. Welch, *Communities of Resistance and Solidarity: A Feminist Theology of Liberation* (Maryknoll, NY: Orbis Press, 1985), p. 35.

2

The Paraiyar of South India: An Exposition of Subjugated Historical and Religious Themes

Then the Primordial man within me exclaimed:
I will lay a stone on my chest
and carve on it
images of my sorrow
songs of pain
that bear witness to my wounds
and welcome tomorrow's sun.
(Bhagawan Sawai)

Chewing trotters in the badlands
my grandpa,
the permanent resident of my body,
the household of tradition heaped on his back,
hollers at me,
'You Whore-son, talk like we do.
Talk, I tell you!'
Picking through the vedas
his top-knot well-oiled with ghee,
my Brahmin teacher tells me,
'You idiot, use language correctly!'

Now I ask you,
Which language should I speak?
    (Arun Kamble)

In conformity with our objective to pursue the inclusive and liberative
prescriptions of the dialogical character of theology as defined in the
previous chapter, this chapter, along with the next, endeavours to reclaim
and reconstruct the communal religious life of a representative Dalit
community, i.e. the Paraiyar of Tamil Nadu, South India. This chapter
has three sections. The first section discusses methodological aspects
related to this study of the history and religion of the Paraiyar. The
second section examines tentative theories on the historical roots of
the Paraiyar community while the third section presents a general outline
of the religion of the Paraiyar.

I. Dalit Historiography: Methodological Reflections

There are at least two purposes that steer this investigatory study of
the history and religion of the Paraiyar. Firstly, it attempts to redress
a predicament that is characteristic of South Indian historiography in
general: the past is documented and interpreted by the powerful, the
literate, and the elite. In the South Indian context this meant that
history was codified, conserved and consolidated by the strategic alliance
between the powerful kings and the influential priests. The sceptre
and pen conjointly functioned as fundamental instruments in the
production, preservation and circulation of South Indian tradition. To
prove this, one only need point to two principal sources that are utilized
in the reconstruction of South Indian society. (a) Inscriptional evidence,
most of which is recorded in temples, is a vital source for Indian
historiographers.[1] Stein, who himself relies heavily on inscriptional data,
tells us that 'most inscriptions are documents recording gifts to Brahmins
or temples from wealthy and powerful persons or groups of a locality.'[2]
The introduction to these numerous inscriptions provides information
about 'the reigning king, his genealogy, conquests and dharmic rule',[3]
because it is in the king's honour that these gifts are bestowed. The
collusion of Brahmins, caste Hindu landowners, and political rulers is
quite obvious. (b) Literature in South India is another source. The
relationship between the king and the court poets and literary figures
is well known. They lived off each other: the king provided them with

gifts and honour while the poets produced literature attesting to the king's wisdom, compassion, righteousness or justice, and generosity.[4]

This work aspires to be deliberately sensitive and attentive to the voice of the subaltern: local, illiterate, and marginalized Dalits.[5] It locates and documents sources of subaltern communities that lived and reflected outside the temples, which were guarded by the Brahmin priests and caste Hindu communities, and alienated by the mechanics of literature, which was the exclusive domain of the twice-born caste communities. It takes seriously the criticism of Kancha Ilaiah that 'Mainstream historiography has done nothing to incorporate the Dalitbahujan perspective';[6] and it prevents the possibility that '[Dalit] history, therefore, becomes non-history.'[7]

The subaltern communities referred to as Dalits are not the lowest in the hierarchy of the Hindu caste society. The Shudras (who are also categorized as the Other Backward Castes and who are not among the twice-born caste group) occupy this position. Rather Dalits are those who are outside the human society as defined by the Hindu system: literally 'outcastes'. My three years of pastoral and community organization work among the Dalits in South India has enabled me to question the generally accepted presupposition that Dalit society and religion is coterminous with Hinduism whether in its classical or popular form. I can still vividly recall the first time I set out as a village pastor to visit my Christian parish in June, 1984. I rode on my motorbike all dressed in a long white cassock to the village that was expecting me to do the evening service. I rode into the village and kept asking the community members where my church was located. All of them assured me that I would not find a church in the village. I confirmed that I was at the right village and protested that they had to be wrong. More curious people gathered around to catch a glimpse of this quite ignorant city-bred Indian who did know their world. Eventually an older women took pity on me and said, 'Sir, How can you be so naive as to look for a Christian church in the main village? This is where we caste Hindus live and the temple is at the center of our space. If you go further down the mud road, about a kilometer or so, you will see the church building as you enter the colony. You must always look for the colony where the Schedule Caste people [Dalits] live. Your church is among them.' The radical disjunction between the caste Hindu communities and the Dalits that is indicated in the woman's comment is indeed reflected in the demarcation of sacred geography. Further, the identification of Christian sacred space with the living space of Dalit communities was revealing. After that incidence I knew where to locate the Christian communities that I was to serve for the next three years: in the colonies outside the scared geography of the temple-centred village. All of my 14 Christian congregations were Dalit-based and, except for the one that was located in the town, all the others were colony-centred.

This attempt to enumerate and document aspects of the tradition of one Dalit community of South India, i.e. the Paraiyar, serves the field of religion in another way too. It rescues distinct subaltern forms of religious symbols and practices from being coopted and assimilated into the homogenizing gaze of the Indian religionists. By respecting the distinctiveness of the religious space of the Paraiyar I endeavour to focus on the particularities of Dalit religion without viewing it solely as a component of Hinduism that spreads from the Hindu temple. It thus facilitates the emergence of a critique of what has been accepted as conventional representation of Hinduism in South India.[8] Along the lines of Guha's objectives for re-writing History, by being attentive to 'undertones of harassment' and 'the note of pain' of subaltern peoples, this listening to the voices of religiosity of the Dalits will (a) 'challenge the univocity' of caste Hindu religious discourse (b) 'put the question of [subaltern] agency and instrumentality back into the narrative' of Indian religion; (c) 'activate and make audible other small voices' that have also been relating and reflecting with the Divine; and (d) interrupt or break up 'the story line and plot' of the dominant religio-cultural worldview.[9]

Secondly, this study seeks to be the true expression of my vocation: as a Christian theologian I am committed to the ongoing refiguration of the religious conceptual framework of South India. For me, this entails the challenge of correlating my Christian convictions with the central elements of the religious schema manifested by the Dalit community as exemplified by the Paraiyars. The Indian-Christian theological necessity of working with the history and religion of the Paraiyar goes beyond my own claims of 'friendship' with and congeniality towards the subaltern peoples. In my explication of theology, I have argued for the relevance and importance of including the world of Dalits in the discourse that initiates Indian-Christian theology. As noted in the previous chapter, Christianity is 'the religion of the Pariahs'[10] since Dalits make up at least sixty per cent of the Christian population. The heritage of the Dalits, thus, is an important resource for any contextual theology in India.[11] In the geographical setting of Tamil

Nadu, which is the focus of this particular chapter, it can be said that indigenous and contextual theology arise from the juxtaposition and negotiatory interaction between Paraiyar and Christian tradition.[12]

The decision to study the religion of the Paraiyar who are not Christian is deliberate. On the one hand, I am presupposing that this will lead towards the common fund of religiosity that is at the crux of the Dalits in South India and has been at the heart of the Christian Paraiyar through the centuries. On the other hand, my experience of living with the Christian Paraiyar has convinced me that elements of Dalit religion are still operative in Dalit Christian communities. However, even while the Christian Paraiyar practice Dalit religious rites and practices at various occasion, they are reluctant to admit it openly, leave alone claim it as their own. Thus, I am only left with the option of studying Paraiyar religion in the knowledge that it surreptitiously spills over into the practice of Christianity in South India. I have personally been intrigued by the reluctance of Christian Dalits to openly live out this dual identity. For example, during a funeral procession, I often noticed the ceremonial role of the drummer in leading the procession, the inclusion of the sacrificial rite of crushing of the lemon (in one case, a young chicken was sacrificed) before entering the cemetery, and the throwing of rice and money all along the way. The reasons for this reluctance to admit to the wedding together of Dalit religious practice and Christian religious belief can be attributed to the powerful teaching by Church leaders.

This study of the history and religion of the Paraiyar aspires to operate counter to that general trend. One early example of a pejorative and judgmental study comes from an Anglican Bishop of Madras. In his analysis of village religion in South India, he writes:

> The only attitude which the Christian Church can possibly take toward it as a working system is one of Uncompromising hostility... The first step towards any religious progress in the villages of South India is to cut down this jungle of beliefs and practices, rites and ceremonies, and clear the ground for the teaching and worship of the Christian Church. When the Outcastes of a village in the Telugu country become Christian, they very often level the shrine of their local deity to the ground and build a Christian prayer-house on the site. That expresses the general attitude of Christianity to the whole system.[13]

This is, however, not to say that there were no other less imperialistic attitudes in studies on Dalit religion. Elmore, writing during the same general period as Whitehead, seems to think that the Dravidian system was less immoral than the Hindu system. By means of a 'closer study' of village religion in comparison with 'Brahmanic Hinduism' he comes to the conclusion that 'while the Dravidian ceremonies are more shocking, their system does not contain so many immoralities as does the Brahmans'.[14] While Whitehead inscribes and evaluates village religion from a self-confessed Christian viewpoint, Elmore's ethnography is much more cryptic. On the one hand, he wants to validate village religion by depicting it as 'less immoral' than Hinduism. On the other hand, his evaluation of both forms of Indian religion is cognizably influenced by a Western framework of morality. Consequently, in the end, Elmore is both unabashedly derogatory in his appraisal of Hinduism and flagrantly condescending of village religion: the former is 'immoral' while the latter is 'non moral'.

This study of the history and religion of the Paraiyar strives to be empathetic. It is driven by a theological conviction that God has created all people in every part of the earth and thus is relating to all creation in love. God reveals Godself to the whole creation continuously and steadfastly. Moreover, in relation to the subaltern communities, there surely is much to be learned from a people so oppressed and marginalized by other human beings; their trust in God may in fact be inversely proportionate to their long, collective, and bitter experience of being let down by others. Nonetheless, despite my claim that I am dedicated to a form of 'advocacy scholarship', I do not wish to refute the charge that this study of the Paraiyar is constricted and swayed by my own internalized structure of what is real, meaningful and relevant, which is, in an intractable and intrinsic way, Christian. Clifford is principally realistic when he suggests that 'ethnographic truths are inherently *partial* — committed and incomplete.'[15] Indeed, very little can reasonably be said to defend an 'immaculate perception' perspective. I am neither Dalit by birth nor an agrarian by upbringing. My interpretation, therefore, emanates from an encounter between the conceptual world of the Paraiyar (local concepts and theoretical grids that are shared by the native community) and my conceptual world (the concepts and categories that I share with my academic colleagues and Christian community).[16] It is my hope that the dynamics of this encounter coupled with the process of inscribing it, through the pages of this book, will be governed by the principles of dialogue, subaltern advocacy, and scholarly integrity. The methodological importance of capturing both the subjection and the subjectivity of the Dalits will be deliberately embraced. On occasions, the emphasis may even be tilted in favour of lifting out the subjectivity of subalternity as exhibited by the culture and religion. Nonetheless, the overall context of subjection of the Dalits (economically, culturally, socially and religiously) must be the frame within which the picture of subjectivity ought to be understood.

II. History of the Paraiyar: An Overview From the Underside

As stated in the previous chapter, Indian society may be explicated by means of the four-fold hierarchical system.[17] However, this general framework fails to take into consideration a large section of the Indian populace which is outside the caste system: the Dalits. The term attests to the element of oppression that best characterizes their history and contemporary context: 'socially outcaste, economically impoverished, politically powerless.'[18] Alongside this, it must be reiterated that the term Dalit has also become 'a positive, assertive expression of pride in Untouchable heritage and a rejection of oppression'.[19]

The Dalits form a substantial proportion of Indian society. According to the 1961 Census, the Dalits numbered 64 million out of a total population of 439 million while in the 1971 Census they were listed to have reached 80 million out of a total population of 548 million.[20] In the most recent Census of 1991, the Dalits numbered 138 million in a total population of 846 million.[21] This means that at the beginning of this decade they constituted about 16 per cent of the Indian population. There is little agreement with regards to their actual population, with their numbers vacillating between 100 million[22] and 200 million; for the purpose of this study it might be best to decide upon the conservative estimate of 150 million, which is based on the figure of 138, 223, 277 determined by the 1991 census. These figures would however be substantially higher if one takes into account the Dalits who embraced non-Hindu religions. The Indian government considers only the Dalits within the Hindu community as the Scheduled castes; Dalits who have converted to Christianity, Buddhism, Sikhism and Islam are not considered a part of this social category since these religions claim to be casteless. This is a major reason to postulate that the Dalit population would be much larger than the numbers suggested by the census of the Indian government. This becomes particularly relevant when one is aware of the fact that between 50 and 70 per cent of Indian Christians come from the Dalit background, which is not atypical of the characteristic of mass conversion movements to other religions as well. Kumar states:

> Between 1871 and 1881 the Hindu population declined by 2.27 per cent, but the proportionate decline was greater for the Paraiyars. The decline was partly due to the effects of the 1876–78 famine, and partly due to conversion.[23]

In Tamil Nadu, according to the 1981 Census, the Dalits comprised 18.35 per cent (8,881,295) of the total state population (48,408,077), which represented almost a tenth of the total Dalit inhabitants in India.[24] The updated 1991 Census of Tamil Nadu records the Dalit population at 10,712,266 in a total state population of 55,858,946.[25] While this indicates that the Dalits constitute 19.18 per cent of the total population of Tamil Nadu, the Dalits of Tamil Nadu represent only about 8 per cent of the total Dalit population of India.

Although the Dalits are said to be drawn from more than 400 different subcastes or *jatis* throughout India,[26] in Tamil Nadu the bulk of them come from three jatis: the Paraiyar account for 59 per cent of the Dalit population in Tamil Nadu; the Pallan constitute 21 per cent; and the Chakkili form 16 per cent.[27] A conservative estimate would put the Paraiyar population at about 6.32 million. Furthermore, in the district of Chingelput (the area covered in this study) 94 per cent of the Dalits are Paraiyars.[28] Therefore, the community is fairly representative of the overall situation of the Dalits, both in the entire district and also in the state of Tamil Nadu, which has a sizable population of Paraiyars. Hanumanthan iterates this when he suggests that the Paraiyar 'can be considered as the typical representatives of the untouchables of Tamil Nadu.'[29]

The historical origins of the Paraiyar are shrouded in obscurity. Nevertheless, a few popular and plausible theories stand out as portentous. In this discussion on the origin of the Paraiyar I lay out some of the germane hypotheses. In so doing, I shall deliberately refrain from indulging in a critique of each of these proposals, although I am aware that there are a multitude of problems implicit in them. It is hoped that the theories of the origin of the Paraiyar will provide some insights into the identity of this community and, by implication, into the overall historical context of South India.

One traditional view maintains that the Paraiyar, in accordance with the laws of Manu (c. 200 BCE to 200 CE), are the descendants of those persons and groups that had been expelled from the caste system because of transgressing caste rules and social regulations. The offspring of parents who marry hypogamously — a lower caste male marrying a higher caste female — eventually became the Dalits.[30] In addition, the descendants of any mixed caste marriage and children born illegitimately were also compelled to join this community of outcasts. It is pertinent to emphasize that according to this school of thinking the Paraiyar are not Dalits because of their low and menial occupations. Rather, they are condemned to these occupations as a punishment for breaching caste laws established and enforced by the caste communities.

The importance of this postulate cannot be explicated apart from an ethnosociological understanding of Hindu anthropology. The native Hindu view of caste, as developed by Mckim Marriott and Ronald Inden in their 'dividual-particle' theory, is based on the belief that all human beings are born with a coded-substance that relates to their caste, sex and personality.[31] These substances are constituted by particles containing the same coding which can be unattached from the body and become annexed to another body. Herein lies the difference from a western notion of the 'individual', which implies a kind of enduring indivisibility of the human person. Because of the potential of dividuation in the Hindu view, physical interaction must be socially controlled to enable individuals possessing the same substance-coding to exchange compatible particles and restrict individuals having disparate substances from coming together. It is crucial that these coded-substances be kept from mixing. This logic feeds the dynamic of Hindu human society which seeks to maintain auspiciousness, order and purity as against its opposite state of inauspiciousness, disorder and pollution. In Dipankar Gupta's words:

> According to the native Hindu theory, individuals belonging to a particular caste share identical particles. These particles are different from the particles that constitute other individuals in other castes. This is why it is necessary to maintain distance between castes, lest these particles comingle... Unlike racial stratification where visible differences govern social interaction, the caste system has to rest eventually on the belief in natural differences.[32]

The mixing of sexual fluids, in an inter-caste sexual relationship, which results in the substantial and unnatural exchange of coded-particles, and the fusion of dissimilar coded-substances, which comes about at conception of human life, rupture the symmetry of the harmonious native system of the Hindu social body. The disruptive coming together of disharmonious particles and substances, can only be ejected from within the contours of the well-ordered Hindu human society. Thus, emerge the Dalits.

The Paraiyar in this schema are those, who, even if unwilling to share in the rationale of the 'native Hindu theory' because it systematically and unfairly disadvantages them, are, nonetheless, constrained to objectingly assent to its practical ramifications in order to live within the confines of the everyday workings of Indian society. The point to highlight through this discussion is the resultant nature of the Paraiyar identity, which is engendered in a cultural and religious system that is foreign to, alienating of and oppressive for them.

A second theory, which contended that the term Paraiyar essentially was a derivative of the Tamil word *parai* (drum), and that it denoted people whose occupation was drum-beating, was first worked out by Bishop Cardwell.[33] A reference to the Paraiyar as a vocational specialization occurs as early as second century AD in a poem by Mankudi Kilar that informs us of three different occupational groups, one of which is the Paraiyar (the drummer).[34]

A correlation between the occupation of drum-beating and the low social status conferred upon this community cannot be easily explained. However, the notion of pollution as advanced by Hinduism and practised by caste communities is a good starting point. Keeping in mind the polluting character of death, it is not difficult to see the connection between the drum and its potential to contaminate a large group of people. Death generates an acute form of impurity; it 'renders even the holy cow impure, fit only to be handled by the Untouchable.'[35] On the one hand, generally the South Indian drum is fabricated out of cow hide. In the case of the Paraiyar, it serves as raw material for drums and in the case of the Chakkili, it is used for making leather merchandise. In either instance because of the specific power inherent within the dead object, more so because of it being a dead cow, it becomes a vehicle that transmits pollution. Consequently, all persons coming in contact not only with the dead object, which is highly polluting, but also with articles or human beings that have been affected by contact with it, are envisaged as sources of contamination. On the other hand, the fact that drums are beaten, as a necessary rite on the occasion of a funeral, by the Paraiyar is another factor that links the drummer with pollution. In my experience, while living and working for three years in a cluster of villages in Chingelput district, I observed that caste people would call only for the Paraiyar drummers on the occasion of a funeral. This idea of pollution emanating from death and its transmission through the participants that are associated with the rites necessary to eliminate the dead object is not something peculiar to the Paraiyar.[36] Srinivas suggests that 'Brahmins who generally work as priests at funerals are degraded by such work, and in some places, rendered permanently impure.'[37]

It is in the above two senses, through the association of death with the drum, that the Paraiyar may have acquired a low social status. It is important to underscore the manner in which the drum symbolizes the occupation, culture, and the overall lifestyle of the Paraiyar. Though all Paraiyar are not drummers, it does not undercut the power of symbolic association whereby all Paraiyar are represented as people of the drum.

A third hypothesis, as K. Rajayyan argues, is that the Paraiyar were the original possessors of the land who had been subjugated by invading caste Hindus. He says:

> The paradox of the glory of the culture in the land [Tamil Nadu] was that it condemned the vast majority of the population as untouchable. Referred to as Dravidas or Adi Dravidas, they were the sons of the soil and the real Tamils. However, by a gradual yet ruthless process of violence and fraud, the caste Hindus deprived them of their possessions and reduced them to the status of landless tenants... [and] treated them as untouchable.

This view has particular significance to the Paraiyar's history because of the nuances that the Tamil word *Parai* is said to demonstrate. In Tamil, the letters *la* and *ra* are interchangeable. The term *Paraiyar* could have its roots in the word *Palaiyar* which means ancient or original people.[38] The Paraiyar are thus believed to be the original inhabitants of the Tamil country and the rightful sons and daughters of the soil. In this context it must also be noted that the word *Paar* means earth or land and so may be said to denote owners or rulers of the land.[39]

Along similar lines, by way of highlighting the racial difference between the Paraiyar and caste Hindus, another hypothesis posits that the term Paraiyar is a derivative of the Sanskrit word *Para* which means foreign. Because the Paraiyar were culturally and racially inconsonant with the Hindu caste people they were designated as the foreign ones.[40] Again, the idea of purity versus pollution may have been construed to differentiate between these conflicting racial and cultural ways of life. The degree of purity and pollution may have varied according to the degree of adoption or rejection of Brahmanic customs and manners; since 'the Paraiyars were stubborn and the least inclined to adopt them',[41] they logically became one of the most marginalized groups in Tamil Nadu.

Finally, one must reckon with Stein's attempt to explain the origins of the Paraiyar through an overall process of territorial augmentation. He suggests that the people of the nucleus areas gradually and collaboratively expanded their jurisdiction and dominion over 'the agrestic' labourers and the tribal and forest inhabitants. The existence of the Dalits and their low social status is not denied in Stein's conceptualization. Nonetheless, he gives the reader the impression that all groups that were involved in the dynamics of social interaction and social struggle were guided by the common purpose of working towards a viable and mutually beneficial fluid polity. In this sense the Paraiyar originated predominantly because of the natural and inevitable social process of 'accretion at the bottom'.[42] Stein's cooperative model of society is founded on the principle of mutual benefit for all caste groups. His fundamental premise is that this cooperative dynamic can be studied in South Indian non-Brahmin society by means of the dual societal division of *valangai* (right-hand castes) and *idangai* (left-hand castes). The Paraiyar, in Stein's schema, belong to the right-hand caste. Conjecturally they may have originally belonged either to the agricultural communities that 'previously cultivated lands deficient in reliable irrigation sources' and who were subtly absorbed into the ranks of dependent agricultural labourers or to the domesticated hill people who were then assimilated into the peasant way of life.[44]

Beck's classic study of right-hand and left-hand castes deals with another region in Tamil Nadu.[45] Nonetheless, her findings problematize Stein's proposal. For our purpose, it would be sufficient merely to emphasize the following pertinent conclusions that she draws: (1) Although there are distinct differences between these two caste divisions, the members of the caste communities of both the right and left factions still comply with the conventional sanctions against commensality and intimate social contact with the Paraiyar.[46] (2) The major portion of agricultural assets, specifically land, is owned and controlled by the caste people and the Paraiyar are predominantly agricultural labourers.[47] (3) The persons involved in the right–left conflict are directed by the 'principle of limited access to primary resources with the specific Hindu view of power and rank.'[48] This unquestionably furthers the interest and the benefit of the caste community since they are the controllers of local resources and the group vying for rank and status within the Hindu system.

The deductions arrived at in the summation of Beck amplify the apparent division between the Paraiyar and the caste communities even if interpreted within the framework of the right-left caste division. The kind of solidarity that Stein conceives of among the segments within each of these relative divisions (right and left hand) is more likely to be the result of coercive control that is cumulatively exercised on the part of the caste people. The idea that South Indian society came into being through natural social processes of cooperation and assimilation, thus, does not do justice to the facts which testify mostly to a multifaceted inequality with regards to social, economic and religious power.[49]

In order to prove the truism that 'there is a caste basis of class and a class basis of caste'[50] in Indian rural society, Dharma Kumar demonstrates that the relationship between the Paraiyar and the caste communities was predominantly based on the ownership and control of land. According to his view, the idyllic notion that agricultural production in the pre-British period was typically self-sufficient, family-labour dependent, and peasant-owned holdings is 'an absurd oversimplification'; rather, he asserts that the South Indian agricultural economy required large numbers of labourers who were, in many instances, recruited from the Dalit castes since 'only members of certain castes could be made serfs or "slaves".'[51] The Paraiyar were traditionally assumed to be one of the serf communities and even in 1901, 64.2 per cent of them were agricultural labourers. It therefore seems illogical to separate caste and economic class.[52] This aspect of the relationship between the Paraiyar and the caste people in terms of utterly dependent labourer/slave and wholly autonomous landlord was observed in 1906 by Dubois:

> The Pariah are looked upon as slaves ... hardly anywhere are they allowed to cultivate the soil for their own benefit, but obliged to hire themselves out to other castes.[53]

From the above theories regarding the historical origins of the Paraiyars three interrelated themes seem to emerge. i) The Paraiyar are an ancient people, perhaps even the aboriginal or original inhabitants of South India. ii) The Paraiyar are a culturally distinct community with the drum as a key symbol of this particularity. iii) The Paraiyar are an economically oppressed and culturally marginalized community, primarily because their particular heritage was not in conformity with the traditions of the Hindu caste communities. With this as the background, the next section explores the religion of the Paraiyar.

III. The Religion of the Paraiyar: Deities, Rituals, and Religious Functionaries

My interpretation of the religion of the Paraiyar draws upon various sources. It brings together (a) unsystematic reflections from my three years of living and working with Paraiyar communities in about 14 colonies (also disparagingly referred to as *ceeri*) around Karunguzhi in Chingelput district (1984–7); (b) documented data from a six-week intensive fieldwork trip in two of these colonies, i.e. Malaipallaiyam and Thottanavoor (June–July 1992); and (c) ethnographies, historical constructions and religio-cultural writings on Dalit communities in South India.[54] This section on the religion of the Paraiyar will attempt to briefly sketch out the general components of their religion by focussing on three themes: deities, rituals, and religious functionaries. It seeks to accomplish one primary purpose: to introduce the reader to the overall features of the Paraiyar's religious life.

Deities

One characteristic that describes the Paraiyar's religion is that it revolves around the worship of a class of goddesses. At a conceptual level, the Paraiyar believe in one supreme, omnipresent Spiritual Being, (that which is or He/She who is) or *Sakti* (Divine Power). All the priests and the devotees who were interviewed asserted that even though they worshipped various goddesses called *amman* (mother), these were only manifestations of the one Supreme Being. In the villages, this supreme being is referred to as Sakti. In practice, however, they tend to worship female manifestations of this supreme being. In Malaipallaiyam the main goddess is Ellaiyamman while in Thottanavoor the goddess that is venerated as the main goddess is Mariyamman. The general consensus among the people I talked to suggests that they believe that Sakti has been revealed to the Paraiyar in seven manifestations as seven virgins who are sisters. However, when asked to enumerate these seven manifestations they either came up short or long of the number seven. When this discrepancy between their claim that Sakti has seven manifestations and their enumeration, which summed up to more than the number seven was pointed out, the typical response was, 'But how does this matter, God is one after all.' This is in keeping with Thurston's comment:

> The names of these goddesses are legion. Each village claims that its own mother is not the same as that of the next village, but all are supposed to be sisters.[55]

Some of the other goddesses they named were Gengaiyamman, Sethu-kaalselvi, Thandumari, Thulukanathamman, Padavattamman, and Muthumariamman. One significant difference between the Dalit goddesses and Hindu representations of the goddess, which will be discussed at length in the next chapter, must be stated in brief: Hindu goddesses are either spouses, consorts or progenies of the Gods (Brahma, Vishnu or Shiva) whereas Dalit goddesses are wholly independent. This is evident by noting the asexuality of Dalit goddesses. The characterization that they are virgins appears to de-sexualize them in a particularly anti-patriarchal way, which may even be interpreted as a critique of Hinduism. But more so, their asexuality keeps them outside the dynamics of the Hindu male gods. Dalit goddesses do not become objects of male gods' sexual pursuits or subjects that endeavour to manipulate and control the passions of these gods. The personal sexuality of the Dalit goddesses is not part of any of their myths and religious narratives. They are overseers of procreation and protection but the working out of their own sexual passion and fertility is not the subject of Paraiyar theological discourse.[56]

Customarily, a devout Paraiyar may have up to a set of five deities to whom s/he pays homage: the chosen deity; the household deity; the lineage deity; the hamlet deity; and the village deity.[57] 'The Chosen God or Goddess' (*ista devam*) is a deity that is venerated because of the individual devotee's particular preference. It can be any one of the numerous deities that has proven to be 'attractive' to and 'efficacious' for a specific religious person. I use these two terms deliberately since these were the determinants by which the Paraiyar chose their personal deity. The word 'attractive' was used to describe why the devotee preferred one god or goddess over another. In one instance a high school educated young man from Malaipallaiyam informed me that the village goddesses were dark and unattractive. He was unwilling to bow down before a female image that was not attractive to him. Instead he sought out a god who has an 'attractive image'. The concept of 'efficacy' was another major reason for a devotee choosing a particular deity. 'Efficacy' has both a personal and a social connotation. In terms of the former, it was an outcome of personal experience in which an individual or family received a blessing from a specific deity. In this case it usually consisted of the realization of a prayer request made to the deity. In terms of the latter, it was more tied up with the fame of efficacy that the deity had acquired in the neighbouring villages. This had to do with the impressive power that was being exercised by a certain deity in a particular region.

There is a great deal of freedom with regard to the deity that can be appropriated by the individual devotee. Three comments can be made concerning the 'Chosen God or Goddess' among the Paraiyar. First, in many cases, 'the chosen deity' is located outside the native village of the devotee. This means that worship of the deity implied a planned trip outside of the village, which involved time, effort and, possibly, expenditure. Second, there are no formal or informal rules governing the possible choice of a deity as 'the Chosen God or Goddess'. Thus, quite a few Paraiyar that I talked with worshipped deities outside the pantheon of Dalit goddesses.[58] Third, the 'chosen deity' is not expected to remain unchanged throughout the devotee's life.

'The household god or goddess' (*viittu devam*) is a deity worshipped by the individual along with one's immediate and undivided family. The class of 'household deities' is often associated with spirits of deceased female family members 'who have died in an auspicious married state.'[59] They are worshipped at 'good times', which mark the life-cycle of a family member (i.e. the maturation of a girl, marriage, and the birth of a child) and 'bad times', which threaten the well being of the family (i.e. ill health of members of the family and infertility of a married woman). The household deities do not have an image or a shrine. However, they are said to be housed in a *kalasam* pot (a kind of tall pot made with clay), which is kept inside the hut. This class of deities are primarily thought of as being in spirit form. Worship of the household deity is performed in the hut and is presided over by the oldest male member of the household.

The class of 'lineage deities' (*kula devam*) is associated with a patrilineage. They have a claim on the whole lineage. Usually they are worshipped at a family festival at least once a year. In both Malaipallaiyam and Thottanavoor, although people would like to celebrate a festival once a year to propitiate the lineage deity, they generally tend to arrange for a festival only when there is a real need to do so. 'The need' to celebrate a festival to this particular deity is determined by either an acute situation that may require the help or appeasement of the deity (usually involving 'bad times' for the lineage) or to comply with the wishes of the older men of the lineage. Both the household and lineage deities are particularly 'concerned with family life-cycle rituals and family crises, with special emphasis being placed on the deities' relationship to maternal fertility and the health of children.'[60]

'The hamlet god or goddess' (colony *devata*) is the common deity of the Paraiyar community that lives in a particular colony. This deity has a contractual (convenantal?) relationship with the colony. 'The village god or goddess' (*kiraama devata*) is a deity that is common to the people who share a geographic space. It supposedly encompasses both the Dalits in the colony and caste Hindus in the main village. However, in the colonies covered by this study, the village deity is primarily the deity of the caste Hindus who live in the village. Because the colony shares the same name with the village, the Paraiyar would be required to fulfill certain roles in the effective worship of these deities. In actual practice, however, these 'village gods or goddesses' do not significantly penetrate into the everyday religious practice of the Paraiyar. This is because the village deity is perceived to be the caste deity. Moreover, given the social and cultural rules that govern interaction between the caste community and Dalits, it is improbable that the Paraiyar will have access to the village deity.

The 'hamlet or colony goddess' of the Paraiyar represents the most public and consensual aspect of their religion. Legends concerning these deities are fairly well known. There is only one goddess that is claimed to be the hamlet deity of a particular colony and is usually housed in a small shrine within the colony. The icon of the colony goddess is represented by a female image that is carved out of black stone. There are no distinct facial features that distinguish the different Paraiyar goddesses. The shrines that house the goddess are a recent phenomenon. Until recently the hamlet goddesses of the Paraiyar were simply located under a tree at a strategic border of the colony. In some other colonies in the region the goddess is represented by a black cone-shaped stone that is planted into the ground under a Margosa tree. In the villages of Malaipallaiyam and Thottanavoor the goddesses are housed in a temple-style building made out of brick and mortar. In Thottanavoor the image of Mariyamman is housed in a one-room temple at the entrance to the colony. Similarly, in Malaipallaiyam, the image of Ellaiyamman is situated in a small building on the border between the village and the colony. Both Mariyamman and Ellaiyamman are represented as black images in a sitting posture with four arms that extend into four hands. Their headgear is in the form of a snake. The horizontal lines of sacred ash on their forehead give the impression that the goddesses are cared for and worshipped regularly. Both goddesses hold the same four instruments in each of their hands: a drum, a soolam, a bundle of rope and a skull.[61] Both temples may also have an image made of black metal, which can be taken out and paraded during the annual festival. A yearly celebrative and collective festival which is held to honour and venerate this deity is probably the most important collective event in the life of the colony.

Religious Rituals of the Paraiyar

The ritual life of the Paraiyar is complex and varied. In order to classify the various rituals of the Paraiyar I have opted to utilize the composition of the worshippers involved in the performance of the ritual acts. I start by discussing individual ritual acts. Next I look at small group settings in which religious rituals are commonly practiced. And, finally, I discuss the colony's collective ritual celebration which takes place annually.

Rituals performed by the individual devotee

Individual *puja* (worship)

Individualized *puja* at a local shrine is the most common ritual performed by a Paraiyar devotee. It may not be done everyday, but many Paraiyar devotees of Ellaiyamman and Mariyamman attempt to perform a puja at least once a week, preferably on a Friday. However, this is not a required routine. On one level, the individual puja reiterates a sense of loyalty that the worshipper has towards the particular deity. It reinforces the profound sense of relatedness between the worshipper and the goddess. On another, more pragmatic, level, the individual puja is performed out of either a pressing need to appease the honour of the goddess so that she would not chastise the worshipper or a specific crisis that demands the goddess's favour and aid.

The individual puja is a fairly simple procedure. The devotee bows reverently before the image of the goddess with both hands folded, places a small offering in front of the icon, circumambulates the image or shrine thrice and leaves with a portion of the offering that was tendered. The question as to what constitutes a proper ritual was frowned upon by my Dalit respondents. They informed me that the goddess is not concerned with correct ritual; rather she is pleased with 'genuineness of devotion'. There is no priest to monitor the devotee's liturgical and ritual practices for individual puja. Interestingly, the prayers are not verbally expressed. It is usually recited in the mind in any language. In the shrines at Malaipallaiyam and Thottanavoor there was no priest, no lighted lamp, nor holy ash that could be taken back by the devotee as a token of blessing from the goddess. However, this aspect of unmediated puja by the individual Paraiyar devotee is not typical of all Paraiyar individual worship. For example, the people informed me that there would be a priest at the shrine every Friday morning during the month which leads up to the colony festival. During those occasions a lamp is lit by the priest and placed in front of the icon of the goddess and the priest gives the devotees a bit of holy ash when they leave the shrine after their puja. This holy ash, as is the custom of Hindus in general, is rubbed on the forehead of the devotee.

Individual supplication at auspicious places or before divinely-possessed persons

At various auspicious times the goddesses make special visitations by manifesting their divine power in chosen geographical locations or through select individuals. When this has to do with a particular location there is a small shrine built on it and individual devotees come to this location to appropriate the power of the deity in order to help meet specific needs. In the case of the divinely-possessed person this power of the deity is vested in a particular human being, who operates as the agent of the deity. He or she becomes the focus of devotion and divine mediation. The individual is chosen arbitrarily; thus, the sub-caste, age, and gender of the person is irrelevant. Because the power of the goddess is manifested and communicated through this individual, he or she is regarded and treated as a divine agent who participates in the power of the deity and mediates this divine power to people who come to them.

In July 1992, I visited one popular divinely-possessed individual in the colony of Vedavakkam. The goddess Muthu Mariyamman manifested herself to this young man and possessed him. From that day onward he became the medium of the goddess. On a hot summer day in July I found my way to a small concrete structure in the middle of many paddy fields. Muthu Mariyamman had chosen this young man who was about sixteen years old. He was not educated and was a caretaker of ducks. From the time the goddess possessed the boy he could tell the future. But more so, in some cases, he had the power of the goddess to influence the future for the betterment of the devotee. She came upon him while he was at the particular paddy field near his home. Since that time his parents have built a small concrete temple in which the goddess's image is housed. Every day the boy sits in front of the image and he speaks the words of Muthu Mariyamman to those who seek her out and come to this temple. The day I visited the boy there were about fifteen individuals who had come to see the boy. All of them were female devotees and they had come by bus from colonies near by. They were prepared to spend the night in the colony if they had to wait a couple of days to see the divinely-possessed boy. Some of them wanted the goddess to remove all obstacles that prevent them from being married. Others were married for a while and had not conceived; they wanted to have a child. One devotee, who had come with her mother, was fourteen years old and had not reached maturity. She wanted to find out when she would reach puberty and what she should do to become a woman. None of them referred to the person they had come to see by name or by any title. When referring to him they invoked the name of the goddess; as if he were nothing more or less than a representation of the goddess.

I entered the main room of the temple and was allowed to stand near the doorway for a few minutes. The boy was seated on the floor cross-legged in a room. There was an image of Muthu Mariyamman in front of him. A lamp was burning in front of the image. He was dressed in a white cloth. He had holy ash on his forehead which was in the form of a dot. He was listening to the woes of a female devotee. He was sitting quite still but did not appear to be attentive. I was not allowed to meet and talk with the boy because I was not a devotee. I was told by others that he could foretell the future and that he could remove the obstacles that prevented the devotee's 'good life.' In fact, I was told that even caste Hindus were attracted to this particular manifestation of the goddess.

Family and Small group based rituals

Rites of Passage: rituals to mark and celebrate stages in the life-cycle of the individual

The Paraiyar tend to mark and commemorate stages in the life-cycle of female members much more conscientiously than their male counterparts. The ceremonies that are ritualized in the life of the child start at birth. The priest invokes the goddess to protect and guard the child and mother from all physical and spiritual harm. This ceremony is performed in the house and usually involves only the immediate family members. However, this ritual is now increasingly not performed because 'the priest costs too much'. Instead the mother, along with some elders, takes the child to the temple or shrine of a 'chosen god or goddess' and informs the deity of the name of the child.

Another significant ritual marks the female's transition from child to adulthood. At maturation, the female is dressed up as a woman and the extended family, clan and friends from the colony are invited over to her home where she is blessed by the older members of family and the elders of the colony. She is displayed in all her womanly splendour and gifts are given to her. In this ceremony, the priest and the drummers of the colony play a significant role; they both announce the good news of a girl's maturation to the community and invoke the spirit of benevolent women who have died to bless the girl-turned-woman. Marriage is also celebrated by the community as a religious event in which the priest and the drummer have a role to perform.

Another ritual that is performed for the pregnant woman takes place in her seventh month of pregnancy. This is usually the time when the woman goes back to her parent's home for the actual birth of the child. This ceremony involves the families of the mother-to-be and her husband along with other friends, relatives and elders from the colony. A final religious ceremony marks one's death. Here the priest, drummers and the cemetery attendant are involved in the rituals.

Religious rites for appeasement or energization of the deity

Sacrifice at a time of crisis has for generations been a common practice among the Paraiyar. There are stories in both Malaipallaiyam and Thottanavoor about the prevalence of buffalo and goat sacrifices. However, this has not been performed at a family or small group level for years. During the time of a crisis or when there is a perception that 'bad times' are incessantly befalling a particular lineage there is a custom whereby a sacrifice is performed to pacify the goddess. It is assumed that either the crises or 'bad times' are brought about by the angry goddess in order to demand attention and worship or the misfortune is the work of demons and other caste gods, who are attempting to defeat and destroy the goddess and her devotees. While, in the former instance, the sacrifice is a gift from the particular family to appease the goddess and evoke her favour, in the latter case, the sacrifice is a way of stimulating the powers of the goddess to subdue and overcome the demons or the caste gods. In the words of Kinsley, 'In either case, it is clear that the goddess demands the blood of a victim, that she needs that blood, either to appease her wrath or to invigorate her in her conquest with the demons.'[62] In most cases a chicken is sacrificed by the oldest member of the family which is then eaten by the whole family.

In a sacrificial rite that I attended in Malaipallaiyam, a family that was beset by constant illness invited the cremation ground attendant to perform the sacrifice. After invoking the goddess Mariyamman to turn her anger away from the family he cut off the head of the chicken with a kitchen knife. He then marked the ground in front of the entrance with the blood as if to draw a boundary beyond which no spirit can enter. He did not stay for the meal that followed in which the chicken meat would have been cooked and 'eaten by the family. Working as cremation ground attendants is a traditional and hereditary occupation in the Paraiyar community. Their duties involve digging the grave and putting the body in it and managing the corpse while it burns on the fire. This role gives them special contact with demons and spirits of the dead and thus qualifies them to perform sacrifices.[63]

Calendrical ritual commemoration of *ammavaasai*

The Paraiyars worship the goddess every *ammavaasai* (new moon day). They do not eat anything till noon on that day. After a bath the women perform a family puja to propitiate the spirit of their dead ancestors. In Malaipallaiyam an informant stressed that this was also a rest day for all the agricultural labourers and that on ammavaasai no one in the colony would use the oxen to plough their land since it was a rest day for even the animals involved in agricultural activity. Although this was the practice in other colonies many years ago, it is seldom practised by all members of the community today. The commemoration of ammavaasai at present is more of a family puja in which women perform the leading role, while men tend to go about their normal routine. A widespread reason for this 'gradual decline in the commemoration of ammavaasai has to do with the fact that increasingly more Paraiyars have become small landowners. As labourers working for someone else they could get a day off to celebrate this festival. Now they have to till and plough their own land since they cannot afford to hire someone else to do the work.

Colony-related and colony-sponsored yearly festivals

Pongal (the harvest festival)

There are two major festivals that are celebrated by the Paraiyar. *Pongal* (literally this Tamil word means to boil or boiling) is the South Indian harvest festival. The most characteristic ritual of Pongal consists in the boiling of sweet rice which is given to the deities, neighbours and livestock. Pongal is celebrated at the beginning of the Tamil month of *Tai*, which falls around the middle of January. Pongal is a colony-related festival which though socially celebrated is not collectively observed by the Paraiyar community. I do not think that it is relevant to my purpose to describe the celebration in any more detail for the following two reasons. On the one hand, and as stated already, this is not a festival that the colony celebrates as a community. It is observed more on a family or clan level. On the other hand, this festival is celebrated more conscientiously and elaborately by the caste Hindu communities in Chingelput district.[64]

The yearly festival to the colony goddess

In the month of *Aadi* (between 15 July to 15 August), almost six months after the festival of Pongal, the Paraiyar hold their most important communal festival. This annual festival which is dedicated to the colony goddess,[65] 'celebrates her link with the people and territory she protects and rules over.'[66] It consists of five phases. Phase one is concerned with the consensual planning of the festival. At the onset of the month of Aadi the elders invite the entire colony to attend a consensus meeting. On the day designated for the meeting the parai drummers go around the colony announcing the time and the place of this community meeting. The consensus meeting has a two-fold agenda: to agree upon the actual date for celebration of the festival and to decide upon the amount that each family will contribute towards the celebration.

The second phase involves a ceremony the night before the actual festival. A few young men come together with the priests and the drummers in front of the shrine of the goddess or at a location where there is water (a lake, river or a well). The young men offer to be the 'ritual assistants' and 'servants' of the goddess throughout the festival. After prayers that are sung by the priest and a series of drum beats, five or six young men are chosen as attendants to carry out the ritual obligations that must be realized through the festival. A black thread called *kapu* is tied around their wrists by the priests. These young men are expected to abstain from sexual activity, eating meat, and drinking alcohol till the end of the festival. One among them will be elected by the goddess to serve as her main servant while the others will assist in some way or another. Interestingly, a black thread is tied to the drum also, symbolizing that the drums also function as instruments of the goddess's power, which will be utilized to fulfill her purposes; thus, the kapu is tied to the *uDukkai* and the *bambai* drums too. At times the goddess will possess certain devotees at this ceremony to point out what preparations have not been done and how they ought to be undertaken before the festival. In certain colonies this ceremony is performed on the morning of the festival.

Phase three occurs on the morning of the festival. It starts at dawn on the banks of the local river, lake or pond. The community members along with the priests and the drummers come together with the young men who wear the kapu in order to invoke the colony goddess to permit, accompany and grace the festival. The young bachelors are dressed in white. After a bath their heads are anointed with oil. They have offered themselves to be the servants of the goddess in the festival. Only one of them is to be chosen the 'goddess-bearer' and they await the moment when the goddess herself, through the action of a 'goddess-possessed' devotee, identifies one of them to be the elected one. The drums are a characteristic and indispensable component of the yearly festival of the goddess. It can be heard for miles around the village, announcing and inviting people to entreat the presence of the goddess. The priest is from the priestly clan of the Paraiyar called the Valluvar. He seems in charge of the festival ceremony. However, he is not the sole authority; the sponsors, the elders of the colony and the devotees constantly instruct and offer suggestions to him about what he must do. The priest, the drummers, and the young boys face a *karagam* pot which is half-filled with water. It is adorned to form a conical shape by placing a coconut on its open upper circumference. The pot is then painted with saffron powder and is covered with mango and margosa leaves. Along with this main karagam pot there is a small clay pot decorated similarly but less elaborately. Next to the main karagam pot is a small lamp that had been lit by the priest. A tray of offerings is kept in front of the pot which contains rice, saffron, flowers and a lemon. On each side of the pot there is a large knife referred to as an *aruvaal* (the instrument that Parasuraman used to behead his mother in the legend of the origin of Ellaiyamman) and a *soolam* (the forked weapon of destructive power that the goddess secured from Shiva).

The priest sings songs in praise of the goddess to the accompaniment of the uDukkai drums. Also drumming along at different times during the process of inviting and invoking the goddess are the various drummers playing the bambai, the parai and the *satti* drums. While the drums beat and the priest sings, the goddess possesses one of the villagers who, after dancing in an ecstatic trance, identifies one of the young men as the chosen one to carry the goddess into the village. Interestingly, the one on whom the goddess descends speaks as if he or she is the goddess herself. The 'goddess-possessed' devotee is questioned and the authenticity of the possession is tested by the priest usually by asking a round of questions. If the 'goddess-possessed' devotee is found to be a hoax, the priest and the drummers start the invocation process afresh. Sometimes an unsuitable or extraneous goddess makes her appearance through a 'goddess-possessed' person; in such cases she is asked to bless the celebration and her help is sought in sending her appropriate sister to make her appearance. When the appropriate goddess possesses one of the members of the group, she usually starts by raising an objection or making a complaint.

In the festival I attended, the goddess Padavattamman was upset that none of her devotees had sacrificed a buffalo or a goat to her for the last several years and that hardly anyone washed and cleaned her shrine on a regular basis. The priest explained to her that this was because of the hard economic times and that they could not afford to sacrifice a buffalo or a goat. The priest also assured her that in the year to come the colony members would be more regular in washing and cleaning her shrine. When the goddess finally agrees to be part of the celebration of her own festival, so as to bless the colony through the year, she also elects her bearer. The one who is possessed does this for her by dancing in front of one of the young men and bowing to him in a state of frenzy. At this point the young man who is identified also starts dancing as though the spirit of the goddess had come upon him and he goes up to the priest to be given the karagam pot which symbolizes the goddess. With the goddess's permission secured and the power of her presence imparted, the priest, the drummers and the devotees follow 'the chosen-bearer' of the karagam pot into the colony.

The procession is headed by the drummers who announce the presence of the goddess and drive away evil demons from her path. Then comes the priest who performs a sacrifice at every border and crossing of the colony. Here the sacrifice is believed to help the goddess, who is coming into the colony, displace and trample over the demons that wait to prevent her from entering the colony. Although the sacrifice at the major border crossings ought to be a male chicken, it is usually substituted by the crushing of a lemon. Two reasons were given for replacing chickens with lemons: the high cost of chickens and the 'social unacceptability' of bloody sacrifices. Finally, comes the 'chosen bearer' of the goddess with the karagam pot which represents the power and the presence of the colony goddess. Next to him is another attendant who carries the smaller clay pot on his head, which represents the male guardian of the goddess. This procession goes around the colony stopping at the strategic border crossing on the North, South, East and West. It then goes to every house in the colony where the women of each household come out and perform a brief puja. They bathe the feet of the bearer of the goddess, decorate the feet with saffron powder, and with a lamp that is lit they make three circular motions around the feet. This lamp is then taken back into their homes as a sign that the goddess has pervaded their homes with her presence and blessing. After every house is visited the procession comes to the shrine of the goddess where the bearer of the goddess is fed the meal that is prepared in front of the shrine. The food that is prepared for the goddess is a kind of porridge made with *ragi*, curds, onions and neem leaves.[67] The 'goddess-bearer' is offered the food first. Soon after the goddess partakes of the food it is distributed to poor members of the colony who have been waiting in a line to share in the porridge. This communal meal ends the third phase of the yearly festival.

The fourth phase takes place at sunset. It starts at the site of the image of the goddess that is kept in the shrine. Usually, as a substitute for the main immovable image of the goddess, a movable image is taken out in a procession through the streets with much fanfare and pomp. The image is adorned with flowers and carried on a temple car. These temple cars vary in kind — from a cart pulled by bullocks to a tractor trailer. Here again the drummers, with the rhythmic beating of their drums, and the priests, singing songs of praises to the goddess, lead the procession which takes the image of the goddess around the colony through the night. Many households perform a puja again when the temple car passes by their house. They bring out an offering and give part of it to the priests. The rest of the flowers, food, and betel leaves and nuts are taken back into the house where they are consumed by the family members as a sign of blessing from the goddess. The procession ends when the goddess has made her journey through the entire colony. She is then returned to the shrine from which she set off. Here the kapus that have been tied around the young men and the drums are removed and the ritual aspect of the festival draws to an end. Having completed all the ritual elements of the festival for that day, the rest of the night is spent in celebration which involves drinking of country liquor for the men and watching an extended street drama for the rest of the colony. More recently these street dramas, which depict traditional mythological themes, are being replaced by a couple of contemporary films. This celebration usually lasts till the early hours of the morning.

Phase five takes place on the day after the actual festival. It is both informal and casual. There is a display of frivolity and gaiety. Members of the colony that have celebrated the festival splash each other with coloured water while turmeric water is used to splash special relatives. The karagam pots are taken to the river or lake and disposed off. Although there is a certain kind of procession that must take place to conclude this phase it is seldom undertaken. Instead a few 'interested parties' take the karagam pots to the river, remove the decorations, and immerse the pots. With this the festival draws to a close.

Religious Functionaries

In an exposition of the persons that sustain the religious mechanism of the Paraiyar, I have deliberately refrained from using the term 'religious leaders'. Instead, I have opted to adopt the label 'religious functionaries'.[68] Firstly, the Paraiyar religion is served by a variety of roles in its multidimensional approach to religious activity. Diverse forms of orchestrating the religious activities of the Paraiyar call for the existence of the coordinated integration of different functions. Second, the knowledge of practising religion is not codified in a text; thus the norms of orthodoxy or orthopraxis are often dialogically reconstructed within particular ritual contexts. For example, during the festival of Gengaiyamman that I observed, the priest was constantly corrected and rebuked by the elders, the goddess-possessed devotees and the drummers for doing things that were unnecessary and unwarranted. Surprisingly, he did not feel threatened nor humiliated; rather he incorporated their suggestions and warnings as he continued to perform his ceremonial role.

The priests (pucari)

Despite the suggestion that the Paraiyar religion is maintained and executed by various functionaries rather than hierarchical leaders, one cannot but be struck by the special role and status claimed by the Paraiyar priests. They belong to a sub-caste called the Valluvar Pandaram.[69] The Valluvar do not live with the rest of the Paraiyar but just outside the borders of the colony. They are also not accepted as being part of the caste community; so they live outside the borders of the caste village. In the villages covered by this study, the Valluvar live in a cluster of four to ten houses geographically located much closer to the other Paraiyar than to the caste community. While there may be as many as ten Valluvar families attached to a particular colony, only one or two male members from this sub-caste are practising priests. This is mainly because the market for priestly functions is limited. Also, the Valluvar neither eat nor drink from or with the other Paraiyar. In some cases offering of food to the Valluvar priest is made in the form of uncooked food ingredients, i.e. rice, millet, vegetables and fruits. Furthermore, the Valluvar do not eat beef.

This appearance of a class that mediates through rituals among the Paraiyar prevents me from agreeing with Ilaiah's claim that 'there is no notion of priesthood among the Dalitbahujans'[70] or that 'No village Goddess or God expects a *yagna* that involves priests'.[71] Nonetheless, one must also resist the temptation of jumping to the opposite conclusion as propounded by Moffatt that this demonstrates the basis of a hierarchy as expressed in the social distance between the caste people that are twice-born (Brahmin, Kshatria and Vaishya) and the once-born (Shudra).[72] Matters are more complex than this with regards to the separation between the Valluvar priests and the other Paraiyar. First, the Paraiyar do not admit to the higher status of the Valluvar. One Paraiyar informant reported that 'the Valluvar are of a lower caste than us'. Another informant backed this argument with what he insisted is 'a commonly known truth': 'According to the government schedule of Dalits, we [Paraiyars] are number 204 and they [Valluvar] are lower down at 274 in the hierarchy.' Second, the Paraiyar do not willingly accept the unquestioning role of the Valluvar even in the performance of their religious rituals. It is quite usual for the priest to alter and redo aspects of collective rituals in accordance with the suggestions of devotees. Third, the caste community associates the Valluvar more with the Paraiyar than with their own communities: The Valluvar are 'divided almost evenly between Untouchables and non-Untouchables by their toRil (services), but the balance of these ties is toward the Untouchables.'[73]

The functions of the priest are connected with the various rituals that have been discussed earlier: individual puja, rites of passage or other household rituals that do not involve blood sacrifices and colony festivals. Along with these the priest's professional duties include 'writing charms for sick people, preparing horoscopes, and making forecasts of good or evil.'[74] The authority of the priests stems from two sources. On the one hand, the priests are from the Valluvar sub-caste. This makes them traditional functionaries of religious practices. On the other hand, the priests are well-versed in the art and practice of religious rituals. This knowledge that is passed down through the generations from father to son, gives the priest the right to preside over religious rites and guide devotees as they seek to peer into their future.

It may be relevant to stress three characteristics of the Paraiyar's priests. First, the priests are intimately tied up with the power of the drum in the execution of their ritual functions. In all collective ritual ceremonies the priest utilizes the rhythmic beat of the uDukkai drums to help him communicate with the deities. Usually the priest himself plays the drums as an accompaniment to his songs and prayers of praise to the goddess. He also uses his drum to entice the deity to possess a devotee. While the priest beats the uDukkai drums he is assisted by another drummer who plays on the bambai drums. Both these drums are key instruments used by the priest in his mediatory relationship with the deities. Second, the traditional priests are male. However, some members in the colony admitted that they have consulted with female Valluvar gurus regarding their future and horoscope. And, third, the tradition of priests being only from the Valluvar sub-caste is being challenged. For example, in Malaipallaiyam there is a priest who is not from the Valluvar community. Though he is not the official priest of the colony festival in Malaipallaiyam, he claims to be the official priest for such yearly festivals in neighbouring colonies. He is a Paraiyar who learnt the prayers and ritual practices from a much respected Valluvar. He also says that people have come to know that the goddess Ellaiyamman has blessed him with special powers to invoke the goddesses and correctly decode their messages and is sought after more than the local Valluvar priest. He abstains from both beef and alcohol. Interestingly, the basis for his authority as a religious specialist stems from his knowledge of the prayers and the practices that make rituals efficacious. Perhaps, his popularity as a priest, who has received special blessing from the goddess, compensates for his not being from a family of priests.

The drummers

The drummers are an intrinsic part of the religious life and practice of the Paraiyar community. They are religious functionaries without whom rituals would be incomplete and inadequate. The drummers as religious functionaries also derive their authority in the same way as the priests. They are knowledgeable in the art of drum-beating (certain drum beats correspond with particular ritual commemorations) and they come from a specific ancestral stock which has practised the techniques of drumming for many generations. They take their role as drummers with utmost seriousness. In the words of a drummer from Endavur,

> Suppose I have already got agricultural work tomorrow, but this evening I am told to play the parai band at the same time tomorrow. I will go do the drumming leaving the agricultural work aside.[75]

However, the only major difference between the priests and the drummers is that they do not claim to be superior to the other Paraiyar. They also have no dietary regulations; they eat beef and are said to consume a lot of alcohol.

In each colony there are at least five drummers, all of whom are male. Although there was no theological reason why a female could not serve as a drummer there was consensus that 'it was not appropriate' and that 'it had never been thought of'. Apart from the priest and his assistant who beat the uDukkai and the bambai drums respectively, there are a set of about five drummers who accompany the priests in the collective ritual ceremonies. While a group of three or four drummers beat on the parai drums, the other one or two drummers play the satti. These drummers as a group are usually positioned away from the priest and his assistant. There can be little doubt that these religious functionaries, although absolutely crucial to the ritual life of the Paraiyar, are today treated with less respect and prominence than the other functionaries.[76]

The divinely-possessed representative of the goddess

Among the divinely-possessed representatives of the goddess, one can distinguish between persons who are transitorily-possessed by the goddess (*saamiyaadis* or god-dancers) and persons who are enduringly-possessed by the goddess (*saamiyaars* or god-persons). Those belonging to the first category are consciously participating devotees at collective festivals. There is the necessity and expectation during these festivals that devotees will communicate the benediction of the goddess to the other members. Therefore, in a sense these functionaries perform an anticipated role in the execution of the ritual. The goddess is invoked by the priests and the drummers and manifests its presence and its word through persons who are temporarily possessed by her spirit. They get roused by the drums and the songs of the priest and with their eyes closed begin to dance with rigid and stiff movements. They speak in a voice other than their own; they speak and act as if their whole body and mind is possessed by the goddess. They speak the word of the goddess: her anger, blessing or wishes are communicated through these divinely-possessed persons. Thus, the possessed individual addresses the devotees as if he or she were the goddess herself speaking to her disciples.[77] After fulfilling her purposes, the goddess leaves and the possessed person falls to the ground and in a while goes back to being himself or herself.

The enduringly-possessed functionary of the goddess is a significant religious functionary in the life of the Paraiyar. They are generally possessed by the goddess in an unusual and unexpected manner. In many cases this possession takes place miraculously without any particular ritual setting. Once this individual is possessed by the goddess in a special revelatory moment, this person becomes the dispenser of the power of the particular goddess that has possessed him or her. The enduringly-possessed servant of the goddess is sought out by devotees from the neighbouring area both as a fortune-teller and a healer. Devotees journey considerable distances in order to encounter the goddess that resides in this individual and to seek her counsel and aid. If the counsel of the goddess is sought, the devotee comes to the possessed servant of the goddess with gifts of flowers, fruit and money. The circumstances of the devotee are shared with the goddess and her counsel is solicited. It usually involves matters pertaining to marriage alliances, job prospects, family unity and harmony. The goddess may ask the devotee many questions. At the end the goddess will offer her words of counsel which may suggest how the future will turn out and what steps must be taken to facilitate the emergence of 'good fortune'. It is quite typical for the goddess to ask the devotee to come back at a latter and more opportune time to get more advice from her.

The enduringly-possessed servant of the goddess is also sought out to help in overcoming a problem, resolving a difficulty or healing an ailment. Again, the devotee encounters the goddess as a supplicant with gifts and then goes on to state the petition and the circumstances that have led her to the goddess. The goddess, through her divinely-possessed servant, offers an explanation that could hint at a solution. The solution usually includes a request from the goddess that the devotee fulfil a specific task, i.e. a minor pilgrimage, a ritual at a local shrine or a certain sacrifice. The devotee goes back home with hope that his or her problem will be taken care of with the help of the goddess when he or she fulfils the obligation that has been requested by the goddess. If things improve, occasionally the devotee comes back to offer his thanks. Sometimes, if things are not better the devotee may come back to plead with the goddess and enquire what more needs to be done. Sometimes, if things are not better, the devotee gives up on this particular manifestation of the goddess.

Both types of divinely-possessed representatives of the goddess can be from any sub-caste and gender. The only criteria for their authority stems from their being unexpectedly possessed by the goddess. This is vouched for by eyewitnesses from the village at the time of possession. In the case of the latter (enduringly-possessed persons), if there is no eyewitness, their possession is verified by the manifestation of the goddesses power in their words and actions, i.e. fortune-telling is unerring and healing power is effectual.

The sacrificer

The person who performs the sacrifice at family-based rituals is usually the oldest male member of the family. When this is done there is hardly any ritual preparation. The animal (as pointed out earlier, it is almost always a chicken) is sacrificed by cutting off its head with a sharp knife and its blood is sprinkled at a particular spot, generally outside the hut. At this time a special prayer is offered by the sacrificer mentioning the reason for the sacrifice and beseeching the goddess's aid.

At community rituals, and occasionally at family-based ceremonies, the sacrificer is from a lineage called Vettiyan. Literally, the word *Vettiyan* means 'cutter or digger'. The sacrificer is the specific Vettiyan who makes his living from digging and guarding the cemetery and officiating at funerals. He is said to be close to the malevolent spirits because of his association with death and the cemetery. In each colony, while there are many families that come from this lineage, only two or three are actually involved with the occupation of maintaining the cemetery and officiating at funerals. However, the Vettiyan's role as sacrificer is getting rare because of the infrequency of animal sacrifices at community festivals and ceremonies.

To conclude, three themes emerge from the above discussion concerning the history and the religion of the Paraiyar of South India. First, the Paraiyar are an ancient people claiming to be the original inhabitants of the land. Second, the Paraiyar are a culturally distinctive community, with the drum epitomizing various aspects of this particularity. And, third, the Paraiyar have a long history of being socially, culturally, and religiously oppressed and marginalized, primarily because their distinct heritage is not in harmony with the traditions of the Hindu caste communities.

In the study of the religion of the Paraiyar I briefly presented an overview of their deities, rituals and religious functionaries. For the purposes of understanding the lay out of the next chapter it is essential to underscore the following: (a) the overall importance attributed to the goddess is a central and pervasive aspect of the phenomenology of Paraiyar religion and (b) the manifestation of the drum as a symbol of the collective identity of the Paraiyar becomes functionally crucial in their religious life.

Notes

1. 'Estimates of the total number of inscriptions collected in India begin at 80,000; one often hears the figure 100,000... The vast majority are in the South, and in the South the greatest number are from Karnataka and Tamil Nadu.' Thomas R. Trautman et. al., 'The Study of South Indian Inscriptions', in *Studies of South India: An Anthology of Recent Research and Scholarship*, eds Robert E. Frykenberg and Pauline Kolenda, (Madras: New Era Publications, 1985), p. 7.
2. Burton Stein, *Peasant State and Society in Medieval South India* (Oxford: Oxford University Press, 1980), p. 46.
3. Ibid.
4. For a detailed and impressive account of the complex relationship between the Brahmin and the king in terms of ritual and ideological interdependency see David Shulman, *The King and the Clown in South Indian Myth and Poetry* (Princeton: Princeton University Press, 1985), pp. 15–46. It does seem as though Shulman presumes that poets in the kings court were on the whole Brahmins.
5. This study is still very much a male's point of view. My conscious attempt

to elicit the response of Paraiyar women was consistently frustrated. I attribute this to two factors. First, the men wanted to influence the direction and content of the discourse. When it came to influencing opinion in the public realm, particularly outside of their own community, they seemed eager to be in control. Thus, they were quick to dominate the discussion even if women were present at the meeting. Second, I was at a disadvantage because of my own gender. Culturally, it did not appear natural for women to discuss their views with me. A successful attempt to fill in this gap can be seen in the work of Margaret Trawick. Her ethnographies lift up the voices of South Indian women. In her book *Notes on Love in a Tamil Family*, Trawick draws from the deep well of women's experience. Even though much of her work manifests an ongoing dialogue with the poetry and prosaic commentary of her male guru, Themolzhiyar, Trawick's documentation and interpretation of the verbal and non-verbal communication between and among the women of his household is substantial and profoundly rich. More specific to the Paraiyar, Trawick has published a few interesting studies based on the songs, stories and voices of Paraiyar women. See Margaret Egnore Trawick, On the Meaning of Sakti to the Women in Tamil Nadu', in *The Powers of Tamil Women*, ed. Susan Wadley (Syracuse, Syracuse University, 1980), pp. 1–34; 'Internal Iconicity in Paraiyar Crying Songs', in *Another Harmony: New Essays on the Folklore of India*, eds Stuart Blackburn and A.K. Ramanujan (Berkeley: University of California Press, 1986), pp. 294–344; and 'Spirits and Voices in Tamil song', in *American Ethnologist*, vol. 15, no. 2 (May, 1988): 193–215.

6. Kancha Ilaiah, 'Productive Labour, Consciousness and History: The Dalit-bahujan Alternative', in *Subaltern Studies IX: Writings on South Asian History and Society*, eds Shahid Amin and Dipesh Chakrabarty (New Delhi: Oxford University Press, 1996), p. 165. The term Dalitbahujan (literally 'the Dalit majority') is used by Ilaiah to include the lower rung of the Sudras (Other Backward Castes) to the 'outcastes'. In this book I am making a case for viewing the break between Dalits and caste Hindus as more definitive than between the twice-born Hindus and others outside this grouping.

7. Ibid., p. 166.

8. I am also conscious that the necessity of such a study is inseparable from my own concord and familiarity with the people that adhere to this religion. Thus, in line with the suggestion of Wilfred Cantwell Smith, the personal quality of this investigation 'derives [in part] from having adherents of that faith as informants and perhaps even as *friends*.' Wilfred Cantwell Smith, 'Comparative Religion: Wither-and Why?', in *The History of Religions: Essays in Methodology*, ed. Mircea Eliade and Joseph M. Kitagawa (Chicago: The University of Chicago, 1959), pp. 38–9. Emphasis mine.

9. Ranajit Guha, 'The Small Voice of History', in *Subaltern Studies IX*, pp. 11–12.

10. L.S.S. O'Malley, *Modern India and the West: General Survey* (London: Oxford University Press, 1941), p. 673.

11. A noted church historian who studied the phenomenon of mass conversions in India suggests that 50 to 70 per cent of Indian Christians come from Dalit communities. See J.N. Picket, *Christian Mass Movements in India* (New York: Abingdon Press, 1933), p. 5.

12. Caplan quoting Richter states that 'between 1880 and 1905 four in every five converts [to Christianity] in the Madras Presidency were outcasts, who came, within a few decades, to comprise a majority of those adhering to the Protestant faith.' Lionel Caplan, *Class and Culture in Urban India: Fundamentalism in a Christian Community* (Oxford: Clarendon Press, 1987), p. 37. In my own parish situation about 95 per cent of the 400 families spread out in 14 village congregations were Paraiyars, which in my own estimation is fairly representative of the Christian populace in Chingelput district, Tamil Nadu.

13. Henry Whitehead, *The Village Gods of South India*, second edition, revised and enlarged (New Delhi: Asian Educational Services, 1988), pp. 153–4. This book was first published in 1921.

14. W.T. Elmore, *Dravidian Gods in Modern Hinduism* (New Delhi: Asian Educational Services, 1984), p. 157. This book was first published in 1913.

15. Emphasis in text. James Clifford, 'Introduction: Partial Truths', in *Writing Culture: The Poetics and Politics of Ethnography*, eds, James E. Clifford, and George E. Marcus (Berkeley: University of California, 1986), p. 7.

16. This is merely a fleshing out of Geertz's call for a mediation between the 'experience-near' and the 'experience-distant'. See Clifford Geertz, *Local Knowledge: Further Essays in Interpretive Anthropology* (New York: Basic Books, 1983) pp. 55–70. Ironically, the debate on the relationship between 'emic' and 'etic' ('the former are internal to a language or culture and are derived from the latter which are posed as universal or scientific') is not extraneous to this project, particularly because it presupposes that the universal cannot be uncoupled from the Christ symbol. Since this theological experiment brings together the rudimentary symbols of the Paraiyar and the Christian, the people who share both symbolic framework are important judges in the possible import of this interpretation. In this sense an evaluation of this proposal by the Christian Paraiyar community is a necessary test. For a cogent and terse explanation and critique of the difference between 'etic' and 'emic' cultural categories, see George E. Marcus and Michael M.J. Fischer, *Anthropology as Cultural Critique: An Experimental Moment in the Human Sciences* (Chicago: The University of Chicago, 1986), pp. 180–1.

17. I am well aware that these are the four general orders of Indian society that allow for an outsider to grasp the most basic structure of the Hindu society. These four *varnas* do not determine every day social interaction. Rather it is the identity of the *jati*, which is specific to a geographical region, that is operational at social, economic, religious and political levels. It is estimated that there are in regional areas in India about 200 caste groups, each of which is further sub-divided into about 3000 sub-castes. For a detailed analysis

of the difference between varna and jati see M.N. Srinivas, *Caste in Modern India and Other Essays* (Bombay: Asia Publishing House, 1962); see also G.S. Ghurye, *Caste and Race in India* (Bombay: Popular Prakashan, 1969).

18. Antony Raj, 'Disobedience: A Legitimate Act for Dalit Liberation', in *Towards A Common Dalit Ideology*, ed. A.P. Nirmal, p. 39.

19. 'Introduction', in *Untouchable: Voices of the Dalit Liberation Movement*, ed. Barbara R. Joshi (London: Zed Books, 1986), p. 3.

20. N.D. Kamble, *The Scheduled Castes*, (New Delhi: Ashish Publishing House, 1982), p. 48.

21. *Census of India, 1991*, volume 11 (New Delhi: Registrar General and Census Commission of India, 1992), p. 15.

22. T.K. Oommen, 'Sources of Deprivation and Styles of Protest: The Case of the Dalits in India', in *Contributions to Indian Sociology (n.s.)*, vol. 18, no. 1 (1984): 45.

23. Dharma Kumar, *Land and Caste in South India: Agricultural Labour in the Madras Presidency during the Nineteenth Century* (Cambridge: Cambridge University Press, 1965), p. 59.

24. *Census of India 1981*, series 20, Tamil Nadu, part xii, p. 279. For a detailed description of the Dalit population according to population density, regional distribution, literacy levels, and work force, see Kamble, pp. 49–71.

25. *Census of India, 1991*, p. 18.

26. See Oommen, 'The Case of the Dalits', p. 45.

27. According to the Census of India 1961 as quoted in Joan P. Mencher, 'The Caste System Upside Down, Or The Not-So-Mysterious East', in *Current Anthropology*, vol. 15, no. 4 (December, 1974): 474.

28. Michael Moffatt, *An Untouchable Community in South India: Structure and Consensus*, (Princeton: Princeton University Press, 1979), p. 65. If we continue to project numbers based on our estimates from the 1991 census, the Paraiyar would number about 1.14 million in Chingelput district. The census records the Dalit population at 1,208,417 in a total district population (Chingelput) of 4,653,593. *Census of India, 1991*, p. 290.

29. K.R. Hanumanthan, *Untouchability: A Historical Study upto 1500 A.D. With Special Reference to Tamil Nadu* (Madurai: Koodal Publishers, 1979), p. 74.

30. Abbe J.A. Dubois, *Hindu Manners, Customs and Ceremonies*, 3rd ed, trans. Henry K. Beauchamp (Oxford: Clarendon Press, 1906), pp. 38–40. Also see a general version of this theory in Oliver C. Cox, *Caste, Class and Race: A Study in Social Dynamics* (New York: Monthly Review Press, 1959), pp. 459-60.

31. For further reading see, McKim Marriot and Ronald B. Inden, 'Towards an Ethnosociology of South Asian Caste System', in Kenneth A. David, ed., *The New Wind: Changing Identities in South Asia*, (Chicago: Aldine Publishers, 1977) and Pauline Kolenda, 'The Ideology of Purity and Pollution', in *Caste and Contemporary India: Beyond Organic Solidarity* (Prospect Heights, Ill.: Waveland Press, 1985).

32. Dipankar Gupta, ed., *Social Stratification* (New Delhi: Oxford University Press, 1991), p. 25.

33. Edgar Thurston, *Castes and Tribes of South India*, vol. VI: P to S, (Delhi: Cosmo Publishers, 1975), p. 77.

34. Srinivasa M. Aiyangar, *Tamil Studies: Essays on the History of the Tamil People, Language, Religion and Culture* (New Delhi: Asian Educational Services, 1982), p. 78.

35. M.N. Srinivas, 'Some Reflections on the Nature of Caste Hierarchy', in *Contributions to Indian Sociology (n.s.)*, vol. 18, no. 2 (1984): 162.

36. Hutton also wants to connect the origins of the Dalits with such ritualistic functions and social taboos. He refers to the grave diggers as those who, because of their association with funeral rites, are feared to be carriers of contamination. See J.F. Hutton, *Caste in India: Its Nature, Function, and Origins* (Bombay: Oxford University Press, 1951), p. 206. I am making a similar conceptual move by adjoining the drum with its role in the phenomenon of death. Also for a detailed formulation of the opposition of the pure and the impure in terms of the Brahmin being linked to the holy living cow and therefore symbolizing the paragon of purity and the Dalit being conjoined to the polluting dead cow and hence representing the model of contamination, see Louis Dumont, *Homo Hierarchicus: An Essay On the Caste System*, trans. Mark Sainsbury (Chicago: The University of Chicago Press, 1970), pp. 146–51.

37. Srinivas, 'Some Reflections', p. 163.

38. Hanumanthan, *Untouchability*, p. 78.

39. Ibid., p. 77.

40. Ibid.

41. Aiyangar, *Tamil Studies*, p. 90.

42. Stein, *Peasant State and Society*, p. 212.

43. Ibid., p. 211.

44. There is a suggestion to this effect in Moffatt's interpretation of Stein in Moffatt, *An Untouchable Community*, p. 41.

45. Brenda E.F. Beck, *Peasant Society in Konku: A Study of Right and Left Subcastes in South India*, (Vancouver: University of British Columbia Press, 1972).

46. Ibid., p. 161 ff.

47. Ibid., pp. 184–6; 195.

48. Ibid., p. 270.

49. In the context of their occupational roles and functions, Srinivas suggests that the Dalits have no choice since if they do not tow the lines imposed by the caste peoples they would be beaten up, probably along with their family, by the dominant castes. See Srinivas, 'Some Reflection', p. 165.

50. K.L. Sharma, *Rural Society in India* (New Delhi: Rawat Publishers, 1997), p. 292. This is an excellent contribution to rural social analysis which combines recent sociological and anthropological sources.

51. Dharma Kumar, *Land and Caste in South India*, p. 190.

52. Ibid.

53. Dubois, *Hindu Manners*, p. 49. For a similar view that construes the relationship of the caste Hindus to the Paraiyar in terms of landlords and dependent labourers see Francis Buchanan, *A Journey from Madras through the Countries of Mysore, Canaras, and Malabar in Three Volumes*, vol. II. Reprinted (New Delhi: Asian Educational Services, 1988), p. 493 f. Also see S. Manickam, *Slavery in the Tamil Country: A Historical Over-view* (Madras: Christian Literature Society, 1982), pp. 40–59.

54. I was pleasantly surprised to find quite an impressive group of anthropologists working on the Paraiyar in particular. I am influenced and greatly indebted to the following sources that deal specifically with the Paraiyar: Robert Deliege, 'Patriarchal Cross-cousin Marriage among the Paraiyars of South India', in *Journal of the Anthropological Society of Oxford*, no. 18 (1987): 223–36, 'A Comparison between Christian and Hindu Paraiyars of South India', in *Indian Missiological Review* (April, 1990): 53–64, and 'Replication and Consensus: Untouchability, Caste and Ideology in India', *Man*, vol. 27 (March, 1992): 155–73; Michael Moffatt, *An Untouchable Community in South India*; Joan P. Mencher, 'The Caste-System Upside Down, or The Not-So-Mysterious East', *Current Anthropology*, vol. 15: 4 (December, 1974): 469–93 and 'On Being an Untouchable in India: A Materialist Perspective', in *Beyond the Myths of Culture: Essays in Cultural Materialism*, ed. Eric Ross (New York: Academic Press, 1980); and Margaret Trawick, also published under the name Margaret Egnore (see earlier note).

55. Edgar Thurston, *Castes and Tribes of South India*, p. 104.

56. For a detailed discussion of the difference between Dalit and Hindu goddesses see, Kancha Ilaiah, *Why I am not a Hindu: A Sudra Critique of Hindutva Philosophy, Culture and Political Economy* (Samya: Calcutta, 1996), pp. 32–5, 71–101.

57. I am using the categorization of Moffatt. For a detailed analysis of these categories as relating to the Paraiyar of Endavur in Chingelput district, Tamil Nadu, see Michael Moffatt, *An Untouchable Community*, pp. 219–89.

58. One informant who was showing me around the Ellaiyamman shrine informed me that he was 'attracted' to Murugan. He told me that he was willing to go to a high-caste temple a few miles away in the town of Madurantakam to do his Puja. He was certain that the priest of that Murugan temple was not aware that he was a Paraiyar since usually Brahmin priests would not like to serve Dalits, even though the temples are legally open to all Hindus, irrespective of caste, since 1939. He informed me that an advantage of worshipping in a busy town is that no one will know or enquire into your caste background. Nonetheless, although his 'chosen god' is Murugan, he takes part in all the village rituals and festivals that honour Ellaiyamman. I asked him how his 'chosen god' would react to his taking part in honouring Ellaiyamman. His answer was in the form of a question: 'But why would he bother?'

59. Moffatt, *An Untouchable Community*, p. 226.

60. Lynn E. Gatwood, *Devi and the Souse Goddess: Women, Sexuality, and Marriages in India* (Riverdale, MD.: Riverdale Company Inc., 1985), p. 140. This motif is closely linked to the perpetuation and protection of the lineage which is dependent on the beneficence of the goddess.

61. For an early enumeration of the worship of Mariyamman and Ellaiyamman, see Bartholomaeus Ziegenbalg, *Genealogy of the South-Indian Gods*, reprinted version (New Delhi: Unity Book Service, 1984).

62. David Kinsley, *Hindu Goddesses: Visions of the Divine Feminine in the Hindu Religious Tradition* (Berkeley: University of California Press, 1986), p. 205.

63. For a detailed discussion of the role of the 'cremation ground attendant' see Moffatt, *An Untouchable Community*, p. 114.

64. For a detailed description of the celebration of Pongal in a caste community of South India see Louis Dumont, *A South Indian Subcaste: Social Organization and Religion of the Pramalai Kallar,* (Delhi: Oxford University Press, 1986), pp. 411–26.

65. I participated in the yearly festival to Mariyamman in Thottanavoor in July, 1992 and had a group interview with the elders of Malaipallaiyam to get information of their yearly festival to the goddess Ellaiyamman.

66. C.J. Fuller, *The Camphor Flame*, p. 148.

67. At times this porridge is served with a curry made from dry fish.

68. This term is much closer to Sullivan's 'religious specialists' or Brubaker's 'primary ritual specialists'. See Lawrence E. Sullivan, *Icanchu's Drum: An Orientation to Meaning in South American Religions* (New York: Macmillan Publishing Company, 1988), pp. 386–465 and Richard L. Brubaker, 'Barbers, Washermen, and Other Priests: Servants of the South Indian Village and its Goddess', *History of Religions*, 19:2 (November 1979): 128–53.

69. Thurston suggests that the Valluvar are 'usually regarded as a sub-division of Paraiyar's. Edgar Thurston, *Castes and Tribes of South India*, vol. VII, T to Z, p. 303.

0. Kancha Ilaiah, *Why I am not a Hindu*, p. 92.

71. Ibid., p. 98.

72. Michael Moffatt, *An Untouchable Community in South India*.

73. Ibid., p. 102.

74. Thurston, *Caste and Tribes of South India*, vol. VII, p. 305.

75. Ibid., p. 197.

76. Later I shall argue that there was a time in which the drum and the drummer were much respected within a cultural valuation that was non-Brahmanic.

77. This is suggested by Moffatt in his study on Tamil Nadu:

> When any human devotee is possessed by a god or a goddess in Endavur, it is said that person 'is' the divine being for the time of the possession; the deity has incarnated itself in a human body, in order to speak directly to the worshippers.

Ibid., p. 236.

3

The Resistive and Constructive in Paraiyar Religion: Ellaiyamman and the Drum as Signifiers of Subalternity

> To me, Dalit is not a caste. He is a man exploited by the social and economic traditions of this country. He does not believe in God, Rebirth, Soul, Holy books teaching separatism, Fate and Heaven because they have made him a slave. He does believe in humanism. Dalit is a symbol of change and revolution.
>
> (Gangadhar Pantawane)

I do not ask
for the sun and moon from your sky
your farm, your land,
your high houses or your mansions.
I do not ask for gods or rituals
castes or sects
or even for your mother, sister, daughters.
I ask for
my rights as a man.
Each breath from my lungs
sets off a violent trembling
in your texts and traditions
your hells and heavens
fearing pollution.
Your arms leapt together

to bring ruin to our dwelling place.
You'll beat me, break me,
loot and burn my habitation.
But my friend!
How will you tear down my words
planted like a sun in the East?
My rights: contagious caste riots
festering city by city, village by village,
man by man.
For that's what my rights are –
sealed off, outcast, road-blocked, exiled.
I want my rights, give me my rights.
Will you deny this incendiary state of things?
I'll uproot the scriptures like railway tracks.
Burn like a city bus your lawless laws
My friend!
My rights are rising like the sun.
Will you deny this sunrise?
    (Sharankumar Limbale)

This chapter seeks to probe and explicate the resistive and creative dynamic that is operant in the religion of the Paraiyar. After some methodological notes, in the first part of this chapter I point to the resistive and creative aspects of the Paraiyar religion by examining one important Paraiyar goddess. In the second part I argue that the religion of the Paraiyar cannot be interpreted without an imaginative look at the symbol of the drum, which can be construed as a 'dominant symbol' of the resistive and creative dimensions of the Paraiyar religious life. The various traces of the drum within the collective life of the Paraiyar community are mapped out and the discussion ends by reflecting upon the contextual ramifications of the use of the drum by the Dalits. The inclusion of this dominant symbol into the discipline of theology enables us to reflect upon the collective experience of the Dalit community. The chapter ends with an extrapolation of certain key features of sub-altern religion as exemplified by the study of the goddess (Ellaiyamman) and the drum.

I. Methodological Shrift

The religion of the Paraiyar is more than a compliant and unreflective internalization of the beliefs and practices of caste Hindus. Many indologists interpret Dalit religion and culture solely through the lenses of caste Hinduism. The latter is taken to be the all-pervading and all-determining social, cultural and religious reality. Therefore, all other frameworks can only be a reflection and a product of the omnipotent nature of the Hindu religious worldview.

In his explication of the worldview of the Dalits, Harold R. Isaac bases his interpretation on such a misconception. He says,

> Because they ['the Ex-Untouchables'] accepted its beliefs and sanctions, they submitted to this condition for more generations than can be remembered. Millions of them still do. Only the great compelling power of the Hindu belief system accounts for this uniquely massive and enduring history of submission.[1]

Isaac goes on to make the case that because of the religious rationalization behind this belief system, the Dalits submitted to it with a 'sense of propriety and even... a certain dignity' since they consider it to be 'their inescapable fate'.[2] Michael Moffatt strengthens and reinforces a similar perspective in his interpretation of the religion and culture of the Paraiyar. He claims that the cultural and religious system of the Untouchables is 'not detached or alienated from the 'rationalization' of the system... [Thus, it] does not distinctively question or revalue the dominant social order'.[3] He goes on to describe the religion and society of the Paraiyar as a 'replication' of the religion and society of the caste Hindus. This notion of the inert, non-resistive and unthinking nature of the Paraiyar is indeed a stereotype posited by the caste communities. This is best captured in a Tamil proverb used by caste people: 'Though seventy years old, a Paraiyar will only do what he is compelled.'[4] Another commonly recounted Tamil proverb complements this notion that the Paraiyar will always be unreflectively placid and uncritically submissive: 'Though the Paraiya woman's child be put to school, it will still say Ayya [sir].'[5]

I do not (nor can I) seek to establish the overall autonomous character of Paraiyar religion. Glorification of subaltern religion as wholly independent and entirely counter to dominant forms of religion cannot be justified both in the light of my own experience and numerous other ethnographical studies that shall be discussed in this chapter. However, I do venture to lift up the creative, dynamic and active side of Paraiyar religion which will enable one to see that the Paraiyar are actors in their own ongoing social drama rather than mere spectators. The Paraiyar are thus self-reflecting human beings who are continually creating their own conceptual religious world which houses their collective existence with meaning and order.

II. Ellaiyamman as an Iconic Symbol of Collective Resistance and Emancipatory Mythography

In order to shed light on the actively resistive and creative aspects of Paraiyar religion, I shall focus on their hamlet or colony goddess Ellaiyamman. As mentioned in the previous chapter, the colony deity is most representative of the communal and corporate religious life of the Paraiyar. Specifically, Ellaiyamman is central to the religious framework of the Paraiyar living in the colonies that were studied in detail. Moreover, the goddess Ellaiyamman is generally distinctive to Paraiyar religion; she has not been coopted by the caste Hindu religious iconographic and mythological imagination. Pupul Jayakar alludes to this special relationship between Ellaiyamman and the Paraiyar. She states,

> The composite female form of the half-Brahmin, half-outcaste was named Ellama, the *grama devata*, the primeval Sakti of the South. She was to be worshipped throughout the country South of the Vindhya mountains by the *pariah* and the outsiders.[6]

Ellaiyamman is, thus, principally a Dalit goddess. She is the colony goddess of Malaipallaiyam. Also, she is inextricably linked to the other predominant Paraiyar goddess, Mariyamman. Most of the myths concerning the origins of the Paraiyar goddesses stem from an elemental or foundational core-myth that involves both Ellaiyamman and Mariyamman. There is no indication that Ellaiyamman is worshipped by caste Hindus either around the villages which were studied or in other parts of South India.[7] The notion that this goddess is the axis of the Paraiyar religion can be inferred from Oppert's etymological explanation: he claims that the name Ellamma is derived from the Tamil word *ellam* (all or everything), making her 'Mother of All'.[8] In the colony of Malaipallaiyam the predominance of Ellaiyamman is preserved by referring to her both as the 'Mother of all beings' and as the eldest sister of all the manifestations of Sakti.[9]

The other common interpretation for the name Ellaiyamman stems from the Tamil word *ellai*, meaning boundary, making her the Mother/-Goddess of the boundaries. Thurston, one of the earliest systematic researchers into Dalit and Tribal religions is South India, referring to Paraiyar religion says:

> Each village claims that its own mother is not the same as that of the next village, but all are supposed to be sisters. Each is supposed to be guardian of the boundaries of the cheri.... She is believed to protect its inhabitants and its livestock from disease, disaster and famine, to promise the fecundity of cattle and goats, and to give children.

He goes on to identify Ellaiyamman as 'the goddess of the boundary [who is] worshipped by Tamil and Telugu Paraiyars'.[10] This is the most prevalent interpretation among the Paraiyar of Malaipallaiyam. They claim that the positioning of the image of the deity at the boundary of the colony suggests that the goddess presides over the colony and safeguards its perimeters. In this case, the image of Ellaiyamman is strategically situated on the boundary that is regularly used as crossing from the colony into the outside world.

One cannot but notice the dialectic nature of the two motifs that can be extrapolated from the Paraiyar's goddess Ellaiyamman: particularity and universality; geographical locatedness and boundlessness; fixity and fluidity; determinedness and openness; resistance and assimilation. I begin by focussing on the particularity of Ellaiyamman within the overall context of the Paraiyar. It is this particularity and distinctiveness of Ellaiyamman that reveals the Paraiyar's resistance to the expansionist and overpowering nature of caste Hindu hegemonic forces.

Ellaiyamman is an iconic representation of the resistance of the Paraiyar to the conquering tendencies of the caste Hindu world. In the last chapter I set forth the historical background against which we can study the Paraiyar. Even though the Paraiyar are an ancient and distinct people, they have had to endure a long and systematic process of economic oppression and cultural marginalization, primarily because their particular heritage was not in conformity with the traditions of the caste Hindu communities. The caste Hindu people and their religious and cultural worldview continuously threatened the Paraiyar. Economically, they were forced into living in non-productive areas, i.e. dry land. They were, and still are, coerced to survive mostly as landless agricultural labourers, wholly dependent on the goodwill of their caste Hindu landlords. Geographically, they were, and still are, cut-off from the caste village community since they live well outside the contours of the village. Because of the location of their living space, they are constantly endangered by the forces of nature — they live in low-land areas, which are periodically threatened by floods, and dry-land areas, which are predisposed to drought — and by the historically successful attempt of the caste communities to annex their land. In the realm of symbolic capital, they continue to be bombarded by religious and cultural mechanisms that seek of marginalize or coopt Dalits. Thus, the Paraiyar have to be vigilant in their endeavour to preserve their own culture and religion.

It is within this historical situation that one must comprehend the characteristic of Ellaiyamman as a deity that protects the boundaries of and for the Paraiyar. She shields and polices the geographic, social, and cultural space of the Paraiyar from the continuous colonizing proclivity of the caste peoples. On a concrete level, Ellaiyamman guards the boundaries of the land that the Paraiyar possess. Her icon, which is situated on the border of the colony, symbolizes this power to resist and guard. Furthermore, as noted in chapter two, during the procession of the yearly festival she is taken to the borders in every direction (North, South, East and West) and a sacrifice is performed in order to energize her powers to guard and protect the colony and its inhabitants at all the strategic points of the geographic boundaries. On a conceptual level, Ellaiyamman guards the cultural and religious particularity of the Paraiyar. In the words of a song of praise sung by the Paraiyar *Pucari* Subramani, 'O Mother Goddess *Ellaiyamman*, grant us the service of your true blessing, for you are the goddess who protects our religion.' By protecting the religion and culture of the Paraiyar, Ellaiyamman safeguards their identity as the indigenous ('original') people of the land, their dignity, their women and children, and their lives. In one of my discussions with the youth of Malaipallaiyam, they brought out the idea that the goddess is situated at the boundary of the colony because she stands as a warning to those who may cast an 'evil eye' on the people (particularly, the women and the children), land and the property of the Paraiyar. In this sense Ellaiyamman represents the divine power of the Dalits which is able and responsible for guarding them against the destructive, possessive and conquering gaze of the Hindu caste peoples.[11] The words of Martin Heidegger, even if referring to the Greek abstraction of the term boundary, is relevant: 'A boundary is not that at which something stops but, as the Greeks recognized, the boundary is that from which *something begins it's presencing.*'[12]

It is pertinent to stress that this notion of protecting the boundaries of the Paraiyar is engendered within the context of the caste communities' conception of the seamlessness of the *uur*. The uur, which is the caste

Hindu's conception of the village, 'is not so much a discrete entity with fixed coordinates as a fluid sign with fluid thresholds.'[13] Interestingly, thus, the uur (the geographical and socio-cultural space of the caste community), which is distinguished from its counterpart, the *ceeri* or colony (the geographical and socio-cultural space of the Paraiyar), represents the pervading frontiers of the caste community. It is this infiltrating and usurping trend that is challenged by the guardian of the boundaries, Ellaiyamman. A portion of a song in praise of Ellaiyamman reveals this cry of the Paraiyar to safeguard aspects of their local, particular, and parochial world from the 'torture of the High caste':[14]

> You are the deity who expels our troubles; come rid us of evil.
> You are present in the neem leaves used for driving out women's afflictions.
> You are present in the fire, the head of our religion.
> You have lived with fame in our village, Malaipallaiyam.
> In Padavethi a buffalo was sacrificed to you, even in Poothukaadu;
> A sacrifice to inspire You, our goddess, to destroy evil.
> You are the goddess who guards our boundaries:
> You protect with your spear;
> You will protect us from 4408 diseases;
> You will protect the Harijans from the torture of the High caste.[15]

There is yet another aspect of the Paraiyar's goddesses that further attests to this idea that the colony deity represents their distinctiveness and particularity in its resistance to the social, economic and religious nexus of the caste people, which threatens to colonize their overall existence: the Paraiyar goddesses remain single, unmarried and unobliged to the Hindu gods. They refuse to be coopted and domesticated by the larger symbols of power as represented by Hindu gods. While there are myths that link Dalit goddesses to Shiva and Vishnu, the independence of Ellaiyamman can be construed as reflecting the underlying desire of the Paraiyar to be distinct, different, even separate. Interestingly, in the case of both Ellaiyamman and Mariyamman, even though one component of their constitutive nature is rooted in being the spouse of a Brahmin rishi, once they come into being as deities they claim independence from their past relationships. Both these goddesses cease to be obliged to the hierarchy of Hindu gods. This buttresses the resistive dimension of the Paraiyar's deities.[16]

In suggesting that the goddess Ellaiyamman symbolizes the resistive character of the Paraiyar in a historical context of the colonizing trend of caste communities, I am not subscribing to a view that the religion of the Paraiyar has not continually been interacting with the beliefs and practices of Hinduism. In fact, Hinduism in its diverse forms and guises penetrates the various domains of Dalit life in South India. Nonetheless, it is not as if Paraiyar religion is a replication of the general ideological and practical manifestations of caste Hinduism. Rather, the religion of the Paraiyar evolved a process of both resisting and refiguring the Hinduism it was faced with so as to serve its own ends.

Thus far, in this discussion of the Paraiyar's goddess Ellaiyamman I have merely focussed on one of the dimensions of the deity: iconic resistance. However, this aspect cannot be studied apart from another dimension that is intrinsic to the goddess — the process of weaving emancipatory mythographies.[17] This process signifies the deliberate and artful manner by which the Paraiyar utilize their goddess to tell their own story, even if through the mythological framework of the caste Hindu. By recasting the myth of the goddess to serve their purposes, the Paraiyar are reimagining their own history, identity and corporate personality.[18] Here the pivotal role of myths in oral traditions must be iterated: 'a myth will be told when other means of recovering the past are either unavailable or impossible. Myths claim to remember what history has forgotten.'[19]

In what follows, I examine one particular locally evolved myth to look for clues regarding the dynamics of the formulation of religio-cultural frames of meaning among the Paraiyar. Through the weaving of these mythographies one can find the creative and imaginative dynamics of an attempt at historicization. One can observe a remarkable process by which the local people, in this case the Paraiyar, reimagine their own communal subjectivity as a counter-history to the hegemonic one. These local myths are mostly oral, multiform, open-ended, and provincial (in the sense of being circulated only among the Paraiyar). They signify the colloquial word. This form of oral transposition of myths is perhaps strategic: it does not risk being codified in written text except by outsiders who are alien to the power system. Because they are not textually inscribed they can be transformed, suppressed, and modified to suit the situation in which they are rendered. For example, a portion of the song to Ellaiyamman that is derogatory of caste Hindus may be omitted or rephrased when performed in front of an audience that has both Dalits and power-wielding caste Hindus. This fluidity is not possible if the myths are preserved in written form. The following mythography which encapsulates the origins of Ellaiyamman may be a good example. It is a version that was sung to me by a Paraiyar religious functionary from Malaipallaiyam[20]:

There were seven girl children born in Uppai. One of these children was abandoned and discovered by a washerman. Since there were seven brothers who fought for this child it was decided that the child would be given to King Varunaraja, who was childless, in exchange for some gold. The queen Vethavalli nurtured the child. The child was named Renuka Parameshwari and was brought up lovingly in the royal household. Renuka attained puberty when she was twelve years old and a grand function was held with the three auspicious fruits (Mango, Jackfruit, and Banana).

There was a miscreant called Naratha.[21] According to Brahma's curse, his head will burst if he does not continually stir up trouble. Naratha sees the rishi Jamarthakini in solitary, deep meditation. He decides to get Renuka married to him. He tells Jamarthakini that he has found a wife for him who can assist him well in performing his worship rites. Together they meet the King with this proposal and the marriage alliance is settled.

The wedding is a grand event and the celebration lasts for five days. The whole town is decorated with flowers and fruits. The bride and the bridegroom are decorated with flowers. And in the presence of Ganapathy (God of all obstacles) they are married. After the wedding the King sends his daughter to the Ashram, which is the home of the rishi. The rishi refuses any dowry. Jamarthakini and Renuka have four children: Anuvaan, Dhanvaan, Vishvathi and Parasuraman.

The family worships Shiva. Renuka assists the Rishi in his performance of the puja by fetching water from the river Ganga. Every morning she walks to the Ganga where a pot of water is miraculously churned out of the river and given to her. Her mind is so pure and chaste that the water is held within the imaginary pot till she brings it to her husband for his worship rituals.

One day while receiving the pot of water at the river she sees the reflection of Arjunan who flies past as Gandharvan. Renuka admires his beauty and at that moment loses her chastity. The water recedes from her pot and she is afraid of being cursed by her husband. She calls for her fourth son (Parasuraman) and asks him to kill her.[22] He refuses and runs back to report this to his father. The rishi is furious and orders Parasuraman to kill his mother.

In the meantime Renuka runs for her life and seeks refuge in a hut in a 'Ceeri' (The hamlet, which is separated from the main village, where the Paraiyar live). The people of the 'Ceeri' hide Renuka in a hut along with an old Paraiyar woman who is to be of comfort to her.

When Parasuraman did not find his mother at the place that he had left her, he began to search for her everywhere. Eventually he traced her to the hut. But in his rage and confusion he beheads and kills both the women. He goes back and reports this to his father. To show his good pleasure to Parasuraman his father grants him one boon. The son asks that his mother's life be restored. The Rishi gives Parasuraman a pot of water and some ash. He asks him to replace Renuka's severed head on her body, apply the ash on her forehead and bathe her with the water in the pot. Parasuraman goes back to the hut and does as he is told. However, in his enthusiasm to restore his mother he mistakenly puts the head of the old Paraiyar woman on to Renuka's body. Now Renuka has the head of the old Paraiyar woman.

She goes home to the rishi but he is unwilling to take her back since she has the head of a Paraiyar. She is sent out into the village to live from the gifts of the people. Here she utilizes her powers to protect all those who nurture her with food, offerings and worship.

Because of her transformed nature the goddess is able to assume various forms. They are imaged in the seven sisters. Of all these forms Ellaiyamman is the most powerful. She does good and protects the people from all evil. She has a troop of devils under her control. She protects the colony in all four directions.

This legend about the origins of Ellaiyamman is closely linked to the mythical origins of Mariyamman. Whitehead recounts a similar story after which he adds, 'The woman with the Brahman head and the Pariah body was afterwards worshipped as Mariyamman; while the woman with the Pariah head and the Brahman body was worshipped as the goddess Yellamma.'[23] Many important themes can be extrapolated from the legend. But this myth primarily points to the complex nature of the relationship between Paraiyar religion and Hinduism. On the one hand, one is struck by the copious borrowing of Hindu story lines, mythological characters and themes. There is a resolute effort by the Paraiyar to work within the symbolic world of Hindu mythology. The setting of the myth reflects a conventional Hindu plot: the divine power emerges through a process of transposition of heads.[24] Furthermore, the mythological characters contained in this myth draw upon easily identifiable figures from common Hindu stories that are fairly well known in South India. The names of Brahma, Naratha, Ganapathy, Shiva, Arjunan, and Parasuraman are common to most South Indian Hindus; and they are invoked to give the story a ring of familiarity. There are also many themes inherent in this mythological song about

Ellaiyamman that are prominent in various Hindu legends: the symbolic alliance between the king and the Brahmin, the invocation of the propitious numerical, i.e. seven, the auspicious marking of the rite of menarche, the efficacy of the holy water of Ganga, the ideal ritualistic pattern of daily puja performed by the rishi with the aid of a religiously devout wife, the blessedness implied in having enough male children, the idea of purity and chastity being a quality of the mind for a devout wife, the commission of matricide as a test for dharmic action, the cutting off of the head because of suspicion that a wife has been unfaithful and the generation of volatile energy that stems from the mixing of incongruous substances.

On the other hand, one cannot but notice the manner in which these themes and mythological characters are utilized with a view towards reinterpreting the collective identity of the Paraiyar in an affirmative way. This remythologizing of the origin of Ellaiyamman functions to valorize the Paraiyar. Through an emancipatory retelling of the story of Ellaiyamman their particular version of history is inscribed and validated. Accordingly, in this myth the Paraiyar are, firstly, presented as being a helpful community; they are even willing to suffer persecution in the service of protecting a refugee.[25] In the context of the caste communities' lengthy, extensive, and calculating effort to dehumanize the Dalits, this version, quite movingly (perhaps in a satirical vein), demonstrates that the Paraiyar are human to such a degree that they manifest this humaneness even when confronted with the distress of caste persons. Secondly, this remythologized version of the emergence of the goddess reinforces the notion that the Paraiyar are the recipients of undeserved violence. They are caught within the various subtle conflicts of the caste community and are affected because it spills over onto the Dalits.[26] What is most interesting in this regard is the association of this victimization with the symbolic figures of women. Both Renuka (caste Hindu woman) and the old Paraiyar lady are represented as the victims who miraculously survive the vengeful power of a male antagonist and then become the foundation of Paraiyar divine power. Finally, this myth reinforces the fact that formidable divine power is generated through being an outcast. Ellaiyamman utilizes this power to protect and guard her subjects from all harm. The discussion concerning the independence of the power of the Dalit goddess from the gods of the Hindu pantheon is relevant at this point. The power of the one that is cast out by Hinduism must be contended with: it is a power which is ejected by caste Hinduism because it cannot be contained and controlled within the workings of its system. On the same count, this inability by caste Hinduism to manage this power outside its systems becomes a resource for Dalits both to preserve their own identity and ward off the infiltration of the religious nexus of the caste communities.

Another definitive element of the legend of Ellaiyamman must be emphasized at this juncture: this Dalit goddess has the head of a Paraiyar and the body of a caste Hindu woman. Commenting on this, Elmore writes, 'the Dravidian goddess, Ellamma, is sometimes represented with the torn-off head of a Brahmin in her hand.'[27] While I did not come across this iconographical or mythological representation, which gives Ellaiyamman control over the torn-off head of the Brahmin woman (Renuka), this further supports my contention that the goddess Ellaiyamman exemplifies this process of emancipatory remythologization. This particular reinscription of the story as expounded by the Paraiyar reimagines the accepted social configurations of South Indian polity by reversing the position of the Paraiyar and the Brahmin. The head that symbolizes power/knowledge of the Brahmin (erudition in the Vedas and schooling in the proper practice rituals: wisdom of orthodoxy and orthopraxis) is replaced with the head that signifies the power of the Paraiyar (brute mundane power in the realm of the material/physical: tangible power to protect and to punish). This is in many senses a symbolic act of subversion: an inversion of the status quo as propagated by Hindu myth and practice.

It is clear from the above discussion that religious remythologization is a domain of specific meaning-making for the Paraiyar. It is the arena of tactful contestation in which the hegemonic outlook of Hinduism is weakened. This process of construing emancipatory mythographies, as just explicated, involves both an interaction with and appropriation of forms from the dominant group and a subtle rejection of it in order to reclaim for the Paraiyar their own human identity and rationale for existence.[28]

This explication of the goddess Ellaiyamman as symbolizing the resistive particularity and the emancipatory remythologization of the Paraiyar gives us a glimpse into the dynamic, creative, calculating and empowering features of the Paraiyar religion. The religious arena for them, thus, is both an arena of continual contestation and conscious reformation: it both discerningly rejects and contextually redefines certain dominant 'conceptions of a general order of existence.'[29]

III. The Drum as a Dominant Aniconic Symbol of the Text of Resistance and Emancipatory Theography

The previous section highlighted the active side of Paraiyar religion. It does not merely represent a passive replication and acceptance of all that was passed on to the Paraiyar from caste Hindu interpretations of religion. Rather, the Paraiyar religion points to an arena of ongoing contestation and transformation of dominant and, sometimes, oppressive cultural and social patterns that are founded on religious narratives (plots?). However, as hinted at earlier, Paraiyar religion is not only the collective art of dismantling and reassembling dominant caste Hindu patterns of meaning for the sake of subaltern communities. It is also a symbolic manifestation of their very own experience of the Divine. Subaltern religion in this sense does not always have to be a response to the experience of the religious as represented by the dominant communities. The response to the Divine as primarily experienced by and symbolically expressed within the collective life of the Dalits (thus, only secondarily mediated through the religious symbol system of the caste Hindu community) is the focus of this section. In order to grasp and thematize the distinct, substantive and subjective dimensions of Paraiyar religion I have opted to focus on the symbol of the drum.

The symbol of the drum primarily depicts the core of subaltern religious subjectivity. However, because of the dominant and ubiquitous nature of caste Hinduism, Dalit religion cannot but express its own distinctness in resistance to the former. The conventional retention and the prevalent utilization of the drum as an essential component of Paraiyar religious practice testifies to a form of deliberate resistance. Within the caste Hindu context, if viewed from the perspective of the theory of purity versus pollution, the drum is derided and demonized as generating and communicating pollution. Yet, the Paraiyar have not dispensed with valuing the drum as a central religious symbol in communicating with the Divine. By preserving this as an essential religious symbol they have symbolically resisted the over-arching valuations of the caste communities. Similar to the logic of Ellaiyamman, the embracing of the drum by the Paraiyar stems from the notion that which is outside the religious rationale of the caste communities is free from its control. Because the drum can be utilized to contain the particularities of the Dalit experience of the Divine it operates as a symbol for emancipatory theography. In other words, the Paraiyar graphically symbolize the Divine (literally, doing Theo/God-graphics) for their own liberation. The drum symbolizes both the distinctiveness of the Paraiyar's religious and social world and its undomesticatability and uncooptability by the caste communities. Thus, it can function to ground the collective religious particularity of the Dalits. A major objective of this chapter is to analyse the distinctiveness of the Paraiyar's religion by unpacking the theological themes resonating from the symbol of the drum. The subsequent chapters attempt to utilize this religious symbol of the Paraiyar to transfigure theology to the emancipatory for all its practitioners, particularly the Dalits.

As already mentioned in the previous chapter, there are many types of drums that are extant in the religious life of the Paraiyar. More specifically, I implicitly alluded to the possibility of the existence of a hierarchy of sorts among the various kinds of drums utilized by the Paraiyar. The uDukkai and the bambai drums, on the one hand, are made of goat skin and are utilized by the priests and their immediate ritual assistants. These are considered to be less threatening to the caste people and are regarded with somewhat more respect in the various collective festivals. The parai and the satti drums, on the other hand, are made from cow hide and are utilized by specialized Dalit drummers who are not priests. The latter drummers are religious functionaries but their role is confined to drumming alone. In this study of the drum I deal primarily with the parai drum. However, I shall not discount the fact that the numerousness of these configurations of drum-types may also be proof that the Paraiyar religion is drum-centred.

The parai drum is a circular, one-sided drum made out of calf leather. The face of the drum has a diameter of about two feet and it is tightly strung around a circular wooden frame carved from a tree trunk. The leather is tightly wrapped around the wooden frame by means of thin leather strips. It usually has a rope that is attached to it which is used to tie the drum around the waist of the drummer. This allows the drummer to utilize both hands to play the drum. The drum is beaten by both hands: a stick held by the right hand and the open palm of the left hand are used in its performance. The beats are produced by the drummer in unison with his fellow drummers: 'when the *parai* drum plays, the four *parais* keep a common rhythmic beat appropriate to the occasion.'[30] Till a few years ago, the drums for Malaipallaiyam and Thottanavoor were produced by one particular Paraiyar sub-caste through a specific process of drying the skin of the calf that was locally procured. However, now the drummers buy their drums from a family in a neighbouring colony known to be experts in drum-making. The drummers I interviewed did not know of ceremonies that must be performed to transform a new drum into a ritual instrument.

The drum is a focal and fecund symbol for comprehending and interpreting the religion of the Paraiyar. It provides the differential with which to perceive their religious traditions. I shall put forward four arguments to underscore and support his proposition.

The substantial presence argument

The drum is central to the religious life of the Paraiyar. In the words of one informant (Govindasamy) from Malaipallaiyam colony, 'only with drums everything is complete.' There is widespread agreement among the Paraiyar that this symbol is what makes the Paraiyar religion unique and complete. In a study on Paraiyar drummers in Sri Lanka, McGilvray highlights the symbolic importance of the drum in the religious life and practice of the Dalit community. He suggests that the *raca meelam* ('King drum') serves as 'a sort of heraldic symbol of the Paraiyar caste as a whole.'[31] Two notable features of the functioning of the drum among the Paraiyar of Sri Lanka are relevant to this discussion. First, the drum 'is carried to all public ceremonies where the Paraiyar provide drumming service.'[32] In fact, wherever the drummers are ritually performing, the 'king drum' is treated with honour and reverence: high caste patrons are expected to provide 'new white cloth' in which to wrap the drum and a 'new reed mat' on which to place it through the performance.[33] The drum, thus, demonstrates the symbolic alliance between the Paraiyar as a community and their particular cultural and religious contribution to society as a whole. Second, the practice of drumming is extremely widespread among the Paraiyar community: 'Virtually every adult male Paraiyar in Tivukkudi is an accomplished drummer or shawm player.'[34]

In contemporary Tamil Nadu, although the art of drumming is not as widespread as in neighbouring Sri Lanka, it is still an important symbol of the Paraiyar's distinct religious power, knowledge and practice. The pervasiveness of the art of drumming is not manifested by the number of male members in the community who play the instrument. In fact, in the regions around Karunguzhi there is a decrease in the number of young Paraiyar males who are even willing to learn to play the drum because they are influenced by the caste Hindus' idea that this is a lowly religious and cultural practice. Nonetheless, the conspicuous and striking prevalence of drumming in the communal life of the Paraiyar can be confirmed by looking into the various aspects of their religious activities. As mentioned earlier, the presence and the power of drumming is integral to all kinds of religious ceremonies. Thus, there is an acceptance that the drum belongs to the celebrative and the afflictive dimensions of human life.

On an individual level, if we take the life of a particular Paraiyar female in her various cyclic phases, the drum finds its place in each of the significant stages: the drums are played for functions that mark (a) the girl's coming of age, (b) the woman's departure from her home to marry someone from another colony, (c) the woman's marriage, (d) the occasion of the seventh month of the woman's pregnancy, and (e) the woman's death.[35] In all these ritual events, the drum is beaten in order to inspire and invoke the goddesses both to protect the person from evils that could befall her and to preserve the individual in health and goodness.

The drum also plays a consistently prominent role in the communal religious life of the Paraiyar. As described in detail in the previous chapter, the drummers are an absolutely necessary part of the annual colony festival to the goddess. They are instrumental in facilitating every phase of the festival. The integral relatedness of the priest and drum and their cooperative functioning in the religious practice of the Paraiyars must also be reiterated. They are together responsible for the mediation between the goddesses and the human devotees.

Various drum beats are associated with specific events in the life of the Paraiyar. The number of the beats that are played by the Paraiyar drummers differs from region to region. The Paraiyar drummers of Sri Lanka claim to possess the largest number of distinct beats. In the words of Mcgilvray:

> There are over 18 distinctive drumming rhythms (*tal[a]llams*) in the Paraiyar repertoire, only 2 of which are inauspicious and are associated with funeral observances. The remaining rhythms are auspicious and varied; they are used in pujas, exorcisms, processions and public entertainments.[36]

In his study in Tamil Nadu, Moffatt lists a much smaller number of drum rhythms that are utilized by the Paraiyar of Endavur. His inference, that Paraiyar drummers 'play at least nine different beats, a distinct beat for each ritual occasion,'[37] is consistent with my personal observations.

In the colonies around Karunguzhi it is generally accepted that there are nine distinct drum beats. However, they quickly add that the drummers do play different beats for every special ritual occasion. Moffatt also characterizes the drum beats according to the classification of auspiciousness: he divides the nine *taalams* (beats) into five 'good beats' and four beats that are 'not for good things'.[38]

In this interpretation, rather than list the different beats according to categories suggested by ethnomusicology, I shall list them by general grouping that I observed as being utilized regularly in the ritual life of the Paraiyar community.

The Processional drum

There are certain auspicious processions that require the drums to accompany the people who are making a particularly felicitous and purposive journey. (i) The procession of the goddess through the colony during the annual festival is one example. At this time the drummers are an integral part of the procession and they play a particular beat that effectively drives demons away from the path of the goddess and lures the goddess to undertake and complete her ritual pilgrimage through the entire colony. (ii) Another common ritual procession takes place on the eve of the wedding when the bridegroom's family and relatives proceed to the bride's home with gifts of sweets, fruits and clothing in order to finalize the marriage alliance. At this time the drummers play a special drum beat referred to as the *varasai melam*. This is a celebrative and auspicious function in which the drum clears all impediments so that 'all will go well' both for the agreed upon alliance and the actual marriage itself.

The divine grace-bestowing drum

Another function of the drum beat is to signify the blessing and the benediction of the goddess's presence and power upon the religious event, particularly focussing on the main actors around which the ritualistic ceremony revolves. I have already alluded to the auspicious nature of the drum in the religious life of the Paraiyar. There are ceremonies in which the drums are beaten in order for the presence of the goddess to grace a particular occasion.

The following four ritual ceremonies are examples of the way in which the drum is utilized to indicate the divine favour of the goddess. (a) The *kalyaana* (wedding) melam is the drum beat played at the wedding ceremony. The bride and the bridegroom are decked in new clothes and garlands and are brought to the center of a *pandal* (a thatched temporary shelter). Here they are seated on a grinding stone which is set on a platform. A kapu is tied to the bride and the bridegroom, usually by the respective prospective mothers-in-law to symbolize that they belong to each other. The bridegroom then ties a *maangalyam* (a yellow thread coated with saffron attached to a small pendant made of gold) around the neck of the bride. After this they both light the family lamp together. Finally they worship the feet of their parents and proceed into their home. The drum beat is played while the bride and the groom make their way to the platform. However, the drum beat is loudly and continuously heard while the bridegroom ties the maangaiyam and when the couple light the lamp and enter their home. It is said to 'help in bringing divine favour and blessedness' for the couple.

(b) The *seemandam melam* is the drum beat that is played when a married woman is seven months pregnant and is ready to leave her husband's home in order to go to her parent's home for the confinement. Drumming during this ceremony serves two purposes. On the one hand, the drums clear the path that the pregnant woman will take in this crossing from the confines of her husband's home to the geographic space of her parent's home. On the other hand, the drum beat is utilized to announce to the community that the married woman who is pregnant has made it safely through the most vulnerable phase of pregnancy. In this latter context, the drum beat is one of appropriating and celebrating the favour of the goddess.

(c) Another kind of drum beat is called *nalangu melam*. It is similar to the seemandam melam and is played when a young bride-to-be leaves her own home to travel to another colony for her wedding. Since it is a custom that the wedding is performed in the bridegroom's colony, the bride-to-be is sent from her own colony with all the blessings of her colony goddess. The drum beat thus performs the role of mediating this favour of the goddess.

(d) Finally, there is the drum beat that is played when a girl comes of age. Again the point of this drumming is, on the one hand, to announce to the community that the auspicious state of womanhood has been achieved by a member of the community. This is particularly important because it declares to the families who may be interested in arranging a marriage alliance with this girl's family that this girl is ready to be considered a woman. On the other hand, the drum beat symbolizes the divine benediction that is mediated to the girl-turned-woman even as she passes from one stage to another.

The invoking and inspiring drum

The drummer utilizes music to invoke and inspire the goddess to display and manifest her power among her devotees. The drum is used in conjunction with the prayers and songs sung by the Paraiyar priests. It is also used as an independent medium by which the goddess is invoked and inspired. When drumming is the sole medium of religious mediation, the drums are beaten rapidly and loudly for a sustained period of time (usually about five minutes) until the effects of the drumming are realized. There are two beats that are identified with this category of invoking and inspiring drums: the *gengai melam* and the *bali melam*.

(a) The gengai melam is associated with the invocation of the goddess Gengaiamman. However, the same beat is played when any of her sisters are invoked to appear and manifest their power before their devotees. It is said that Gengaiamman is attracted and lured by this drum beat; thus the goddess is addressed and controlled by means of this drumming. It was fascinating to see the way in which the drum beat is used at the colony festival at the time when the goddess is invoked to bless and participate in the yearly festival. The drums are central to this festival. Most significantly, the drums are played in rhythmic unison when the goddess descends on her chosen servant: it facilitates this revelatory appearance of the goddess.

(b) The *bali melam* (the drum of sacrifice) is used at times of public sacrifice of an animal. As noted earlier, although the Paraiyar talk about regular sacrifices that involved buffalos and goats in the past, presently the most common sacrificial animal is a male chicken. Also, there is general agreement that the *bali* beat is not really necessary when a male chicken is sacrificed since it is not a 'substantial sacrifice' on behalf of the whole colony. The bali drum beat, therefore, is not a frequently heard beat because communal and public sacrifices are less common now. For example, the Paraiyar of Malaipallaiyam and Thottanavoor have not sacrificed a goat publicly for the last five years.

There are two interpretations regarding the purpose of the bali melam. According to one theory, animal sacrifice is made in order to appease the goddess; the drum, in this case, is beaten to invoke the divine being to be present at the sacrifice performed in her honour. Here it is assumed that the presence of the goddess, which is mediated by the drums, is required for the efficacy of the sacrifice. Another interpretation is that the goddess is inspired and invigorated through bloody sacrifice so as to conquer competing demons. Here the drum is a medium of invocation that entices the demons to be present at a particular sacrificial rite; it is also a medium that energizes the 'urgent' and 'wrath-filled' power of the goddess which is needed to overcome and subdue these demons at the site of the sacrifice.

The protecting and exorcising drum

There is general consensus among anthropologists, indologists, and religionists that the Paraiyar are involved in the drumming that occurs during funerals for both the caste communities and the Dalits. Mcgilvray suggests that 'funeral drumming is certainly the most symbolically potent embodiment'[39] of the Paraiyar's dual hereditary occupation, which consisted of drumming and funeral work. The caste community consider the Paraiyar's role to be irreplaceable during their own funerals. In the areas surrounding Malaipallaiyam and Thottanavoor they are said to entice the Paraiyar drummers with 'more money and more rice' so that they do not reject this important ritual component of the caste funerals.[40]

The *saavu melam* (literally the death drum) is a beat that the drummers identify as a specialized melam. It is played at funerals. The drummers start at the house where the dead body is laid out. After the individual dies, the body is bathed, wrapped in a single cloth and laid out on a simple wooden cot outside the dead person's hut. On the day of the funeral, which is almost always the next day (the body cannot be preserved any longer in South India because of the hot and humid weather throughout the year), the priest along with the drummers comes to the site where the body is laid and offers his prayers while the drummers stand near the dead body and play for extended periods. Again, there is no variation in the beats; it consists of regular, even beats. The drummers, along with the official priest, lead the procession to the cemetery. The drummers continue to play their saavu melam in unison as they lead the dead body, which is carried on a disposable mat weaved out of palms by four men holding on to its four corners. The procession comes to a halt at the intersection of the colony and the cemetery. This crossing is usually marked with a stone that symbolizes the presence of the guardian of the cemetery, Arichandran. After a sacrifice (usually a male chicken or a lemon) to Arichandran, the drummers lead the body into the cemetery to be either cremated or buried.[41]

After the funeral the drummers lead the family back to their home where they are paid in cash and kind.[42]

Drumming at the funeral is said to accomplish two things. First, the drums are supposed to bid and contain the spirit of the dead person. There is a belief that the dead person's spirit leaves the body at death and hovers around the house. It is without an inhabitation and awaits to occupy a person or a place familiar to the spirit. The drum functions to coax and direct the spirit to leave the house and go in peace to the cemetery where it may be under the directive of the spirit world. In this sense the drums are instruments of exorcism: they exorcize the spirit of the dead person from the lives of the family and its dwelling space and guide it along to a space that is destined for spirits of the dead.

Second, drumming during funerals is believed to keep other demons away. The death of an individual brings out the malevolent spirits in an unusual way. The spirits are both disturbed and awakened by death. It is at such a time that the drummers are mostly required. Drumming is associated with divine power; and this divine power is needed to control the demonic spirits. The drums are utilized to keep the demonic powers away from the physical space occupied by the family as well as the colony. This practice of utilizing drumming as a means of communicating with, controlling and exorcising demons is recorded by Dumont in his study of the Kallar of South India:

> The beneficent possession of his god descends on him. For hours or perhaps days, he plays a great variety of rhythms on his drum (the knowledge of these rhythms determined the specialization...).... After a varying length of time – generally several hours, but sometimes as much as a week, it is said – the demon begins to answer his questions.[43]

With regard to the Paraiyar, this aspect of drumming as a means of containing, controlling and exorcising the spirits, whether divine or demonic, is consistent with the themes of drumming that have been examined thus far.

The announcing drum

One of the practical functions of drumming is implicit in many of the situations that have been described: it is utilized as a means of communicating to neighbouring villages that a certain event is taking place. The distinct beats generally convey the nature of the event taking place in the particular colony. For example, when the people who live at a radius of about 3 or 4 kilometres hear the saavu melam they know that there has been a death and will enquire further as to who has died. Along similar lines, the drum is also used for calling people together within the colony for a community consensus meeting. As mentioned in the previous chapter, at the time of the annual festival drummers go around the colony in order to call the community members for meeting to arrange for the festival.

The relaxing dance-drum

The drum is used to facilitate communal merry-making. A beat called the *kummi melam* is an example. *Kummi* is a type of communal dance that is performed with sticks. Usually kummi is performed by women but it is not exclusively so. The drums play a rhythm to which the dancers move. While there is mention of this beat and its context of dancing among the Paraiyar, they were unable to recall when they last performed the kummi dance. My informants profess that 'people do not have the time to dance'. Moffatt also refers to a drum beat that is utilized in a dance that makes fun of a sub-community called the Kurivikaran. This again points to drumming as a means of relaxing entertainment.

The cultural and economic association argument

The parai drum is also expressedly linked with the cultural and economic sphere of the Paraiyar. On the one hand, the Paraiyar are a beef-eating society. Notably, Dalits are the only beef-eating community among those that are generally designated under the term Hindu. Culturally, thus, this is a food habit involving contact with the flesh of the cow which is abhorrent to caste Hindus. Interestingly, the drum, which is made from the cow after its flesh has been eaten, symbolizes the cultural characteristics of the Paraiyar. When I lived in Karunguzhi I was surprised that the butcher who delivered beef to our house came from a town 20 kilometres away. His visit required both anonymity and secrecy. Moreover, he had the meat wrapped up as though he was delivering a gift. When I asked him why he was so secretive about his mission, he answered, 'I do not want your caste neighbours to know that you eat beef because they will think that you are a Paraiyar.' On the other hand, the livelihood of the Paraiyar depends on the carcasses of dead cattle: they are the designated cattle scavengers. They eat the flesh of the dead carcass and skin it in order to procure its skin. The holy cow which symbolizes aspects of the sacred (purity?) among the caste Hindus is reversed when it becomes the dead cow which symbolizes aspects of inauspiciousness (pollution?) in the hands of the Paraiyar. By ingesting the meat and by dealing with its carcass and skin the Paraiyar symbolize inauspiciousness to the caste communities. The parai drum, which is made from the leather of young calf, becomes the most explicit and fitting symbol of the degradation of the Paraiyar. The once-holy, but now-deceased, cow represented by the drum is debased and taken to be representational of the culture and occupation of the Paraiyar by the caste Hindus.[44]

This, nevertheless, is not representative of the Paraiyar's perspective. While the Paraiyar accept that the drum is something of a paradigmatic symbol of their economic and cultural situation, at the same time, they continually refuse to admit to its degradation and debasement. Rather, they remythologize the significance of the drum to tell noble tales. One such tale, recorded by Moffatt, subscribes to the idea that the parai drum was actually the 'big drum', which more accurately signifies its prestigious connotations:

> Among themselves, and in relation to a non-Indian anthropologist, the Harijans do articulate some minor reinterpretations of their *toRil.* One Harijan, for example, tries to say that the 'real' name of the *paraimelem* ('parai drum') was the *'periya meelum'* ('big drum'). *'Parai'* and *'periya'* are not that close in spoken Tamil, though folk etymologies common in Tamil villages frequently work with differences this great. The shift from *'parai'* to 'big', however, would represent the detachment of one Harijan artifact from a word now solidly stigmatized and its reattachment to a more generally and vaguely prestigious term.[45]

The historical association argument

The drum is a symbol with which the Paraiyar have been historically associated for many centuries. As a religious symbol it has its roots in pre-Aryan times. The drum, thus, is a common symbol that connects the Paraiyar with the ancient peoples and cultures of South India. In his reconstruction of the *Sangam* age of the Tamils (fourth century BCE to fourth century CE) N. Subrahmanian focusses on the *murasu* drum as a religious symbol. According to him the parai drum that is used by contemporary Paraiyars 'seems to be a variant of the Murasu'.[46] In his discussion of the drum in the Sangam age he situates it within the arena of their religion.

Three facets of the drum as thematized by the ancient Tamils of the Sangam age manifest themselves in the Paraiyar's understanding of drums. First, the drum is taken to be a representative of the Divine.

'The Tamils of the Sangam age attributed divine qualities to the drum and so bathed it in holy water, garlanded it and worshipped it.'[47] This integral connection of the drum with the Divine is also assumed in the annual festival of the goddess that is celebrated by the Paraiyar. At that time, as mentioned in the previous chapter, the drum is tied with the kapu so as to actually represent the Goddess:

> These [drums] and the various images to the goddess used during this [festival] day, 'are' the goddess's power and her being. They are not mere symbols or representations of her, standing for her in some abstract way.[48]

Second, the drum is considered as an auspicious religious symbol. In the Sangam age the drum was a much sought after auspicious object. For example it 'was sent to the battlefield on an auspicious day to ensure victory in battle.'[49] Moreover, it was thought to be so auspicious that 'the drum like the other royal emblem, the Umbrella, was a cherished booty in a battlefield; and he that could capture these emblems was a hero.'[50] This acknowledgement of the auspicious nature of the drums is a distinctive peculiarity of Paraiyar religious practice. The drum is utilized for religious, cultural and social occasions. The caste communities utilize the drum mainly for inauspicious rituals whereas the Paraiyar use it for both auspicious and inauspicious ones.

Third, the drum is accepted as a symbol of proclamation and protection. In the Sangam age 'the drum was a symbol of protection and was called the tutelary drum.'[51] It also announced the beginning of war and conflict and thus enabled people to prepare for war. In the case of the Paraiyar, the drum also symbolizes protection from divine and human forces that try to afflict them.[52] It is also utilized as an instrument that proclaims and announces communal news that have religious significance. Particular drum beats are associated with specific tidings and people prepare to participate in the rituals that are appropriate, for example, the death beat in the case of a death or the festival beat which indicates to the people to get ready to celebrate the goddess's festival.

It is pertinent that some caste Hindus in Tamil Nadu actually acknowledge that the Paraiyar's association with the drum stems from a favour granted to them as a community by the goddess. Drumming is thus a symbol of their high-calling which they squandered because of their greed. Moffatt captures the essence of this original high status of the Paraiyar as drummers in the following local myth:

> In those days the Colony people were higher in caste. Therefore Kali gave

them the right to announce, to beat the drum, and to honor the dead. The *uur* people had to pay them a fee for this, so they had both honor and income in those days. One day, Kali asked a Colony person to beat the drums and to declare: 'Let the unripe and let the ripe fall' (that is, let the young and the old die). The Harijan added two or three more phases: 'Let the bud and let the flower fall' (that is, let the unborn and let the small children die). He did this in order to get even more income. Kali became angry with him and said, 'since you have changed my pronouncement, you are hereafter lower castes.' Since then others have looked down on them as low, because they attempted to increase their income in this crude way.[53]

The myth clearly brings out the notion that the practice of drumming was considered a respectable and worthy profession. It also establishes a link between the goddess and the drum. The drum in this case, is a gift of power to the Paraiyar to influence matters concerned with protection, production and procreation. These three attributes we may recall are associated with the Dalit goddess.

The Paraiyar's continued use of this religious symbol (the drum) is an act of judicious preservation. The Paraiyar claim, that they are the indigenous people of South India who were over-powered and enslaved by the invading groups,[54] is symbolically expressed through the drum. Despite the painfulness of its representational ramifications among caste communities it is retained as a memorium of the ancient heritage, culture and religion of the Paraiyar. Even if the drum is used by the caste Hindus against the Paraiyar in order to emphasize their inauspiciousness and pollutedness, it is for them a nebulous, though corporeal, reminder of their traditional religio-cultural prominence and power.

The etymological argument

There have been many imaginative attempts to decipher the meaning of the term Paraiyar. The most widely accepted and popular etymological theory is that it comes from the Tamil word parai which means drum. In fact, to date the Paraiyar are the drummers for religious rituals of both the Dalits (for auspicious and inauspicious occasions) and the caste Hindus (for inauspicious occasions). One local young man from the Paraiyar community in Thottanavoor proposed that the term Paraiyar comes from the two words that together accurately depict the people of his community. Accordingly, the Paraiyar got their name from being the *aiyar* (priest) of the parai (drum). His creative etymological interpretation thus suggests that the Paraiyar are literally 'the priests of the drum'. Levi-Strauss suggests that in India there seems to be an intimate and singular relationship between a caste group and its totemic object. In his words,

> This heterogeneity [of caste/clan names] is most apparent in India where a high proportion of totemic names are names of manufactured objects, that is, of products or symbols of functional activities which...can serve to express distinction between social groups.[55]

In consonance with this view, it is permissible to suggest the existence of a primal and inherent relationship between the drum and the Paraiyar.

In the earlier section of this chapter, I suggested that the Paraiyar goddess serves the Dalits in two ways: she protects them from the colonizing tendency of caste Hindus by her iconic resistance and provides them with the impetus to continually refigure their own framework of religio-cultural meaning through a process of remythologization. This section has documented the fact that the drum is the heart-beat of the religious life of the Paraiyar community. In so doing, I have also pressed for the analogously daring claim that the drum be interpreted as an aniconic symbol that artfully and discriminatingly functions to manifest the substantive and subjective elements of Paraiyar religiousness.[56] This substantive and resistive symbol of the drum is nothing other than the power of the Dalit goddess herself. The words of the Dalit poet, Shiva Ingole, are relevant here:

None but I [The Ancient Mother]
have tattooed songs of liberty
on the bare torsos
and planted drums of defiance
on the lips
of womenfolk here.[57]

It is ironic that a symbol which has been the target of centuries of denigration, defamation and vilification can be foundational to the sustenance, nurture and empowerment of the Paraiyar. The capacity of the drum to galvanize resistive and emancipatory forces in order to retain the particularity of their collective identity is the hallmark of the religious creativity of the Paraiyar. This resistive potential of religion being put to emancipatory use is hinted at in the words of a third century BCE Ashoka edict: 'the sound of war drums has become the call to religion.'[58]

IV. The Dominant Symbols of the Paraiyar in Context

Before concluding this discussion, two contexts through which the symbol of the drum can be further explicated need to be highlighted. At this time I shall merely allude to these contextual pointers in order to situate the drum within the overall world of the Paraiyar in its interrelatedness with the caste communities. In so doing, I shall also suggest its relationship with the symbol of the goddess Ellaiyamman.

First, the drum can be appreciated as a fitting counter-image of the Paraiyar when viewed against the backdrop of the Hindu conception of the sacred Word. It is a pragmatic and constructive counter-symbol in response to the tyranny of the sacred Word of the Hindus. The Dalits have been systematically and effectively marginated by the sacred Word both in its written form (the Hindu scriptures) and in its oral form (the mantra and ritualistic prayers that were handed down in Sanskrit). For instance, there is a commonly held belief among the Paraiyar that they would be severely punished if they attempted to hear or study the Hindu Vedas. There are different versions of the brutality of this punishment that range from cutting off of the Paraiyar's tongue to being beaten by the caste council.[59] Learning of Sanskrit by the Paraiyar was also a punishable offence. Thus, they were severed from the ritual and religious know-how of the caste Hindus. Till this day, learning Sanskrit is incongruous with being a Dalit: it 'is a dreadful anomaly to the traditional mind.'[60]

It is in the midst of this oppressive context of the sacred Word that one must understand the appropriateness and potency of the symbol of the drum. The divine sound is claimed by the Paraiyar in a context in which the sacred Word is terrorizing. An example of this intimate relationship between the divine and the drum among the Paraiyar is communicated in the following lullaby by a Paraiyar woman. One can notice the centrality of the drum in mediating the sound and presence of the Lord. The sound of the drum seems to resound from the interior of the temple, the place from where the Word would normally emanate. The sound of the drum in this context can be interpreted to be a comforting and protecting divine presence: it enfolds the baby in a such a way that the baby can sleep in peace, security and wholeness.

For you, lullabying and caressing,
(I) have laid you in your cradle.

For you the conch shell sounds, boy,
My little brother, in the temple of your Lord,
Your drum sounds, boy,
My darling in the temple of the supreme.[61]

Second, the drum can be seen to represent divine power, which is fundamental to the Paraiyar. Here it is relevant to remember that the universal and supreme divine Spirit of the Paraiyar is Sakti (Divine power). On the one hand, the symbol of the drum keeps the incessantly infiltrating powers of the caste community away from the Dalits by exerting its own power. In a sense it can be said that the drum, which is symbolic of the Paraiyar as a people and the sacred forces they represent, is feared by the caste community. They will not come into contact with it and they will not dare to slight it in certain rituals in which it is utilized for their welfare. By posing a threat to the caste community the power that is mediated by the drum can, thus, further the cause of protecting the Paraiyar. Interestingly, the rhythmic thudding sound of the drum penetrates, in its own reverberating way, boundaries that are imposed by caste regulations so as to periodically remind all those in its surroundings of its vital and tangible existence. In a social world where pollution can be transferred through touch and even by sight, the drum is a call to the caste communities to hear the sound and the existence of the other communities (the Paraiyar in this case) and their divine power.

On the other hand, for the Paraiyar, the drum symbolizes the mediating and empowering presence of the divine. In one sense, the drum plays a role analogous to that of the sacred Word for the caste communities: it communicates the divine to the individual and/or the community and empowers the worshippers. In another sense, the drum's relationship to functional power may be different from the Word's relationship to the power of knowledge — a correlation, perhaps, between actualization and realization.

It must be restated that in symbolizing the presence of the sacred, the drum represents divine Sakti (a female principle). In the various religious rituals and festivals of the Paraiyar, the drum manifests the persuasive power of the divine. It elicits, rouses, evokes, stimulates, mesmerizes, celebrates and captivates in a sense that is invitational to and affirming of the Paraiyar. This may be construed as being dissimilar to the coercive power of the sacred Word as experienced by Dalits; albeit one must not deny that the Word can be made to function in a persuasive manner. For our purpose, it is germane to underscore the fact that the Paraiyar do not worship or sacrifice to their goddesses in order to attain or gain wisdom. Their worship of the Sacred has much to do, with the concrete efficacy of divine power. This 'restlessness' of Sakti as symbolized by the activity of energy-producing thudding of the drum can be contrasted with the 'stillness' and 'passivity' of the caste Hindu's conception of Wisdom as preserved in the sacred Word.[62]

From the above discussion a correlation between the drum and the goddess, which is implicit in the religion of the Paraiyar, may be contrasted with an association between the sacred Word and the great male gods, which is represented in caste Hinduism. The drum represents the Dalit goddess in her unco-optable and uncontrollable form; while also serving as a vehicle for her characteristically female energy/power (Sakti). However, apart from this suggestion of the tacit nature of this set of drum–goddess and word–god relationships, more detailed information on caste Hinduism and Dalit religions is necessary to establish such a theory. At this juncture we can mainly assert that Paraiyar religion conjointly retains the dominant symbols of the independent goddess and the ancestral drum as means of depicting their particularity in the face of the pervading dimensions of the great gods (Brahma, Vishnu, Shiva) and the sacred Word (Vedas) of caste Hinduism.

V. General Features of Subaltern Religion

Before concluding it would be fruitful to discern general features of subaltern religion by sifting through some of the arguments concerning the Dalit goddess (Ellaiyamman) and the drum. The first explicit finding about subaltern religion was suggested as a methodological hunch earlier: symbolic capital of subaltern communities as manifested in their religion is not entirely controlled by the dominant communities. Thus, religion among the subalterns is not mere 'false consciousness' that is wholly the fabrication of the dominant classes to delude, mesmerize, and control the dominated classes. Rather, it becomes a site of contestation in which the subaltern communities reconfigure their own subjectivity. In other words, despite the overall impetus of subjection of the Dalits, religion-making exhibits the orchestration of subaltern subjectivity. Resistance to the domineering religious production of the caste communities and creative emancipatory resymbolization of their own religious particularities are 'weapons of the weak'[63] that mark the religious subjectivity of the Dalits.

Here one is forced to move away from the interpretations of one dominant Marxist school that posits 'religion as ideology'. This rationale is best exemplified in the following excerpt from *The German Ideology*:

> The ideas of the ruling class are in every epoch the ruling ideas: i.e. the class which is the ruling material force of society, is at the same time its ruling intellectual force. The class which has the means of material production at its disposal has control at the same time over the means of mental production, so and thereby, generally speaking, the ideas of those who lack the means of mental production are subject to it.[64]

Rather, the emerging school of 'Cultural Marxism' seems a more relevant framework within which to interpret subaltern religion as encountered among the Paraiyar of South India.[65] On the one hand, it allows us to causally and conceptually loosen the bond between the base ('essence', which consists of the material/economic productive relationships) and superstructure ('appearance', as best exemplified by the epiphenonemon of religion, which as an ideological construct hides the exploitative nature of the structures). In so doing, the realm of religion-production gains some degree of independence from the domain of material production. A much more flexible, diversified and multiplex dynamic is read into an overall domination–subjection relationship. On the other hand, it brings back the dimension of agency to the subaltern people. Religion possesses the capacity to function as a counter-symbolic factory whereby subaltern communities reject the hegemonic symbolic universe of the dominant communities and conjure up one of their own. The act of 'making' their own symbolic worldview in the face of severe domination becomes the basis of hope, not just for their resistance but, more importantly, for the working out of their common subjectivity.

A second feature of subaltern religion, which offers insight into various dimensions of its resourcefulness and versatility, must be mentioned. Subaltern religion is characterized by the interweaving of at least the following factors: copious, though judicious, borrowing from the dominant religious tradition; calculating, though provisional, piecing together of all available symbolic resources; and creative, though alternate-mode, imagining of their own collective religious experiences. We cannot glorify Dalit religion as being completely independent of and, thus, at all points contradictory to caste Hinduism. This binary structure of opposition of subject–object, foreign–native, colonizer–colonized, self–other, and Hindu–Dalit, even while useful to analytically dissect the problem, hardly does justice to the complexity of the relationship between caste Hindu and Dalit religion. Let us look at the three elements of subaltern religion just mentioned to warrant the claim of its resourcefulness.

First, we have seen much ingenuity in borrowing from the dominant symbolic system with a view to claim, debunk or transfigure it for subaltern purposes. Here the inbetweenness of subaltern subjectivity must be stressed. There is no evidence for constructing Dalit subjectivity as solely a kind of counter-identity to the dominant caste communities, nor is there the possibility of moving away from all that has been Dalit and Hindu into a new and yet unexplored imaginative religious world.[66] Rather, among the Paraiyar there is a forging of subjectivity by wedding together some ingredients that can be retained as signs of Dalit particularity with some components that can be skillfully appropriated as signs of human universality from the larger caste Hindu worldview. 'Soft boundaries' are seen to exist between subaltern and dominant cultural interaction, which enhances the points of relatedness.[67] Here the notion of 'hybridity', as popularized by Homi K. Bhaba, may be helpful. Instead of viewing the dynamic of the colonizer with the colonized in terms of a one-way process of the oppressors obliterating the oppressed, he lifts up the cross-fertilization dimensions of survival that characterize subalternity.[68] Hybridity, thus,

> lays emphasis on the survival even under the most potent oppression of the distinctive aspects of the culture of the oppressed, and shows how these become an integral part of the new formations which arise from the clash of cultures characteristic of imperialism.[69]

In the context of the Paraiyar, this means that the resistance of Ellaiyamman cannot be accentuated without at the same time taking into consideration the annexation of many Hindu religious themes and theological motifs in enunciating this goddess's mythography. Similarly, the religious reflection around the symbol of the drum, which testifies to the distinctive subjectivity of the Paraiyar, cannot be interpreted without alluding to the fact that the drum also continues to play a role in the inauspicious rituals of the caste community. The point to highlight in this complex symbiosis is the subaltern-centred dynamic of this process of hybridization within an overall ethos of the forces of domination and subjection.

Secondly, we notice the manner in which subaltern religion makes use of all and sundry in its religious construction. Bits and pieces are collected from various sources through numerous ways: some religious resources are discarded as irrelevant, many others are useful pieces annexed conveniently from the dominant communities' framework, while some are discovered from years of their own collective life experiences. They are all employed to put together a jigsaw-like religious configuration. Here I am reminded of the local village 'junk salesman' who rides around on his bicycle calling out for people to sell him their junk. He will take anything: some he will pay for and others he will offer to get rid of. Nothing is really wasted. The things he can sell to others he sells; the things he can creatively assemble together to make something useful he gradually works with; and the things he cannot sell or put to use immediately are stored in a corner, just in case he may have need of them at some point in the future. What he eventually constructs is based on what object is required for a particular purpose and the materials that he happens to have available to make this product. The bottom line when putting something together is functionality and not artistic perfection. The resourcefulness and versatility of subaltern religion as observed in the life of the Paraiyar operates on similar lines. It is an economical symbolic resource system. All fragments of religious resources are put to use; nothing is irredeemable. The versatile putting together of a variety of religious fragments is a subaltern art. Comprehensiveness and unitary cohesiveness are sometimes not possible; instead fluidity, temporary relevance and partial enhancement of communal subjectivity are settled for.

Thirdly, the alternate modality that is put to creative use in subaltern religion further attests to its resourcefulness. The drum, within the context of their being severed from the sacred Word, and the independent goddess (Ellaiyamman), within the context of the predominance of the Hindu gods (Brahma, Vishnu and Shiva), manifest the Paraiyar's creative utilization of differential modes from the dominant community in their religious representation. This alternate-mode of religion-making must be understood against the backdrop of the earlier observation that subaltern religion situates itself within the overall complex dynamic of judiciously borrowing from and calculatingly employing the religious capital of the dominant communities. Taking the drum as an example, I argued that it symbolized the voicing of the subaltern in a mode that was not fully co-optable and comprehendible by the dominant communities. The dexterous exploitation of its capacity for expressing subaltern religiosity, coupled with the dogged determination to preserve the resounding of the Divine as experienced by the Dalits, testifies to the confidence and creativity in continuing to use a modality that was distinctly different from that of the dominant community. This

imaginative utilization of the drum by subaltern communities as a
distinctly different mode from the dominant ones is recorded among
the Black slaves of the United States. In the words of Wilson:

> In South Carolina they lived with it [the drum] and feared it. They ex-
> perienced the power of the Spirit-calling drum. That's why in 1740, after
> the Stono Rebellion, the South Carolina colonial assembly outlawed hand
> drums... The law was: You play, you lose your hand. Maryland, then
> other colonies, quickly followed suit with similar 'no-drumming-in-public'
> laws.... But Africans did not stop... In the 1930s Amer-Africans told govern-
> ment interviewers from the works Progress Administration about doing
> their rituals with hand drums. How did they do it, if drums were outlawed?
> Simple: take your everyday mortar or water barrel, put a rim and skin
> on it, and there's your drum, anytime you need it. And for safety's sake,
> it was instantly dismantlable. Others buried their drums in the earth after
> use.[70]

There is no evidence that caste communities of South India banned
the playing of drums. On the contrary, they wanted Dalits to play
the drum for the observance of their own inauspicious rituals. Nonetheless, I am merely attesting that the drum was retained as a alternate
mode of representation by the subaltern community as a viable and
effective resource in dealing with the dominant community.

A final feature of subaltern religion can be garnered from this study
of the Paraiyar: the realistic element of tacitness and subtlety that
ensures the survivability of dimensions of subaltern religion within an
overall context of dominating forces. The explicitly combative and
radically oppositional symbolization of subaltern religious expression
does not appear to operate on the ground. Such a construction primarily
obscures the active operation of everyday social, political, cultural and
economic power. John Friske rightly contrasts the radical and explicitly
confrontational nature of protest in avant-garde art with the more
ambiguous and resent-through-participation approach that characterizes resistance in popular culture.[71] Avant-garde representations express what the dominant communities think ought to be the case from
their distanced and romanticized perception of the subaltern; whereas
subaltern representations pursue lasting changes in the social order which
are more likely to emerge through resistance that is combined with a
vested insertion into the very processes that produces dominant systems
of meaning.[72] The resistance and contestation of the religious legitimacy
of the dominant caste communities by subaltern communities is clearly
evidenced in this study of the Paraiyar. However, I am simultaneously

asserting that this disputing posture is communicated within a stance that also conveys compliance. The overt acting-out of conformity by the subaltern communities is laced with a subtle and tacit subversion, which may not even be detected by the dominant community. Commenting on 'the mentality of subalternity', Bhadra perceptively writes,

> It is well known that defiance is not the only characteristic of the behavior of the subaltern classes. Submissiveness to authority in one context is as frequent as defiance in another. It is these two elements that together constitute the subaltern mentality.[73]

This complex interweaving of domination and subordination, on the one hand, and compliance and resistance, on the other, is capable of realistically holding together both the camouflage of submissiveness, which characterizes the overt behavior of subaltern ritualized religion, and the 'sly civility', which characterizes its emancipatory yearnings through subtle contestation and reinscription.[74] Among the Paraiyar, even while they manipulated the drum to voice their own religious subjectivity, they continue to play the subordinate role of playing the drum for the inauspicious rituals of the caste communities. Similarly, even while they construe their goddess (Ellaiyamman) as an independent figure from caste Hinduism, they continued to pay homage to the many manifestations of Hindu gods. This overt acting-out of the rituals that implies subordination is a form of submissiveness, whereby the subalterns act out the agenda of the dominant communities in order not to lose their role in the arena of symbolic production. Having established their location at this strategic fulcrum, even if by farce and play-acting, these same conditions, resources, and practices of domination become the foundation for defiance. Overt mimicking of dominant religious doctrines and practices by the subaltern can thus also be said to be fertile ground for the germination of resistive strategies. As Bhadra says,

> the idioms of domination, subordination, and revolt...are often inextricably linked together... If this is true, it follows that subordination and domination is seldom complete, if ever. The process is marked by struggle and resistance.[75]

Notes

1. Harold R. Isaacs, *Idols of the Tribe: Group Identity and Political Change* (Cambridge: Harvard University Press, 1989), p. 158.
2. Ibid., p. 159.

3. Moffatt, *An Untouchable Community*, p. 3. Through a detailed analysis and interpretation of the religion of the Paraiyar in comparison with the caste community in Endavur, Moffatt attempts to prove that there is a certain commonality in the structure of religious belief and ritual practice: 'Every fundamental entity, relationship, and action found in the religious system of the higher castes is also found in the religious system of the Untouchables.' Ibid., p. 289.

4. Thurston, *Scheduled Castes and Tribes*, vol. VI, p. 117.

5. Ibid.

6. Pupul Jayakar, *Earth Mother: Legends, Ritual Arts, and Goddesses of India* (San Francisco: Harper and Row Publishers, 1990), p. 44.

7. Ilaiah notes that the counterparts of the Paraiyar in Andhra Pradesh, i.e. the Madiga, have a similar relationship to Ellamma: 'as a community they celebrate only the festival of Ellamma who is their kuladevata (caste goddess).' *Subaltern Studies IX*, p. 175.

8. Gustav Oppert, *The Original Inhabitants of India* (Delhi, Oriental Publishers, 1972), p. 464. First published in 1893.

9. This conception that the term Ellaiyamman derives from the view that she is considered to be the 'Mother of all' was articulated by a Paraiyar priest. The notion that Ellaiyamman is the eldest of the sisters among the manifestations of Sakti was expressed by a few devotees. This feature of being the oldest among a line of siblings must be understood within the social and cultural context of South India where age and position of birth determine the status of the person. The role and status of the oldest is qualitatively higher than the rest of the children born into that same family.

10. Edgar Thurston, *Castes and Tribes of South India*, vol. VI, p. 105.

11. This conception of the 'evil eye' (*dishti*) is not uniquely distinct to the Dalits. It is a fairly general South Indian belief that harm and misfortune is caused by the envious and covetous gaze of the beholder. The view articulated by the Paraiyar youth is a contextual and communal interpretation of this common belief. For further details pertaining to the evil eye in South India see C.J. Fuller, *The Camphor Flame: Popular Hinduism and Society in India* (New Delhi: Viking, 1992), pp. 236–40 and David F. Pocock, *Mind, Body and Wealth: A Study of Belief and Practice in an Indian Village* (Oxford: Blackwell, 1973), pp. 28–33.

12. Quoted in Homi K. Bhabha, *The Location of Culture* (London: Routledge, 1994), p. 1. Emphasis in text.

13. Valentine Daniel, *Fluid Signs*, p. 104. Daniel delineates the meaning of two Tamil words that denote the village: while *uur* implies a emotional and cognitive conception *Kiraamam* designates the geographically determined territory. In contemporary Tamil Nadu, the latter conception (Kiraamam) is fairly fixed because of government documentation of geographical space. However, the former conception (uur) is active in its expansionist vein and it is

this conceptual caste worldview that threatens to usurp the distinctness of the Paraiyar social, cultural and religious space.

14. This is part of an opening prayer of adoration sung by a local Paraiyar pucari K. Pallaiyam. The song is sung to the beat of drums. I am aware of the fact that my own interpretation of the central idea of the characteristic of iconic resistance is confined to the relationship between caste Hindus and Paraiyars. I do not deal with the other facet of guardianship that the goddess epitomized: protection against disease, death, and natural calamity.

15. It must be noted that Mariyamman has the very same function. She has the powers to 'guard the boundaries of her territory, to protect all those inside these boundaries against disease in humans and cattle, particularly epidemic disease, and to bring rain for those who worship her.' Moffatt, *An Untouchable Community*, p. 247.

16. I find the concept of 'spousification' suggested by Lynn E. Gatwood, a useful one for determining the dynamic of resistance and assimilation of the local indigenous traditions to the more prevalent Sanskritic traditions. She explicates three categories based on the degree of spousification of local goddesses:

> First are the untouched, apparently permanently unspousified Devis... The second category consists of Devis who undergo temporary spousification ... but whose popular symbolism remains essentially Devi-like ... [And] A third and more complex category, that of partial spousification, involves more than minimal manipulation.

Gatwood, *Devi and the Spouse Goddess*, p. 156 f.

17. This notion of weaving an alternate mythography, as a way by which people deny and defy the construction of unitary and universalizable history, is expressed by Ashis Nandy in his interpretation of how the victims of colonization express their own historical perspectives in the midst of the dominant Western colonial discursive practice. See Ashis Nandy, *The Intimate Enemy: Loss and Recovery of Self Under Colonialism*, (Delhi: Oxford University Press, 1983). Also see Gyan Prakash, 'Writing Post-Orientalist Histories of the Third World: Indian Historiography is Good to Think', in *Colonialism and Culture*, ed. Nicholas B. Dirks, (Ann Arbor: The University of Michigan Press, 1992), pp. 353–88.

18. A profound theo-anthropological postulate underlies this interpretation: Dalits are thinking and self-reflexive human beings. If we agree with Kaufman that 'that which most sharply distinguishes human beings from other forms of life ... is their historicity, their having been shaped by and their having some control over the process of historical change and development', then we must attribute this element of self-reflexivity to the Paraiyar [Kaufman, *In Face of Mystery*, p. 127]. They do have their own active and creative manner of collectively representing their historicity, which is closely intertwined with their experience with what they take to be the Divine Power. Ellaiyamman as the goddess of the Paraiyar is a pivotal symbol of the source (and the

hope of protection) of this distinct physical and conceptual space: she conserves their geographic space by guarding their particularly as a community and she represents their conceptual space as self-reflective human beings.

19. Brian K. Smith, *Classifying the Universe*, p. 58.

20. K. Pallaiyam is a Pucari who travels around the area performing priestly roles. He claims to have the power to induce the goddesses to descend upon people. This legend was translated and edited with the help of Roja Singh who lives and works in Karunguzhi, which is about a mile away from Malaipallaiyam.

21. Hiltebeitel refers to him as the 'inveterate troublemaker Narada'. See Alf Hiltebeitel, *The Cult of Draupadi: Mythologies From Gingee to Kuruksetra* (Chicago: The University of Chicago, 1988), p. 191.

22. Parasuraman himself is identified with the qualities that are a product of mixed unions, which are quite compatible with the characteristics attributed to Dalits. According to Shulman

> In the myth's earliest version, there is no mention of Parasuraman's divine identity: he is simply the startling, unruly product of a horrifying mixed union... Brahmin and kingly blood flows in almost even quantities in his veins, and he acts accordingly, in a tragic life guided throughout by conflicting impulses. (We shall ask ourselves to what extent the dread 'mixing' of genetic strains is the true source of his trouble.)

It must be kept in mind, however, that 'by the time of the major Puranic versions, of course, our hero [Parasuraman] has become the avatar of Visnu.' David Shulman, *The King and the Clown*, p. 110. In this Dalit version, Parasuraman is really the hero who uses his boon to produce the Dalit goddess. Perhaps, it may be interpreted as a vindication of mixed unions! I say this in the awareness that there is a school of thought that believes that Dalits are the products of inauspicious mixed unions. See Simon Casie Chitty, *The Castes, Customs, Manners and Literature of the Tamils* (New Delhi: Asian Educational Services, 1988), pp. 53–4; 133. First published in 1934.

23. Whitehead, *The Village Gods*, p. 116. For variations of this account with regard to Mariyamman see Wendy D. O'Flaherty, *The Origins of Evil in Hindu Mythology* (Berkeley: University of California Press, 1976), p. 351; E.R. Clough, *While Sewing Sandals* (New York, Hodder and Stroughten, 1899), p. 85 ff; Thurston, *Castes and Tribes*, vol. VI, p. 306 ff; Moffatt, *An Untouchable Community*, p. 248 f.

24. Thomas Mann, *The Transposed Head: A Legend of India*, trans. H.T. Loew-Porter (New York, 1941).

25. This is a counter-point to the usual stereotype that the Paraiyar is 'a double-dealing, unreliable person'. This quote is attributed to H. Jensen, a missionary who worked among them in South India. See Thurston, *Castes and Tribes*, vol. VI, p. 118.

26. This is consistent with Deliege's conclusion:

Recent analyses of Untouchables' myths of origin clearly reveal, contrary to Moffatt's own interpretation, that Harijans consider their low degraded position as a result of a mistake, some trickery or an accident. Robert Deliege, *Man*, p. 166.

27. Elmore, *Dravidian Gods*, p. 7. Also see Oppert, *The Original Inhabitants*, p. 464.

28. A version of the Mariyamman myth of origin suggested by a Paraiyar pucari further illustrates the process of emancipatory remythologization. This version was translated and edited with the help of Roja Singh from a compilation of oral sources furnished by K. Palaiyam, Gunadayalan and GunaSeelan. The latter two work as community leaders in the villages of Pasumbur and Vallarpirrai, respectively. The story is very similar to the myth of Ellaiyamman. However, it refers to the other woman who was restored – the one with the head of Renuka and the body of the Paraiyar women. She is worshipped as Mariyamman and her legend continues thus:

> Renuka who now has the body of the Paraiyar woman returns home. The rishi is not willing to accept her in her changed form and curses her. She becomes the bearer of the 'Pearl', which is the name given to small pox. Renuka has authority over this agonizing disease. She brings this disease upon the rishi who begs for healing. She offers him healing if she be permitted to go to the four worlds of Shiva, Vishnu, Brahma, and Yama. He enables her to visit the Four worlds. She goes to Shiva and causes a disease on him. In exchange for healing she receives his Soolam (a forked weapon) and his cow. She inflicts Vishnu and gets from him his Conch shell and wheel. From Brahma she gets consent for converting her name. She is no longer Renuka but assumes the name Mariyamman (the changed Mother). She then inflicts Yama with a disease. She requires that Yama's wife arrange for a huge festival for her. She agrees' to this and asks her to remove the 'pearl-like' disease in return.

Again one can notice the process of emancipatory remythologization at work in the story as remembered by the Paraiyar. There is a deliberate attempt to work within the categorical and symbolic framework of Hinduism and yet recast it to advantage the collective identity of the Paraiyar. Thus, the goddess of the Paraiyar, Mariyamman, is able to subdue all the major caste Hindu deities and annex segments of their powers. The divine powers of Hinduism are brought under the powerful and inauspicious curse of the goddess of the Paraiyar. The domain of Mariyamman expands toward universality; even the underworld is under her control.

29. Clifford Geertz, *The Interpretation of Cultures* (New York: Basic Books, 1973), p. 90. It is quite obvious that my methodology of the study of religion is dependent on the work of Geertz. However, I think that this study attempts to throw light on the social forces that operate in the forging of religion. According to his critics, this is an aspect that Geertz does not explore. See

Talal Asad, 'Anthropological Conceptions of Religion: Reflections on Geertz', in *Man*, vol. 18 (1983): 237–59 and Brian Morris, *Anthropological Studies of Religion: An Introductory Text* (Cambridge: Cambridge University Press, 1987), pp. 318–19.

30. Moffatt, *An Untouchable Community*, p. 198.

31. Dennis B. McGilvray, 'Paraiyar Drummers of Sri Lanka: Consensus and Constraint in an untouchable caste', in *American Ethnologist*, vol. 10, no. 1 (February, 1983): 101.

32. Ibid.

33. It will be significant to notice that this honour of providing a new mat for the 'king drum' is not extended to the drummers who perform the ceremony; they are usually given cloth for a new turban, but are not given new mats to sit on during the performance. Ibid.

34. Ibid., p. 103.

35. See Moffatt, *An Untouchable Community*, p. 198–200.

36. Mcgilvray, 'Paraiyar Drummers of Sri Lanka', p. 103.

37. Moffatt, *An Untouchable Community*, p. 199.

38. Ibid.

39. Mcgilvray, 'Paraiyar Drummers of Sri Lanka,' pp. 101–2.

40. There was a discussion initiated in the mid-1980s by social activists as to why the Paraiyar drummers are invited to the caste communities' religious ceremonies only during inauspicious times such as funerals and whether this stereotyping of parai drums could be countered if the drummers refuse to perform at caste funerals. Although many colony people favoured such an attempt at collective resistance by withholding the services of drummers for caste funerals, this was not financially feasible. Interestingly, this enabled the drummers to increase their bargaining power and increase the fee for their performance.

41. The Paraiyar do not have any theological reasons to help them decide between cremation and burial because they believe that the spirit of the dead person has already left the body at death. The decision between cremation and burial is primarily a matter of economics. Cremations cost more than burials because of the price of firewood. The economic factor, however, does have its social status ramifications; thus, it is more prestigious to have a cremation because it shows the colony that the family is prosperous and loves the dead one in an extravagant manner.

42. There is variance in this practice. While sometimes the drummers play their drums on the return procession to take the male family members back to their house, most often the drummers conclude their role at the funeral site and receive their payment at the cemetery soon after the cremation or burial.

43. Dumont, *A South Indian Subcaste*, p. 451. I am well aware that this is not the same as the Paraiyar drummers: Dumont is referring to the uDukkai and not the parai drums; also the Pramalai Kallar are not on the same social level as the Paraiyar. Nonetheless, it establishes the fact the drums are utilized

as a medium of controlling and exorcising the demons. An argument can be put forth that the Paraiyar are the only community that will take on this role at the inauspicious time of death.

44. It must be kept in mind that the parai drum is beaten by hand by the Paraiyar drummers; this may be interpreted as leading to constant defilement by touch. It is also relevant to point out that there are other drums that are utilized by high-caste persons in the village. However, these drums, i.e. the uDukkai, the bambai and the *tavul*, are made out of goat's skin. See Moffatt, *An Untouchable Community*, pp. 111–14. For a detailed explanation of the opposition of the pure and the impure with regards to the Brahmin being linked to the holy living cow and the Dalit being conjoined to the polluting dead cow, see Louis Dumont, pp. 146–51. Srinivas's critical and constructive response to Dumont stresses the economic and cultural factors that contribute to the Dalits association with the dead cow. See M.N. Srinivas, 'Some Reflections', pp. 160–6.

45. Moffatt, *An Untouchable Community*, p. 119.

46. N. Subrahmanian, *Sangam Polity: The Administrative and Social Life of the Sangam Tamils* (Madurai: Ennes Publications, 1980), p. 82.

47. Ibid.

48. Moffatt, *An Untouchable Community*, p. 253.

49. Subrahmanian, *Sangam Polity*, p. 83.

50. Ibid.

51. Ibid., p. 82.

52. Hart's words in explicating the role of the drum in ancient Tamil society is relevant here: The drummers and bards were rendered dangerous by the gods who were thought to reside in the drums and lutes, and by the occupations, which involved controlling dangerous forces by playing [drums] during battle. George Hart, *The Poems of Ancient Tamils* (Berkeley: University of California Press, 1975), p. 122.

53. Moffatt, *An Untouchable Community*, pp. 126–7. This is not a well-known myth in the areas I worked in where there is a general belief that the drum is a 'lowly' musical instrument, mainly because of its association with the dead cow. However, this myth is quoted primarily to highlight that the historical association between the Paraiyar and the ancient people of South India through the symbol of the drum is not incomparable with the caste mythology of the origins of the Paraiyar.

54. According to Aiyangar, 'The high honour of founding villages in the South [of India] during the remote period belonged to the sylvan ancestors of the Paraiyar.' Srinivasa M. Aiyangar, *Tamil Studies: Essays on the History of the Tamil People, Language, Religion and Culture* (New Delhi: Asian Educational Services, 1982), p. 81. A similar view is expressed in K. Rajayyam, *History of Tamil Nadu: 1565–1982* (Madurai: Raj Publishers, 1982), p. 275. For a variety of myths that extol the high honours of the Paraiyar in ages past see

Robert Deliege, 'Les mythes d'origine chez Paraiyar', *L'Homme*, vol. 109 (1989): 107–116.

55. Claude Levi-Strauss, *The Savage Mind* (Chicago: University of Chicago, 1966), p. 121.

56. This is quite consistent with the view that local religiosity was generally expressed in aniconic forms. In the words of Diana Eck:

> The most ancient non-vedic cultus was almost certainly aniconic. Stones, natural symbols, and earthen mounds signified the presence of a deity long before the iconic images of the great gods came to occupy the *sancta* of temples and shrines.

Diana L. Eck, *Darsan: Seeing the Divine Images in India*, second revised and enlarged edition (Chambersburg, PA: Anima Books, 1985), p. 33 f.

57. Shiva Ingole, 'Ancient Mother Mine', in *Poisoned Bread: Translations from Modern Marathi Dalit Literature*, ed. Arjun Dangle (Bombay: Orient Longman, 1992), p. 68.

58. Quoted by Ter Ellingson, 'Ancient Indian Drum Syllables and Bu Stone's *Sham Pa Ta* Ritual', in *Ethnomusicology: Journal for the Society of Ethnomusicology*, vol. XXIV, no. 1 (January, 1980): 448.

59. These are local and contextual versions of Dharam Sutra XII 4, 5: 'if a Shudra listens intensively to a recitation of the Veda his ear shall be filled with molten tin or lac. If he recites the Vedic text, his tongue shall be cut out. If he remembers them his body shall be split in twain.' Quoted in L.R. Balley, 'India Needs a Cultural Revolution', in *Untouchable: Voices of the Dalit Liberation Movement*, ed. Barbara R Joshi (Zen Books: London, 1986), p. 149.

60. Kumud Pawde, 'The Story of My Sanskrit', in *Poisoned Bread*, p. 96. This essay is a touching and honest portrayal of the author's situation: she is a Dalit who becomes a Sanskrit teacher. Although this autobiographical reflection is from the state of Maharashtra, it still rings true of the social context in Tamil Nadu.

61. Trawick, 'Internal Iconicity in Paraiyar Crying Songs', p. 338. I have left out a term (My Eye) she uses to refer to the baby because I think this is a mistranslation of the Tamil word *Kannaa* which means something like 'the object of my eye'. It is an endearing expression much like the English term darling.

62. Karin Kapadia, *Siva and her Sisters*, p. 159.

63. James C. Scott, *Weapons of the Weak* (New Haven: Yale University Press, 1985). I am indebted to this valuable book for the general line of argument that I work out in this section, specifically to its break with the school of thought which assumes that symbolic production is completely controlled by the elite who also control economic production.

64. K. Marx and F. Engels, *The German Ideology* (London: Lawrence and Wishart Publishers, 1965), p. 62.

65. This school can be said to originate from interpretations of the work of Antonio Gramsci (1891–1937), particularly by teasing out his distinction between 'common sense' and 'good sense'. While the former refers to the received mode of making sense of the world, which is dominated by elite ideology, the latter refers to the sediments of resistance and autonomy that are part of subaltern communities. See, David Forgacs, ed., *An Antonio Gramsci Reader: Selected Writings 1916–1935* (New York: Schocken Books, 1988), pp. 342–62. For examples of this approach see, E.P. Thompson, *The Making of the English Working Class* (New York: Panteon Books, 1967) and *Customs in Common* (London: Merlin Press, 1991) and Raymond Williams, 'Base and Superstructure in Marxist Cultural Theory', in *New Left Review* (no. 82, 1978): 3–16 and *Problems in Materialism and Culture: Selected Essays* (London, Verso, 1980).

66. The latter was the mistaken direction of Dalit Christians as argued in chapter one. They were attempting to use the symbolic world of the Christian religion to distance themselves from their Dalit heritage and forge something completely new. The lack of success of such a movement is clear from the Dalit Christian call to make a liberative and contextual theology.

67. Claire Detels, 'Soft Boundaries and Relatedness: Paradigm for a Postmodern Feminist Musical Aesthetics', *Boundaries 2*, vol. 19: 2 (Summer, 1992): 184–204.

68. Bhabha, *The Location of Culture*, pp. 171–97.

69. 'Introduction', in *The Post-Colonial Studies Reader*, eds: Bill Ashcroft, Gareth Griffiths and Helen Tiffin (London: Routledge, 1995), p. 183.

70. Sule Greg Wilson, *The Drummers Path: Moving the Spirit with Ritual and Traditional Drumming* (Rochester, VT,: Destiny Books, 1992), p. 21.

71. For a critical interpretation of popular culture, which offers a viable alternative to the dismissive attitude of the same by the Frankfurt school, see John Friske, *Reading the Popular* (Boston: Unwin Hyman, 1989) and *Understanding Popular Culture* (Boston: Unwin Hyman, 1989).

72. As summarized by Kelton Cobb, 'Reconsidering the Status of Popular Culture in Tillich's Theology of Culture', in *Journal of the American Academy of Religion*, vol. LXIII/1 (Spring, 1995): 78.

73. Gautam Bhadra, 'The Mentality of Subalternity: Kantanama or Rajdharma', in *Subaltern Studies VI: Writings on South Asian History and Society*, ed. Ranajit Guha (New Delhi: Oxford University Press, 1989), p. 54.

74. Here I am drawing on the work of Homi Bhabha as he deconstructs the working of colonial discourse. I am arguing that a similar process of 'mimicry', which Bhabha identifies in the discourse of the dominant community, is also part of subaltern communities. Thus

> what the native rewrites [or repetitively performs] is not a copy of the colonist [or Caste community] original, but a qualititatively different thing-in-itself, where misreadings and incongruities expose the uncertainties and ambiguities of the colonist [or Caste community] text and deny it an

authorizing presence. Benita Parry, 'Current Theories of Colonial Discourse', in *The Post Colonial Studies Reader*, p. 42.

75. Ibid.

4

Drumming up Representational Space for Subaltern Religious Expression in Indian-Christian Theology

Uninitiated as yet to the mysterious lispings of a language belonging to the cradle-phase (as it were) of humanity, these primitive drum-beats meant next to nothing to the present chronicler. The study of modern branches of learning filled him with a certain mistrust. Although he was familiar with geology and paleontology, sciences also concerned with the remote past, they shed a different light, on aspects of life other than the human field revealed by archaeology and anthropology. His studies were concerned more with the dumb dawning of life, with the vital or mechanistic force which asserted itself over inert matter within the course of millions of years, while the cautious, conservative approach was also distinctive and alien to the understanding of the throbbing drums. (Nataraja Guru)

Musical notes, with all their power to fire the blood and melt the heart, cannot be mere empty sounds and nothing more; no, they have escaped from some higher sphere, they are the outpouring of eternal harmony, the voice of angels, the Magnificat of saints. (James George Frazer)

The life of the individual and of the species depend on the rapid and/or accurate reading and interpretation of a web of vital information. There is a vocabulary, a grammar, possibly a semantic of colours, sounds, odors, textures, and gestures as multiple as that of language, and they may be dilemmas of decipherment and translation as resistant as any we have met. Though it is polysemic, speech cannot identify, let alone paraphrase, even a fraction of the sensory data which man...can...register. (George Steiner)

From the arguments advanced in the previous chapters, there appear to be two distinct key symbols around which my interpretation of Dalit religion revolves. These symbols, i.e. the goddess (Ellaiyamman) and the drum, are interlinked. Nonetheless, I shall work with one of these symbols (the drum) in the rest of work. The justification for this is three fold. First, the drum is a safer and more neutral symbol to work with in doing constructive Christian theology. It would be a more acceptable starting point for doing liberation theology since the drum is a universal symbol. Sound is a means by which culture and religion are communicated the world over. Therefore, the practical issue involving the receptivity of the symbol by the Indian-Christian community influences my choice of the drum. Second, I must admit that I myself am still ambivalent about the use of the goddess symbol for doing Christian theology. While this may very well be a result of the evolvement of my thinking along patriarchal lines, it can also be attributed to my not being situated within the promising school of Feminist Christian theology. Third, I believe that whatever can be done with incorporating the symbol of the goddess into Indian-Christian theology can best be done by bringing together the following: systematic documentation of the experiences of Dalit women; interpretation of the liberative and domesticating aspects of religious themes in goddess representations; and teasing out courageous and progressive resources already available in feminist Christian theology. Since it was not easy for me to gain access to women respondents, and since I lack substantial knowledge in the emerging field of feminist theology, the avenue that I have conceptually opened up can be more fruitfully taken up by women researchers and theoreticians.

In this chapter I venture three things. First, I seek to interpret the drum in its relatedness to other Indian traditions. Here I want to underscore the harmonious relationship of the symbol of the Paraiyar with other local religious traditions. In this discussion, the subaltern turn of this symbol will be noted. Second, I shall argue that the symbol of the drum presents theologians with a complementary mode of religious representation. Here I shall contrast two modes of thought and rep- resentation (subaltern-based orality and dominant-funded literacy) and suggest that the drum can be posited as a paradigmatic symbol of the facets of orality just as the word exemplifies the aspects of literacy. Third, I shall isolate the various themes that can be explored by reflecting upon the drum as a paradigm of religious representation.

I. The Drum as Thematized in other Local Religious Traditions

It is important to begin with a clarification of the scope and task of this section. Even if it is the case, I am not setting out to argue that utilizing drums for religious practice is a universal and archaic phenomenon. Rather, in this segment I want to point to a few examples of the use of drums in religious practice among the people of South India. In so doing I want to attest to the shared dimension of the Paraiyar's collective religious experience with people of their geographical region. There are principally two theological reasons for wanting to sustain this argument. First, it establishes that the Paraiyar do not differ radically from the religious perceptions and imaginations of the people that live around them. In the context of the long history of vilification of the Paraiyar as less-than-human, this underscores the common human roots of religious perception and construction. If viewed in this light, the drum as a symbol of religious expression is not a primitive symbol that needs to be superseded by other symbolic representations. Thus, even while being a root symbol of the religious expression of the Paraiyar, elements of the drum as a shared religious symbol appear to exist among a few diverse groups in South India.

Second, by alluding to the shared nature of the Paraiyar's religious symbol, the trend to associate the drum as an instrument of evil is countered. By marking the use of the drum as a symbol of religious use among other Indian traditions, I am confirming that its association with the Divine is generally attested to by the people of this region. The drum, thus, is related to the apprehension of the Divine and connected with the mediation of divine power. Before proceeding to discuss these other religious examples let me highlight one underlying set of factors that link the three examples I discuss in the following pages: the South Indian religious strands that I cite are known to have evolved through interactions with subaltern communities and are predominantly connected with the oral tradition.

One early and well-organized South Indian religious tradition was represented by a collective of saints called the Alvar.[1] These poet saints lived between the sixth and the tenth centuries of the common era. They composed devotional poems that were set to music and sung to the god, Vishnu. The Alvar represented a branch in popular Hinduism which resulted in the philosophical thought of Ramanuja (CE 1077–1157).[2] Interestingly, the Alvars' poetic songs arose out of a social and religious movement that was significantly inclusive. The Alvar theologized out of the religious energy that flowed out of the *Bhakti* (devotion) movement that brought together the caste Hindus and the Dalits in South India. In the words of Carman, 'The Alvars came from a number of castes; some were Brahmins, some Sudras, and one was an outcaste. The small Vaisnava community that treasured their memory and sang their hymns was also made up of different castes.'[3] Furthermore, even though the poems were eventually written down, they were used most often in song form by the devotees. Much of the devotional material of the Alvar was utilized by the devotees in singing devotional praises to Vishnu.

Although the theme of the drum is not dealt with by the Alvar in general, one female Alvar, Andal, does discuss the drum in her work.[4] Notably, in her famous work, the *Tiruppavai*, Andal (born C E 850) structures the whole poem around young maidens who petition Lord Krishna to bestow upon them his auspicious drum (parai). The focus on the parai drum as an auspicious means of mediation by the Alvar community must be specially noted. In this thirty song poem, Andal starts the first verse with the young maidens stating the purpose of the vow they are about to undertake — the aim is to gain the ritual parai drum from Krishna. In the next four verses (songs 2–5) the maidens extol the benefits that the land and the community will receive by their keeping of the vows as they prepare to be given the drum. After ten verses (songs 6–15), in which Andal describes the maidens bathing in the river in order to become 'awakened', the maidens proceed to the house of Krishna's cowherd wife (Nappinnai) so as to enlist her help in gaining access to Krishna (songs 17–20). In the next nine verses the maidens ask Krishna for the drum (songs 21–25) and profess to him that the drum symbolizes more than just God's blessings upon the land and the community. The maidens specify (songs 26–29) that they want both material blessings as well as the gift of the honour of serving their Lord. The last song (song 30) ends with Andal verifying that the young maidens had indeed obtained the drum.[5]

Three points must be highlighted with regards to this brief summary of the *Tiruppavai*. First, the idea that the drum is a symbol of god's power and the gift of god to god's devotees is central to the poem of Andal. Second, the drum that is signified in the *Tiruppavai*, as the symbol of god's divine favour to the devotees is the parai, which is the central religious symbol of the Paraiyar. And third, the parai drum, which is sought by the young maidens, represents both a material blessing to the land, community and the devotees and a devotional privilege of serving the Lord in utter devotion. This indicates that the drum is tied up with both the material things of the world and to god that implies being god's servant.

A second South Indian religious tradition that theologized in the midst of active involvement with the subaltern communities (the Dalit and *asat* (impure) Sudra communities) was led by Sri Narayana Guru (died in 1928). Although grounded in the philosophical school of Sankara, Sri Narayana Guru's movement worked with and for the rights of the Dalits in the West coast of South India. One of his disciples, Nataraja Guru (1895–1973), directs our attention to the power of the drum even as religionists seek to come to terms with the truth revealed by the ancient ones. Quoting the words of his mentor he writes, '"Do you hear?" the melodious-ringing Guru voice was heard to enquire, "Do you hear that distant drumming?" It has been like this not for a few years; it has been like this for ever!'[6]

The integral association of the sound of the drum with the mediating voice of the Divine is situated within the religious tradition of the people of South India. This is not something alien to the people of South India; rather it is reflective of the ancient days, the eternal and pristine echoing of the Divine. In line with this stream of theologizing, Nataraja Guru further expands upon two dimensions of the drum. On the one hand, the sound of the drum is interpreted as being the Word of wisdom that is prior to the spoken and the written word. It is a form of the 'Word-language' of South India that is rooted in the religious history of the people of ancient India. A link between the Word of wisdom and the drum is purported. In the words of Nataraja Guru:

> And so in this enlightening intelligence springing from unitive wisdom, consisting of the universal and perennial human values involved in that Word-language which extend back of and beyond the spoken and written languages, the sound of the prehistoric insistent drumming heard from across the river on this occasion ought to have had a meaning and significance of its own. This thudding drum-beating itself revealed a state of mind with an implicit behaviour language which spoke across the gulf of time.[7]

On the other hand, even though the sound of the drum is conceptualized as being prior to the spoken and the written word, there is conscious insistence that drumming is also a medium of Divine mediation that functions complementarily with the spoken and the written aspects of the Word of wisdom. Guru goes so far as to refer to it as 'the suggestive language of the drums'. Here I want to stress that the drum is not simply interpreted as an ancient religious form that mediated the Divine in ages past, which has evolved into a more modern and developed symbolic system of the spoken and the written word. Rather, according to this particular school of thought, the sound of the drum is a distinctive, contemporaneous and viable medium of tuning-in to the mediating wisdom of the Divine:

> Instead of depending upon the evidences buried in the earth or recorded on stone, pure memory should be able to delve directly into the past by means of sympathy and insight ... even as in the case with electro-magnetism, one can tune-in and gather the immediate echoing response when the right wave-length of frequency is touched.[8]

A third South Indian religious strand in which the drum is of central importance is the tribal tradition. Eric J. Lott discusses the 'explicit' importance of the drum in 'primal' forms of Indian religion: 'That the drum is of primary sacred importance to most Indian tribal life can hardly be denied.'[9] He summarizes the religious meaning of the drum among tribal cultures in the following words:

> In most tribal life the drum occupies a decisive role, its rhythmic beating often being the primary expression of the sacred in tribal tradition in most parts of the world.... [The] tribes of Southern India, of Orissa, of the North East of which I have some knowledge definitely take the drum to be the most potent instrument of sacred power.... The most general significance of beating the drum among these tribals is not only to drive away evil forces threatening the welfare of the tribe, but also to re-invigorate the life of the tribe. For example, the drum gives strength and confidence enabling the tribe to make war with its enemies. Tribal fertility too is in a number of cults related to drum beating.[10]

The significance of the drum as an instrument of sacred power, which mediates protection and provision for the community, is quite similar to the relationship between Sakti (Divine power) and the drum in the Paraiyar's religious tradition. Furthermore, the association of the drum with the well-being, health, and strength of individuals and the community points to the divine powers that are intrinsic to this religious symbol. The drum, thus, is not only an instrument that deals with and controls evil forces. It is also a medium for tapping into the beneficial and auspicious powers of the divine.

146 • *Dalits and Christianity*

II. The Drum as an Organizing Symbol of the Culture and Religion of Subaltern-based Orality

A manifest theme that holds together all three traditions that were described is linked with imagining the drum as a means of mediation between the Divine and human beings. This mediation involves both dimensions of material protection and provision and spiritual blessedness through relationship and service to the Divine. Also, it stresses both the priority and the complementarity of the drum to the spoken and/or written word. Nonetheless, a latent function of the symbol of the drum that is detectable in the discussion must be reasserted: the drum brings together human communities in South India, which are related to and plugged into movements that are, at a minimum, inclusive of Dalits and, at a maximum, centred around Dalits. The incorporation of various communities that evolve in relatedness with the Dalits, in an otherwise caste-ridden ethos, points to the agency of the drum in subaltern community-making of sorts.

In light of the evidence of the significance of the symbol of the drum in the religious reflections of other South Indian traditions, I want to move from my earlier inference in the previous chapter, that the drum is a dominant symbol in the religious framework of the Paraiyar, to the assertion that the drum is an 'organizing symbol' that loosely knits together a community of subaltern-based oral communities. The drum, thus, becomes a heuristic device which organizes and interprets the sets of premises that underlie a subaltern-based culture or philosophy, which is rooted in orality.[11]

The drum can be construed to be representational of a particular mode of thought and symbolization that is an essential component of the human dialogical symbolic intercourse of the Paraiyar community in South India. Furthermore, even while the drum depicts the particularity of the collective religious experience of the Paraiyar, it extends itself in relatedness to other Dalit and Dalit-identified communities in South India. In so doing, the drum gathers together the interconnected collective religious experiences of a complex cluster of communities that share at least two characteristics: relatedness to subaltern movements and rootedness in the culture of orality. By positing the drum as an organizing symbol of the religious tradition of the Dalits, thus, I simultaneously carve out reflective space for this subaltern- based oral 'community of communities' within the realm of theology; the voices that have not been substantially circulated so far within its theories and practices can be affirmed, appreciated and included.

As explained in chapter one, I am convinced of the multimodalities of thought[12] and representation.[13] However, in this discussion, for the sake of confinement of scope and clarity of argumentation, I shall focus on its most general two-fold characterization. I cannot extricate myself from the interrelated, flexible, non-binary, intricate, non-hierarchical, and anti-essentialist nature of the two-fold description of the relationship between dominant and subaltern religions that I established in interpreting the religion of the Paraiyar. In order to work within the confines of those directive, as explicated in the previous chapter, I shall resist the tendency to set up structural or substantive dualisms. The soft or fuzzy bifurcation that is suggested will be fleshed out in detail shortly. At this point it will suffice to simply state that this two-foldness should be understood as a functional and pedagogical device to offer general and permeable frames of analysing the multifaceted nature of human construction.[14]

S.J. Tambiah presents us with a general overview for this discussion from an anthropological perspective.[15] Drawing upon the work of various philosophers, psychologists, anthropologists, linguists and religionists, Tambiah demonstrates the existence of at least two orientations by which human beings frame their thinking about reality around them — participation versus causality.[16] After an extensive, thorough, and critical analysis of the various theories relevant to the issue of how human beings order their reality, Tambiah concludes with a convincing depiction of his categorization, i.e. participation versus causality modes of orientation. He states:

> While much of the discourse of causality and positive science is framed in terms of distancing, neutrality, experimentation, and the language of analytic reason, much of the discourse of participation can be framed in terms of sympathetic immediacy, performative speech acts, and ritual action. If participation emphasizes sensory and affective communication and the language of emotions, causality stresses the rationality of instrumental action and the language of cognition.[17]

Tambiah's arguments get to the core of an important and appropriate conceptual distinction. However, I object to the restrictive association of the causality and participation modes of orientation with science and religion respectively. It does not take into consideration the multimodalities that exist within the realm of religion itself. Walter Ong,[18] Jack Goody[19] and David Olson[20] have efficiently and effectively argued for an analogous two-fold categorization — orality and literacy. They have captured the dynamics of the two-fold nature of this modality, which Tambiah sketches so skillfully, within the realm of society, culture and religion. Through an examination of work done on 'primary oral cultures' and primarily 'chirographic [writing] and typographic [print] based' cultures, they delineate the characteristics of two orientations.[21]

Reflecting upon my own interpretation of the religion of subaltern communities, and along with the many critical voices that object and respond to the numerous problematics that emanate from the literature on orality and literacy, it is pertinent at this point to register my own qualifications and provisos, which go well beyond my precursory caveat. I deliberately and affirmatively stress these because they are both in continuity with the interpretive stance of the religion of the Dalits and important to the direction of my reconstruction of the dynamics of two-foldness in general.

First, even while suggesting a two-fold manner by which modes of ordering can be classified, in theory, I am open to the possibility of the existence of a multiplicity of modes of ordering. I reiterate Tambiah's words that 'it is possible to separate analytically at least two orientations to our cosmos,'[22] which implies the existence of many other orientations.

Second, I contend that the drum represents more than just orality since it is inclined towards gathering up other modalities of thought that resist literacy. Thus, it includes the practices of reflection and representation that are symbolic, even if not verbal. In this specific context, which focusses on the Paraiyar, it represents the mode of reflection that is intimately linked to sound. Interestingly this 'verbomotor' alliance between emanating sound and physical playing of music through somatic involvement is a characteristic of orality:

> The oral word ... never exists within a simply verbal context, as a written word does. Spoken words are always modifications of a total, existential situation, which always engage the body. Bodily activity beyond mere vocalization is not adventitious or contrived in oral communication, but is natural and even inevitable.[23]

Ong even cites the example of drumming to make his point about the close and inextricable connection between orality and accompaniments involving somatic involvement. This is a point at which the drum as an organizing symbol becomes quite comprehensive. The drum expresses and represents the orality of a tradition in its affinity with other non-verbal means of communication, specifically music.

Third, the drum expresses the oral character of culture and religion in its interactive appropriation of and resistance to literacy. Orality is not synonymous with subalternity. The religion and culture of the Paraiyar fundamentally exhibit dimensions of orality. However, this is not unaffected by the more than hundred years of literacy that has existed in South India among the Dalits. Neither is it separate from the other forms of institutional and ideological structures of power that promote literacy in rural India. Orality then is a form of thought and representation that prevails through an interaction with the currents of literacy and various other institutional and social effects of power. Correspondingly, the drum expresses and organizes the diverse forces of orality as they interact with and resist the forces of literatization and its type of social transfiguration. This accurately depicts the situation in South India where the Paraiyar retain their oral and non-verbal symbolic patterns in the context of increased literalization through the school system, which in some cases is associated with Christian mission.

This elasticity in the definition of orality is also reflective of recent constructive modulations in theoretical studies on the relationship between orality and literacy.[24] Current anthropologists and cultural and literary theorists are reinterpreting the complex relationship between orality and literacy in any given community. Fundamentally there is a general acceptance that the 'divide' between the relationship of orality and literacy is much more accurately depicted in terms of a 'continuum'.[25] Contemporary cultural and social settings around the world are cited as examples of the interlaced, mixed and diverse interaction between elements of orality and literacy.[26] It is within this context of the interpenetrative and mutually transformative relationship between orality and literacy that the drum is posited as an organizing symbol of orality.[27]

Thus, in conformity with my exposition of Paraiyar religion in particular, and subaltern religion in general, it would be appropriate to transfigure the categories of orality and literacy somewhat differently. The contextual categorization seem much more to present orality as a subaltern-based orientation, which is integrative of other non-literary modalities of thought and representation, and interactive with, though resistant to, the dominant and co-optive forces of literacy. The symbol of the drum is most suited to portray these aspects of subaltern-based orality. By the same token, literacy is constructed as a broad orientation which interacts with and utilizes many forms of orality. But, as a whole, it tends to take writing and print as the norm through which all other media can be evaluated and transformed.

It is not possible to go into the numerous distinctions that contrastingly mark out these two orientations. It may be most helpful for the purpose of this study to broadly dwell upon the main differences which can be discerned in subaltern religion as we have encountered it. In the ensuing exposition I shall concentrate on explicating subaltern-based orality as a sound-centred orientation that is interactive with and resistant to the expanding forces of literacy. Whatever is juxtaposed to this, as a sight-centred orientation of literacy, is grounded in the research of scholars who have dealt with qualitative and quantitative research in oral and literate societies. Since the corpus of this research does not spring out of the South Indian situation, and since no data on how literate caste Hindus construct religion in India has been presented, it must be admitted that the discussion of literacy is provisional and hypothetical.

The difference between subaltern-based oral religion and dominant-based literate religion is contingent upon the respective ways in which they 'make use of the sensorium, that is, of the various senses: seeing, hearing, touching, smelling, tasting.'[28] Literacy associates the generation, acquisition, preservation and dissemination of knowledge principally with seeing. Through print, literacy engraves knowledge in space: 'with literacy, people tend to take objects in three-dimensional visual space as their model of what is "really real" and tend to regard other kinds of experience, and other forms of knowledge, as derivative or even unreal.'[29] Subaltern-based orality, on the other hand, allies itself with hearing: 'the crucial feature of an oral culture is the centrality of sound to all thought and communication.'[30] In the sphere of religion, the written word (scripture) with its emphasis on sight through reading best symbolizes the various dimensions of literacy; whereas, the drum with its rootedness in sound through hearing captures the numerous aspects of orality as have been redefined in this book.

Sound can be said to have three properties that are linked with the ways in which the drum symbolizes subaltern-based orality:[31] it unites communities by connecting 'interiority to interiority';[32] it situates human beings in context-dependent, present actuality, which is participatory; and it fosters collaborative and eclectic patterns of community behaviour.

The first major characteristic of sound is that it 'unites groups of living beings as nothing else does.'[33] Being based on sound, subaltern-based orality is 'aggregative' and 'incorporative' of the yearnings and strivings of others in a manner that knits them together from within.

On the one hand, Ong suggests that sound is 'closely associated with the sense of interiority of our selves ... [S]ound gives us at the level of the senses the most acute awareness of other persons and their relationship to our inwardness.'[34] On the other hand, he argues that sound also establishes 'patterns of distance and closeness necessary for communal behaviour and provide signals that determine appropriate responses from others.'[35] The sound of the drum does just that: it both integrates the interior longings of multiple subaltern communities ('special sensory key to interiority')[36] and initiates such people struck by the cords of unity to move from this networked interiority towards expressing collective responses.

This 'incorporative' and 'aggregative' feature of orality can be explained in terms of oral societies' affirmation of the open-ended nature of collective memory. Here we must move away from the misconstruction that oral people are the paradigm of rote learning. Often the art of memorization and repetition are projected as hallmarks of oral cultures as they adopt, circulate and transmit their wisdom from generation to generation.[37] However, Jardine reminds us that 'in tests measuring ability to memorize lists, nonliterate people actually did worse than literate ones.'[38] This only goes to prove that even though oral people are well acquainted with the process of memorization, they build into it an openness to the inclusion of variation. 'Oral people [in fact] can scarcely memorize verbatim, since there is no "text" to memorize from.'[39] Rather, that which is creatively integrated takes the form of being 'aggregatively' interweaved into that which is memorized. The drum in this context symbolizes both the secure storing away of the remembrances of the marginalization of the Dalit-centred oral people of South India and the open-endedness of subaltern-based oral communities in the process of solidarity-seeking.

In the arena of religious discourse, Goody has suggested that this difference be comprehended by noting the characteristics of 'incorporation' and 'exclusion'. The former is a feature of oral religions that appear both 'flexible' and 'symbiotic' in their development, whereas the latter marks out literate religions whose boundaries are continuously determined through a process of logical and analytical reasoning with reference to the dictates of the written word.[40] Thus, while oral religions are 'subject to change and absorption rather than to rejection and conversion',[41] literate religions are fuelled by exclusion and mastery in the effort to categorize and analyse in order to convert everything else to the 'new measuring stick, the written word'.[42] This element of inclusiveness was noted in the religion of the Paraiyar in its interaction with the religion of caste Hindus. The Hindu deities' mythographies, religious myths and legends were reinterpreted and transformed to tell Dalit truths about their history and collective identities.[43] The open-ended and improvisatory oral recounting of the myths and the songs (using the 'aggregative' method) was also pointed to in the study of Paraiyar religion.[44] Furthermore, the incorporativeness of the subaltern through the drum, which symbolizes the weaving together of interior yearnings of subaltern-based communities, highlights this characteristic of orality.

It must be restated that this incorporativeness and aggregativeness of subaltern-based orality is not without a resistive streak to the exclusive and co-optive character of the forces of literacy. However, it must be added that the resistive dynamic is not construed in purely oppositional terms: it is constituted by a crafty resolve to engage, utilize and transform elements of the dominant community for emancipatory ends. This resistiveness to the tendency of dominant-allied literacy is captured by the symbol of the drum in two ways. First, the ever-expanding infiltration and co-option of the worldview of caste Hinduism in its 'Vedas as norm of Hindu orthodxy' form is resisted. Here one must be careful not to present Hinduism as purely a textual religion. Even in the classical or Brahminical expressions there is an oral dimension built into the theory and practice of Hinduism. Recent scholarship on Brahmanic Hinduism is quite cognizant of the interplay of the dynamics of these textual and oral forces. The canonicity of the Vedas, thus, is interpreted from both a 'detextualized' perspective, in which their oral/mantra status ('primordial impulses of speech') is emphasized, and a textual viewpoint, in which the 'right reading' of the text is paramount.[45] Nonetheless, one cannot ignore that even this oral dimension of the Vedas is literacy-centred: it answers writing and is answered by writing. Furthermore, the origins and development of much of caste Hinduism is maintained by the priests of the temple who bring together in their theory and practice the language (Sanskrit) and content (even if transmitted orally) of the Vedic text. This is reinforced by the commonly held view that one of the characteristics of a Hindu is that s/he consents to the authority of the Vedas.

Second, the drum is also resistive of the dogma that the Christian Bible (the closed printed canon, consisting of the sixty-six books) is the sole medium of communication and manifestation of God in all realms of life. From the viewpoint of subaltern-based oral communities, the drum reminds us that there is mediation between the Divine and the human that is at times before, beyond and beside the written Word, which cannot always be transposed into the medium of writing. Thus, the many dimensions of the senses must not surrender their respective ways of knowing and reflecting upon what is known to the sense of sight.

A second characteristic of sound is that it situates human beings in the middle of 'present actuality'. It exists only in the present moment, enfolding the hearers into the living now: 'sound surrounds us and comes to us simultaneously', giving us a greater sense of the actual moment and situating us in the midst of all that goes on in the present.[46] This explains why oral cultures are 'situational' and thus much closer to 'the human lifeworld'. A.R. Luria's monumental work documents and interprets the nature of 'operational thinking' (primarily characterized by being concrete and situational) among orality-based communities in areas of what used to be 'the Soviet Union' in the 1930s. On the one hand, he reports that persons from an oral culture did not think in abstractions when they were asked to identify shapes such as circles and squares. Instead, they would identify circles in terms of a plate, a sieve, a watch or a moon and squares in terms of a house, a door or mirror. On the other hand, he also indicates that definitions that arise for an object out of a process of abstraction were not known to exist among oral people. A tree cannot be abstractly defined apart from it being an apple or elm tree. Ong concludes his discussion of Luria by summing up as follows:

> An oral culture does not deal in such items as geometrical figures, abstract categorization, formally logical reasoning processes, definitions, or even comprehensive descriptions, or articulated self-analysis.[47]

He goes on to differentiate between 'oral organization of thought' and 'text-formed thought'. The former bespeaks of the particularity of the oral cultures while the latter inscribes the particularity of literate cultures.[48]

I want to resist the idea that abstraction and logical reasoning are not operant among subaltern-based oral communities. In order to debunk this misconception that oral communities are in some way pathological, it will be best to continue to recast this argument in different parlance: while oral cultures are 'empathetic and participatory', literate cultures are 'objectively distanced'. It is noteworthy that for both Tambiah and Ong there is a difference between orientations of thinking based on whether knowledge is participatory or distanced.[49] On the one hand, for people in oral cultures 'knowing means achieving close, empathetic, communal identification with the known'.[50] On the other hand, the very art of writing and textuality creates a possibility which does not exist in oral cultures: 'Writing separates the knower from the known and thus sets up conditions for "objectivity", in the sense of personal disengagement or distancing.'[51]

At a more general level, this difference can be subsumed under the categories proposed by Goody in his attempt to distinguish between oral religions that are 'particularistic' and literate religions that are 'universalistic'. His argument maintains that the move from particularism to universalism in the domain of religion is directly related to the possibility of 'decontextualization' and 'generalization' which is an outcome of the mechanics of writing. He says:

> Written formulations encourage the decontextualization or generalization of norms... In written codes there is a tendency to present a single 'abstract' formula which overlays, and to some extent replaces, the more contextualized norms of oral societies... First, when the codes (more especially the alphabetic ones since they are more easily adopted) are associated with religion, they often extend beyond the bounds of any particular state to embrace the whole community of the faithful. Secondly, in their very nature written statements of the law, of norms, of rules, have had to be abstracted from particular situations in order to be addressed to a universal audience out there, rather than be delivered face-to-face to a specific group of people at a particular time and place.[52]

The participatory, situational, empathetic, and face-to-face nature of subaltern-based oral religion can be perceived through the symbol of the drum. The drum performs the present. It resounds in a manner that invites people to live with an acute sense of the complexity of 'present actuality': pain and sorrow of living as a subaltern community under the symbol of the drum; nurture and hope of being intimately related to the Divine through the instrumentality of the drum, even in the midst of being ejected from the written word of scripture; and celebration of a life of togetherness that is experienced because of the unitive call of the drum. Drumming is a non-abstractive and non-analytical mode of being involved in religious activity. The people absorbed in the dictates of drumming (both the drummers and the devotees) are participating in a religious activity that is particular (in the sense that each beat is a call to participate in a specific ritual activity) and immediate.[53]

A third characteristic of sound is that it tends to foster its own community structures which engender certain skills, capacities and proclivities. Sound-based communication makes oral cultures highly communitarian. For example, on the one hand, the drum can be said to project the intense sensitivity to and respect for all dimensions of human collective creativity. The drum is rooted in communal productivity. In its own subaltern way, it is related with different occupations that use their various senses. The drum as a symbol of subaltern-based orality is a product of the labour of an interrelated productive community.[54] It cannot be usefully put to work apart from the collaborative productive labour of the subaltern community: the Dalit scavengers, responsible for removing the dead cattle; the Dalit tanners, responsible for skinning and preserving the cow hide (the local tanner has a native technique of tanning which involves tasting the solution that must be used for cleaning and drying the hide); the Dalit artisans, responsible for the crafting of drums from hide and wood; and the many Dalit drummers, responsible for transforming thudding into music. It must be underscored that the senses of touch, smell, sight, hearing and taste are all employed in the production of the drum. And these senses are operative in its playing as well. The drum is indeed an organic symbol that reflects the interrelated productive character of the subaltern-based oral communities. All these community skills are integrated for the sake of plugging into the fullness of the Divine. In contrast, written words tend to disassociate from the cycle of productivity in society. Words that are inscribed into a book are permitted to float free from the multisensory real world of human production. It also allows for an individualistic and fragmented disposition:

> In a chirographic culture, where the material for thought are permanent and objective, people can analyse situations and issues in the privacy of the minds, and they develop more individualized and [less organic] ways of thinking.[55]

It objectifies a text, which is distanced from the everyday touch, smell, and taste of the lives of the people who give their blood, sweat and tears for economic productivity.

On the other hand, because drumming has to be generated and sustained by a concrete person, or many concrete persons, it tends to call for a more interpersonal and relational ethos.[56] In keeping with this, leadership in oral societies tends to be more collaborative and eclectic whereas in literate cultures it tends to be identified with people who are proficient in matters pertaining to the script. Goody attempts to demonstrate how this medium of communication, i.e. the technology of writing, has influenced society in the areas of religion, economics, politics and law. In his analysis the escalating and domineering role of the class of the possessors and promoters of writing technology is evidenced.[57]

In the discussion of the religion of the Paraiyar, the cooperative manner by which religious functionaries performed their roles has been highlighted. The priests, the community elders, the goddess-possessed devotees and the drummers dialogically reconstructed many collective rituals; since orthopraxis was not fixed according to one written text it remained fluid and collectively construable. The leadership among the Paraiyar in religious ceremonies was noted to be defused and multiplex.[58] Moreover, it was described as not being tied up with the written text that is taken to be the norm for all religious theory and practice.

This is quite unlike the religions of the literate. 'With writing a new situation arises since the priest has privileged access to the sacred texts ... of which he is the custodian and prime interpreter.'[59] When one looks at the collusion between the mechanisms of the church or temple and educational institutions in India there seems a kind of control on the field of knowledge which is affirmed to be textual. This has generally been attested outside of the South Indian context: 'religions of the Book are often associated with the uses and extent of literacy.'[60] Within the religions of literacy, thus, central importance is given to the authority of those who are proficient in the sacred text and who are also committed to its being established as the decisive norm of all religious theory and practice. This undercuts the multifaceted dimensions of social intercourse that are a characteristic of oral religions, and homogenizes these pluriform functionaries by making them accountable to one medium, i.e. writing.

It has been suggested rather simplistically that this divergence between orality and literacy can be reduced to the difference attributed between all other worldviews and the 'western' one. While it may be the case that western culture is comprehensively entrenched in a writing and print based system, in the Indian situation there can be little doubt of the existence of both types of orientations within one geographical and historical setting.[61] On the one hand, my analysis of Indian-Christian theology points to the slighting of the world of the Dalits, which resulted from the caste communities' text-based orientation of doing theology (literacy-mode of collective reflection). Indian theology wedded together the philosophical wisdom of caste Hindu communities (mainly as contained in their sacred scriptures) and the story of the Christ even as recorded in the Christian scripture.[62] On the other hand, based on my extensive description of the religion of the Paraiyar, with the symbol of the drum at its hub, I am pointing to religious elements that constitute a whole canvas of subaltern-based culture of orality. This orality of the Paraiyar was discussed both in terms of the oral religious mythographies concerning the goddess Ellaiyamman and the creative symbolic, even if non-verbal, religious utilization of the drum. When one couples that depiction with my subsequent description of the religious reflections on the symbol of the drum in other South Indian traditions (particularly those which were influenced by, and interacted with, Dalit peoples), one can begin to appreciate the meaningfulness of positing the drum as a metasymbol that gathers together fragments of the symbolic world of the cultures and religions of sub-altern-based orality.

Just as the Word (in this context its written form) can be made to epitomize the various dimensions of the culture and religion of literacy among the theological practitioners of dominant communities in India, the drum can be introduced as representational of the religious symbolization of the subaltern communities which most comprehensively comprise the richness of their oral-based culture and religion. In this vein, the drum as an organizing symbol represents the various features of human modes of thought and representation that are engendered by subaltern-based orality: it unites communities by connecting inte-riority with interiority; it situates human beings in context-dependent, present actuality, which is participatory; and it fosters collaborative and eclectic patterns of community behaviour.

III. Stretching and Striking the Drum for Theology's Sake

I proposed that theology is critical and constructive reflection on human dialogical symbolic intercourse in its attempt to make sense of, find meaning in, and determine order for living collectively under the Divine. I then went on to elaborate upon two major drawbacks that prevent Indian theology from functioning in terms of the design of this defini-tion. First, I argued that Indian-Christian theology is non-dialogical and non-representative of the symbolic interaction of the whole community. It generally ignores and excludes the history, culture and religious tradition of the Dalits. Second, I suggested that Indian-Christian theology, through this exclusion of the voice of the Dalits and espousal of the interests of the caste communities, becomes an instrument of hegemony: a means of ideological co-option.

The foregoing analysis of the two-fold modes of thought and orientation helps us flesh out significant clues to this dynamic. On the one hand, Indian-Christian theology is not equipped to deal with the cultural and religious resources that are represented by orality. Its agenda is set by and dependent on the norms and framework laid out by the practitioners of the culture of literacy. Theology has been script-and text-centred in its discourse and thus is unable to contain the mode of thought and reflection of the Dalits that is oral in orientation. This development of theology as a discourse of the forces of literacy has been brought about by two colluding factors. First, James Massey reminds us that '[t]he roots of Indian Christian theology lie in the experiences of mostly upper caste/class Christian converts.'[63] Thus, the caste Christian theologians' chief agenda was understandably driven by the quest to 'relate or interpret their new faith or experience in Indian thought forms.'[64] The most obvious characteristic of these Indian thought forms is that they are 'based on Brahminic religion and culture', documented and contained in the sacred texts of Hinduism.[65] Second, the Indian-Christian community is influenced by western notions of biblicism: 'To limit the words of God to one particular text book and to believe that this alone is God's word amounts to burying God's voice in the printed papers.'[66] Antony Mookenthottam's 'pluridimensional method' for working towards 'A Theology in the Indian context' is a case in point, since it brings together texts of both the Indian religions and Christianity in order to do contextual theology. In his own words, Mookenthottam analyses and reinterprets the 'Truth in the Indian scriptures' and the 'Truth in the Christian scriptures' with a view to apply this to and solve 'concrete problems in Indian theology'.[67]

On the other hand, Indian-Christian theology utilizes literacy as a medium by which other media that are symbolized by the multidimensionality of subaltern-based orality are co-opted and overcome. This trend is so well established that Samartha, a noted contemporary Indian-Christian theologian, entreats theological colleagues to be wary of 'writtenness' when divorced from 'spokenness': 'It uses language as an instrument to define, control and manipulate Truth.'[68] Here one notices that the medium is inextricable from the message: literacy is the medium and textuality encodes, translates and communicates the message. My own effort attempts to go a step further. It expands the category of 'spokenness' by linking up aspects of non-verbal representation with the spoken dimensions of the word (subaltern-based orality). Thus, it advocates an interpretation of the forces of orality (an expanded notion of 'spokenness') for their own sake and in their interaction with and resistance to literacy-centred orientations of 'writtenness'.

Projecting the drum as an organizing symbol for the various dimensions of subaltern-based orality assuages the tendency of pedestalizing 'writtenness', which has dominated Indian theology. Additionally, in the domain of theology, the drum may be introduced as more than an organizing symbol that gathers up, represents and circulates the various dimensions of the culture and religion of orality. It also functions as a 'theological interpretant'. According to Neville, an interpretant 'means a sign that interprets another sign as standing for an object in a certain respect.'[69] With regards to theology he goes on to say:

> An interpretant of God is required if God is to be experienced as anything at all. Or rather, to experience divine matters as divine, it is necessary to have some interpretants explicating 'God' or proper alternatives in which divinity can be experienced.[70]

Neville posits creation *ex nihilo* as a fundamental theological interpretant for understanding and explicating divinity in its comparative religions context.[71] My own situation has more to do with excavating a fundamental theological interpretant that both allows the Indian Christian community to recognize and validate 'proper alternatives in which divinity can be experienced' and challenge theologians to construct their dialogue within the framework of such conceptual and analytical devices. I thus suggest that the drum is 'a well-constructed, archeological deep, experiential interpretant of God [/the Divine]'[72] that forces Indian-Christian theology to both comprehend and utilize the religious collective experience of subaltern communities in its effort to make theological reflection more inclusive and liberative.

In submitting the drum as a theological interpretant I am deliberately digressing from and, perhaps, disputing two premises that are intrinsic to Neville's methodology. On the one hand, whereas Neville argues stridently for the abstract character of theological interpretants, I have opted to designate a concrete symbol to that position.[73] I maintain that such a move is in keeping with the tangible, organic and productivity-related character of the representational world of subaltern-based orality. On the other hand, while Neville prefers to delineate one key conceptual category (creation *ex nihilo*) as a theological interpretant to organize and illuminate diverse themes from different world religious, I admit to the provision of at least two such interpretants, i.e. the word and the drum. Two possibilities emerge in transforming the drum from an organizing symbol of the culture and religion of subaltern-based oral communities into a theological interpretant through which alternatives of the Divine can be experienced and reflected upon in the arena of theology as I defined it. On the one hand, the drum can be taken to represent the particular non-linguistic (as in script-dependent language) modes of reflection that must be accommodated on its way to being celebrated within Indian-Christian theology. On the other hand, the drum can supply Indian-Christian theology with themes from its multisensory collective experience that can be transposed into the linguistic mode in order to become a resource for its inclusive dialogical discourse.

The drum voices the different modes of expression found in the culture of orality for Indian-Christian theology

An important point that we have discovered in the sphere of theology is that the process of thought and reflection among human beings also uses media that are both distinct from writing and syndicated with non-verbal forms of musical expression. In a general critique of the tendency to concentrate on the written text, Sullivan's exhortation to scholars working in the field of religious studies is timely: 'come to grips with alternate construals of meaning as they are found in other cultures.'[74] He further prompts religionists

> to unfasten the bonds placed on inquiry by culture-bound notions of the text and give fair hearing and sight to the imaginal expressions that lie outside the singular expression of writing.[75]

By the reclamation of the drum, Indian theology is beckoned to interact with music as an autonomous medium of reflection and construction of meaning. In the specific context of doing Indian-Christian theology (in the light of our exposition of the social intercourse of the Paraiyar), the construals that emerge from the creative renditions of drummers become a call for the inclusion of non-discursive, theophonic voices in any theological conversation. Here music is treated as a somewhat independent symbol system that reveals the meaningful, mediative and expressive reflections of human beings in their collective relatedness to each other, the world and the Divine.[76] James Frazer demonstrates this link between music and the construction of religion:

> Indeed the influence of music on the development of religion is a subject that would repay a sympathetic study. For we cannot doubt that this, the most intimate and affecting of all the arts, has done much to create as well as to express the religious emotions, thus modifying more or less deeply the fabric of belief to which at first sight it seems only to minister. The musician has done his part as well as the prophet and the thinker in the making of religion.[77]

In chapter three I discussed the specific context in South India that has contributed to the Paraiyar's learning to utilize and develop drumming as a means of communication and representation of meaning: they were severed from hearing and reading the sacred Word of the caste Hindu communities. In this chapter I went on to trace the existence of this mode of theophonics among other subaltern-based communities in South India. Even outside the South Indian context, there is ample evidence that the utilization of the drum for purposes of communication with, and reflection on, the Divine is not uncommon.[78] The distinctiveness of the drum as a semiotic system in its own right has been explored and expounded upon. Sebeok captures this assertion aptly:

> These surrogates are noteworthy objects of study not only for this ability to represent spoken language, however, but also as semiotic systems in their own right. Like some other surrogates, such as writing, drum and whistle systems frequently become partially independent of spoken language due, on the one hand, to the different contextual pressures exerted on them and, on the other, to the systemic requirements of the surrogate itself.[79]

Pursuing this option (theosymphonics?) would no doubt be a fascinating and productive way to study and interpret the religious themes of the Paraiyar and other drum-related subaltern communities. Three reasons can be stated for encouraging such an ethnomusicological study: it would force religionists to come to experience Paraiyar's and other subaltern communities' themes on their own terms; it would expand the scope of theology constraining it to deal with different modes of representation;[80] and it would redefine the composition of participants in theology's reflection on the social intercourse of the community. However, apart from suggesting this as a fruitful direction for theology, this option lies beyond both the competence and the scope of this book.

The drum engenders religious themes proffered by subaltern-based orality for Indian-Christian theology

Theology can also be enriched by transposing themes that are significant to orality into forms of literacy. In this case it involves a literary (written) extrapolation of the religious resources reverberating from the symbol of the drum in Paraiyar and Dalit-related religions. Accordingly, I undertake an explication of the complex interweaving of the dimensions of orality by focussing on the meaning produced and ascribed to the drum and drumming in the religion of the Paraiyar in its relatedness with other local subaltern-based traditions. The religious themes are reconstructed from the meaning and significance given to drums and drumming by the community; these are then interpreted within and through the confines of discourse. Their meaning are thus interpreted through and translated to the symbol' system of language, without disparaging and invalidating the integrity and creativity of oral-based symbolic interaction.

Having undertaken this option I shall endeavour to do two things. Briefly, on a formal level, I shall summarize the ways in which the drum brings into the realm of Indian-Christian theology the three dimensions that were identified as being part of the characteristics of orality: The drum represents the dimensions of religion that are aggregatively integrative of the interiority of subaltern communities; participatory through closeness to the context; and eclectic and multisensory. On a more material level, I shall then extrapolate religious themes that are expressed by the specific symbol of the drum within the Paraiyar's tradition in particular, though quite related with other subaltern communities in general. While the former performs a complementary function by bringing into theology aspects of orality that have been ignored by the agenda of literacy, the latter performs the supplementary function of gleaning themes from subaltern religion by analysing the symbol of the drum.

Formally, the drum brings to the arena of Indian-Christian theology characteristics that are tied up with the culture and religion of orality. In so doing it provides a broader framework by which the particularity of the Dalits can be incorporated into the critical and constructive reflection that I defined as being the task of theology. Specifically, the symbol of the drum within the realm of Indian-Christian theology represents the incorporative, immediate (as in 'present actuality' rather than non-mediated) and eclectic aspects that characterize Dalit religion. First, the drum represents aggregative inclusivity (not without its resistive streak towards the co-optive characteristic of the domination and unisensory mode of literacy) as it widens the scope of theological reflection by bringing in various religious resources that are expressed in diverse forms. In this discussion the various modes are projected by the advancement of the two organizing symbols of the drum and the word, which represent diverse, though interrelated, orientations of thought and reflection, i.e. orality and literacy. For its part, the drum symbolizes the fact that all resources do not have to be subsumed into the universality of the word in its written form. Second, the drum represents in the sphere of Indian-Christian theology the significance of participatory and close-to-context ways of knowing and reflecting. The drum best conveys the immediate characteristic of the religious imaginations of the Paraiyar which was retained and celebrated in a context in which they were denied access to (distanced from) the sacred Word of the caste Hindus. Third, the drum suggests the importance of eclecticism in the doing of Indian-Christian theology. This is true of both the eclectic media through which meaning is synchronized in the community and the diverse leadership of those who are involved in producing religious meaning. Just as the drummer, the priest, and the elders among the devotees become the sources of meaning-making among the Paraiyar, theological reflection must also be sensitive to the various media (music, art, architecture, weaving, landscaping, drama, literature, etc.) through which human beings express their relationship with the Divine.

Materially, the themes that are extrapolated from the drum as utilized by the Paraiyar allow us to put into discursive circulation the distinct, substantive and creative religious experience of one major Dalit community in South India. An imaginative and thematic recapitulation of the drum in the collective religious life of the Paraiyar will contain at least the following three components: drum as a medium of divine-human communication (invokes, contains, and dispenses power); drum as an instrument of linking the subalternity of communities for resistive and emancipatory ends (call to fight invading troops, evil forces, and colonizing caste forces); and drum as a symbol of exemplifying and managing communal subaltern suffering.

Drum as vehicle of Divine-human mediation

In our study of the religion of the Paraiyar we noted that the drum makes their dealings with the Divine 'unique and complete'. Further, we ascertained that within a historical and social context that severed the Dalits from the sacred language (Sanskrit) and sacred literature of the caste Hindus, the choice of the drum as a medium for communication was practical, calculating and ingenious. In harmony with our interpretation of subaltern-based orality, there are two particularities that must be noted when interpreting the drum rather than the word as a notable and vital vehicle of mediation between the Divine and the human.

First, the drum suggests both the inexplicable and the unutterable aspects of communication between the Divine and the human. The surplus of meaning is pregiven in the sound of the drum rather than something that needs to be teased out of the structure of the inscribed text. In the case of the Paraiyar, on the one hand, from the human side of communication, this stems from their communal expression which is riddled with so much pain and oppression that it cannot really be expressed adequately in mere words. Moreover, mediation with the Divine via the drum, in the context of the multidimensionality of oppressive forces that characterize the history of the Paraiyar, also guards against the manner in which words that are verbalized within this intimate Divine-human communication can be misinterpreted by caste communities and utilized against them. On the other hand, from the Divine side of this communication, this inarticulatability on the part of human beings, signifies the dimension of mystery that is an intrinsic component of the relationship between the Divine and the human. The drum is a tangible reminder of that dimension in Divine-human relationality that is cryptic, incomprehendable, uninscribable and incommunicable in human language. This is stressed in the analyses of the surplus and supplementary dimensions of meaning built into the orientations of subaltern-based orality as symbolized by the drum.

This naturally leads to the second aspect of the Divine-human mediation: the drum symbolizes the dimension of Divine power that is closely tied to materiality. In our study of the drum as symbolizing the mediating and empowering presence of Divine power among the Paraiyar, the difference between the operation-centred character of the Paraiyar's use of power and the knowledge-centred character of caste communities' use of power was delineated. For the Paraiyar, the drum is an instrument of mediation between the Divine and the human that channels the efficacious power of the Divine in order to acquire material gains. Thus, the spirit that is invoked and mediated through drumming is contained and coaxed to exercise its power in a manner that brings forth material rewards for the devotees and the community: physical and mental health and wholeness; financial security and bounty; and harmony, sufficiency and well being for the family and the community.

Through the drum, thus, theology is invited to ponder upon the dialectics of upholding the sense of mystery of Divine-human communication without neglecting the very materiality from which and for which this mediation occurs. Here one must pause to stress the rich paradox of this suggestion: while subaltern religion and its relationship with Divine power has generally highlighted material benefits, this does not imply that their relationality with the Divine is devoid of the central aspect of mystery and ambiguity. The drum lifts up the inexplicable and unutterable nature of Divine-human relationship in conjunction with its materiality.

Drum as instrument of resistive and emancipatory religious and communitarian identity

In chapter three we considered the various ways in which the drum symbolized the text of resistance and emancipatory theography of the Paraiyar. Three central ideas can be restated to capture the essence of that discussion. First, the pervasive and deliberate utilization of the drum in the various aspects of the religious life of the Paraiyar's within the context of its being propagated as a symbol of inauspiciousness and degradation by caste Hindus, attests to its communal resistive capacities. Second, the drum substantively represented the unique and particular collective religious experience of the Paraiyar. The drum as a central religious symbol reveals the creative religious and cultural capital that is particular to the community. Third, the drum was transfigured through a process of creative resistance by incorporating a level of vested compliance to the symbolic universe of the dominant caste communities. Thus, the drum, as a creative symbol of the particularity of the Paraiyar, enacted its ongoing emancipatory potential through a process of creative resistance and reconciliatory engagement.

Traces of the resistive power of religion were also noted in the religion of other local subaltern-based communities earlier in this chapter. Again, through a calculating process of realistic and negotiatory interaction with the religion of the dominant communities, the drum symbolizes subaltern-based oral communities' collective resolve to resist in their own way the demonizing and colonizing tendencies of caste communities' religious grids of interpretation. An important theme emerges: the power of the Divine manifests itself in subtly resisting forces of hegemony that aspire to demonize or colonize human beings. In this case we have documented this specifically in relation to the lands, culture, religion, bodies, and communal identity of the Paraiyar. David Tracy reminds us that this is quite typical of religions in general:

> Despite their own sin and ignorance, the religions, at their best, always bear extraordinary powers of resistance. When not domesticated as sacred canopies for the status quo nor wasted by their own self-contradictory grasps at power, the religions live by resistance.[81]

The drum, no doubt, symbolizes the resistive and emancipatory power of the Divine as the Paraiyar confront, contest and combat the demonizing and colonizing proclivities of the caste communities. However, it is also an instrument for resisting and conquering evil and demonic forces that threaten the overall stability and well being of the Paraiyar community. In the discussion of the various kinds of drum beats we established that the effective role of the drum during funerals, processions and sacrifices had to do with its ability to resist and overcome the demons that threaten the well being of the community.[82] In addition, the drum was associated with the call to resist invading human powers: the call of the drum was a call to war. Here the drum is taken to be a symbolic call to gather the community together in order to prepare them to resist invading groups of enemies. Finally, we noted the drum's role in resisting the co-optive tendencies of literacy. It keeps the multisensory and multidimensionality of sound-based (subaltern orality) religious reflection alive within a predominantly sight-based (dominant literacy) milieu.

In sum, the drum brings together the many facets of human resistance in the communal striving for emancipation that is intrinsic to the existence of subaltern people. The Divine and the human co-operation of resistance and liberation is symbolized in the drum. Most notably it manifests the crucial role that the Divine plays in aiding their communal resistance and emancipation against both human and spiritual oppressive powers. In the case of the former, this is exemplified in the calculating and multifaceted manner in which the Dalits have been assisted by the drum to resist the attempts by the caste communities to demonize and colonize them. In the case of the latter, this is manifested by the drum's ability to impede the demonic forces that aspire to disrupt the life and well being of Dalit communities. However, the negotiatory and subtle character of subaltern resistance must not be overlooked. The overall objective of realizing Dalit emancipation is possible only through small and fragmented gains implicit in the process of resistance-in-and-through-negotiation, which allows for a process that is necessarily reconciliatory and potentially liberative.

Drum as means of exemplifying and managing communal suffering

A third major theme that the drum is intimately tied up with in the life of the Paraiyar is communal suffering. The drum is both a symbol of the corporate suffering that the Paraiyar had to endure through centuries and a means by which they cope with this suffering which is characteristic of their communal existence.

In chapter two, in the reconstruction of the historic origins of the Paraiyar, I pointed to the deep-rooted and widespread acknowledgement of the correlation between the occupation of drum beating and the low social and cultural status conferred upon this community. The caste Hindu conception of pollution underpins the ideological reinforcement that is necessary to fuel this general theory. On the one hand, the drum is made from cow hide which is highly polluting. On the other hand, the Paraiyar drummers are connected with death and funerals, which is also a major source of pollution.[83] The Paraiyar, thus, as a community associated with cow hide and funerals become the despised and outcast community, and the suffering they have endured for centuries is symbolically and factually rooted in the drum. Nonetheless, it is this same symbol of oppression and humiliation that is utilized as the means by which suffering is managed and contained. The source and the emblem of communal suffering of the Paraiyar becomes the cornerstone of their struggle to cope with and overcome subjugation. The symbol of pathos (the drum), which I have contended is the organizing symbol of the religion of the Dalits, also functions as the symbol that reveals the Divine presence among the subaltern people. The resounding of the drum is tied up with the genesis of the Divine among the Dalits. Suffering is indeed the womb of epistemology: to experience, participate in, and establish truth is to be drawn into the reverberation of the drum that instantiates communal suffering of the Dalits. The Divine and human meet at the fulcrum of suffering; and the drum symbolizes this encounter. This explains the fact that the drum represents both the synchronization of the collective suffering of the Dalits and the source of their communal relaxation and celebration. To put it theologically, when the Divine is revealed at the core of a people's communal suffering it allows for the birthing of hope that can even be experienced as celebration — a celebration that God is faithful in the midst of forsakenness and that if God is within the throes of pathos, then He will act to emancipate such communities.

Before concluding this section let me explicitly state a religious truth that can be said to be subaltern-based orality's contribution to theology. Through the progression of these religious themes, which have emerged from our reflection on the drum one must not ignore the existence of a certain dialectic dynamics. This has been pointed out at various junctures through the discussion of both Paraiyar and subaltern religions, on the one hand, and subaltern-based orality, on the other. In this section as well, in deliberating on the religious themes of the symbol of the drum, this dialectic is quite noticeable. While discussing the first theme, i.e. the drum as an instrument of Divine-human mediation, we must hold together two dimensions of divine power, which is characterized by its ambiguity (as it proves faithful to the idea of mystery) as well as its concrete materiality. The conjoining of mystery and materiality lends itself to an existential paradox that reflects the Dalits representation of the Divine. The second theme of the drum as an instrument of the resistive and emancipatory communal spirit cannot but be also interpreted in the context of the Paraiyar's compliance with the overall social framework of the Hindu system. Here the example of drumming is in itself paradigmatic: whereas the Paraiyar were the drummers for the caste Hindus only for inauspicious functions, they used drumming for both auspicious and inauspicious functions in their own communal life. They were thus willing to accept their own inauspicious role as drummers within the larger context of the overall caste Hindu framework without giving up their own resistance (symbolized by their continued use of the drum for their own auspicious communal rituals) to such a restricted religious grid. In explicating the third theme of the drum as a means of exemplifying and managing suffering, we must also keep in mind that this same instrument which is integrally related to suffering is also used to pronounce news of peace and victory in war and for the purposes of communal relaxation.

To conclude this lengthy discussion, let me recapitulate the main conceptual moves that have been made. First, I started with a brief interpretation of the drum in other South Indian religious traditions.

This discussion enabled an accentuation of the harmonious relationship of the drum as a dominant symbol of the Paraiyar with other local subaltern-based oral (religious) traditions. The central point that converged in the discussion may be stated as follows: On the one hand, the drum in various strands of South Indian religious traditions is associated with subaltern communities, which are Dalit-identified and Dalit-related; on the other hand, the drum gathers together (integrates) the liberative yearnings of subaltern-based oral communities within the context of a dominating and co-optive orientation of literacy.

Second, the symbol of the drum presents theologians with a complementary mode of religious representation. In this extended section, two modes of thought and representation were submitted, with a plethora of qualification and modifications: subaltern-based orality and dominant-funded literacy. I then made a case that the drum can be posited as an organizing symbol of the various facets of orality just as the word exemplifies the many aspects of literacy. Three aspects of orality were culled and commented upon keeping in mind its potential resourcefulness for doing theology: it unites communities by connecting interiority with interiority; it situates human beings in context-dependent, present actuality, which is participatory; and it fosters collaborative and eclectic patterns of community behaviour.

Third, I suggested the ways in which Indian–Christian theology would be enriched by propping up the drum as a theological interpretant. On the one hand, I demonstrated how the drum can voice the different modes of expression that are characterized by the culture of orality for the inclusive, dialogical and liberative purposes of Indian-Christian theology. Music was the specific mode of expression that was represented in this study of the Paraiyar; but this expanded the reflective space within the realm of theology to incorporate a multiplicity of expressive and reflective modes. i.e. dance, art, weaving, architecture, etc. On the other hand, I extrapolated formal principles and material resources for Indian-Christian theology by positing the drum as a theological interpretant. This helped to both capture and circulate religious themes that are proffered by the culture of orality that have been ignored by the discourse of Indian-Christian theology.

Notes

1. For information on the Alvar, see Vidya Dehejia, *Slaves of the Lord: The Path of the Tamil Saints* (Delhi: Munshiram Manoharlal Publishers, 1988);

Norman Cutler, *Songs of Experience: The Poetics of Tamil Devotion* (Bloomingdale: Indiana University Press, 1987); and John Carman and Vasudha Narayanan, *The Tamil Veda: Pillan's Interpretation of the Tiruvaymoli* (Chicago: Chicago University Press, 1989), pp. 13–33.

2. I am aware of the problems involved with dating the life of Ramanuja. Here I accept the dates suggested by Carman. For a comprehensive discussion of Ramanuja's theology, particularly in its context of the *Bakthi* tradition, see John Braisted Carman, *The Theology of Ramanuja: An Essay in Interreligious Understanding* (New Haven: Yale University Press, 1975).

3. Ibid., p. 25.

4. I am thankful to Eric J. Lott for bringing this to my attention. See note number 9 for information about the source.

5. This summary is based on the interpretation of the *Tiruppavai* by Vidya Dehejia, *Antal and Her Path of Love: Poems of a Woman Saint from South India* (Albany, NY: SUNY Press, 1990), pp. 1–71. For an English translation of the Tiruppavai, see Norman Cutler, *Consider Our Vow: An English Translation of Tiruppavai and Tiruvempavai* (Madurai: Muthu Patippakam, 1978). For a substantial critical study of the Tiruppavai, see C. Jagannathachariar, *The Tiruppavai of Sri Andal: Textual, Literary and Critical Study* (Madras: Parthasarathy Swami Devasthanam, 1982).

6. Nataraja Guru, *Life and Teachings of Narayana Guru* (Fernhill, India: An East-West University Publication, 1990), p. 93. Emphasis in text.

7. Ibid., p. 91. In another passage Narayana Guru reiterates the primeval character of religious drumming:

    > Ancient drumming, extending far behind recorded history, beat out a perennial message which is transmuted and scientifically restated, after passing through the vicissitudes of history, through Guru after Guru.

    Ibid., p. 243.

8. Ibid., p. 92.

9. Eric J. Lott, 'The Divine Drum: Interpreting a Primal Symbol', in *Sri Andal: Her Contribution to Literature, Philosophy, Religion and Art*, ed. M.N. Parthasarathi (Madras: Ramanuja Vedanta Centre, 1986), p. 40.

10. Ibid.

11. Most notably Stephen Pepper's work on 'World hypotheses' attributes the variances in different philosophies to their being grounded in six foundational 'world hypotheses' or basic metaphors: animism, participation, formism, mechanism, contextualism and organism. See Stephen Pepper, *World Hypotheses* (Berkeley: University of California Press, 1942). For a similar argument in terms of 'Key Symbols' and 'Key metaphors', see Sherry Ortner, 'On Key Symbols', in *American Anthropologist*, 75 (6): 38–46. I am influenced by the conception of 'organizing Metaphor' proposed by James W. Fernandez. I use the term organizing symbol because the drum can only be used as a metaphor in a metaphorical sense, which further complicates the manner of

its usage; see 'Persuasions and Performances: Of the Beast in Every Body and the Metaphors of Everyman', *Daedalus*, 101, no. 1 (1972): 39–80 and 'The Mission of Metaphor in Expressive Culture', *Current Anthropology*, 15, no. 2 (1974): 119–45. I am aware that from the 1980s onward Fernandez has pushed anthropologists to study and analyse metaphors within the context of other tropes in culture. Nonetheless, he does appear to argue for a qualitatively distinct role ('mission') for metaphors in 'expressive cultures'. See *Persuasions and Performances: The Play of Tropes in Cultures* (Bloomington: Indiana University Press, 1986), pp. 28–72.

12. Much work in this field has focussed on the individual and his/her mind as a physical, psychological and social entity. The most compelling and systematic case for the theory of multiple intelligence has been put forward by Howard Gardner. He dissects the working of the mind and points to seven distinct and independent, though interactive, frames: linguistic, logico-mathematic, spacial, musical, bodily-kinesthetic, interpersonal and intrapersonal. See Howard Gardner, *Frames of Mind: The Theory of Multiple Intelligences* (New York: Basic Books 1983). Another attempt to construct a multiple and interacting systems theory of thinking comes from Robert J. Sternberg, 'The Triarchic Theory of Human Intelligence'. Here the relationship of intelligences are explained in an integrative manner between the following three areas: intelligence and the internal world of the individual; intelligence and the external world of the individual; and intelligence and experience. See Robert. J. Sternberg, *The Triarchic Mind: A New Theory of Human Intelligence* (New York: Viking Press, 1988) and *Metaphors of the Mind: Conceptions of the Nature of Intelligence* (Cambridge, UK: Cambridge University Press, 1990), pp. 261–99.

13. In the discipline of philosophy Nelson Goodman's work deals with both the multiple versions of the worlds that are made by human beings and the multimodal way by which they are constructed. See Nelson Goodman, *Ways of Worldmaking* (Indianapolis: Hackett Publishing Company, 1978) and *Of Mind and Other Matters* (Cambridge, MA: Harvard University Press, 1984). Also see Nelson Goodman and Catherine Z. Elgin, *Reconceptions in Philosophy* (Indianapolis: Hackett Publishing Company, 1988).

14. This dialectical and interpenetrative nature of the interplay of a two-fold representation can be consistently noticed in my interpretation through this entire book: Caste and Dalit communities; theology (written words about God) and theographia/theophonia (graphic/sounds about God); dominant and subaltern communities; orality and literacy; expansive and constrictive poles of Christology.

15. Stanley Jeyaraja Tambiah, *Magic, Science, Religion, and the Scope of Rationality* (Cambridge, UK: Cambridge University Press, 1990).

16. For a bird's eye view of the various schemes involved in reflecting upon this two-fold categorization let me briefly name the different diadic modes

conceptualized by scholars through this century. For a further explication of these in reference to Tambiah's schematization see ibid., pp. 84–110.

Author	Participation	Causality
Levy-Bruhl	mystical mentality	logical mentality
Freud	primary processes	secondary processes
Gregory Bateson	iconic/digital coding	verbal/analog coding
Sazanne Langer	visual forms	word forms
Carol Gilligan	female orientation (ethic of care & responsibility)	male orientation (logic of justice)
Sudir Kakar	Indian personality	Western personality
Nelson Goodman	exemplification	denotation
Karl-Otto Apel	interest for social, morally relevant praxis	interest for technical praxis
Piaget	language of complexive classification	language of dimensional classification
Foucault	doctrine of resemblance	doctrine of representation
Wittgenstein	form of life	explanation

17. Ibid., p. 108.
18. Walter J. Ong, *The Presence of the Word* (New Haven: Yale University Press, 1967); *Interfaces of the Word* (Ithaca: Cornell University Press, 1977); and *Orality and Literacy: The Technologizing of the Word* (London: Routledge, 1988).
19. Jack Goody, ed., *Literacy in Traditional Societies* (Cambridge, UK: Cambridge University Press, 1968); *The Domestication of the Savage Mind* (Cambridge, UK: Cambridge University Press, 1977); *The Logic of Writing and the Organisation of Society* (Cambridge, UK: Cambridge University Press, 1986); and *The Interface between the Written and the Oral* (Cambridge, UK: Cambridge University Press, 1987). Goody is an anthropologist who tests out his theory between oral and literate cultures in specific settings mostly in Western Africa. Also his work takes into considerations the sphere of religion. Notably he is able to revise the duality of Levi-Strauss, Levy-Bruhl, Horton, et al., in such a manner that the technology of writing becomes a central agent in the cognitive and organizational difference among types of peoples:

> The differences between written and oral languages of registers, limited as it is, displays some striking similarities to another difference which has been talked about in vague cultural terms. This is the difference between what Levi-Strauss refers to as the domesticated and the savage, what others refer to as primitive and advanced, or as simple and complex, hot and cold. Some major differences touched upon in this discussion can reasonably be attributed to the advent of writing.

Goody, *The Interface between the Written and the Oral*, p. 290 f.

20. David R. Olson, 'From Utterance to Text: The Bias of Language in Speech and Writing', *Harvard Educational Review*, vol. 47, no. 3 (August 1977): 257–81; 'Mind and Media: the Epistemic Functions of Literacy', *Journal of Communications*, vol. 38, no. 3 (Summer, 1988): 254–79 and *The World of Paper: The Conceptual and Cognitive Implications of Writing and Reading* (Cambridge, UK: Cambridge University Press, 1994). Also, see Olson, ed., *Social Foundations of Language and Thought* (New York: Norton Publishing House, 1980) and Olson, Torrance N. and Hildyard A., eds, *Literacy, Language and Learning* (Cambridge, UK: Cambridge University Press, 1985).

21. Walter J. Ong, *Orality and Literacy*.

22. Ibid., p. 105. Emphasis mine.

23. Ibid., p. 67 f.

24. From a reflection based on the culture of literacy in the Modern West, Godzich encourages us to be careful about glossing over the aural nature of much of our consumption.

> What we need to consider is the coexistence of the oral and the written in a culture that is primarily audative, where, in other words, even the written is received for the most part in an aural form. Such a culture ... differs from the more purely oral [and] ... from the more purely written.

Wlad Godzich, *The Culture of Literacy* (Cambridge, MA: Harvard University Press, 1994), p. 79. From studies based on the culture of orality, ethnographic reports are increasingly revealing the ways by which literacy is being collectively and creatively manipulated to serve the interest of oral practices. Specially, see Don Kulick and Christopher Stroud, 'Conceptions and Uses of Literacy in a Papua New Guinean Village', Niko Besnier, 'Literacy and Feeling: The Encoding of Affect in Nukulaelae Letters'; Maurice Bloch, 'The Use of Schooling and Literacy in a Zafimaniry Village'; and Caroline H. Bledsoe and Kenneth M. Robey, 'Arabic Literacy and Secrecy among the Mende of Sierra Leone', in Brian V. Street, ed., *Cross-cultural Approaches to Literacy* (Cambridge, UK: Cambridge University Press, 1993), pp. 30–134.

25. See W. Frawley, ed., *Linguistics and Literacy* (New York: Plenum Press, 1982); M. Nyystrand, ed., *What Writers Know: The Language, Process and Structure of Written Discourse* (New York: Academic Press, 1982); D. Tannen, ed., *Spoken and Written Language: Exploring Orality and Literacy* (Norwood, NJ: Ablex Press, 1982); J. Cook-Gumperz, ed., *The Social Construction of Literacy* (Cambridge, UK: Cambridge University Press, 1986); K. Levine, *The Social Context of Literacy* (London: Routledge and Kegal Paul, 1986); K. Scousboe and M.T. Larsen, eds, *Literacy and Society* (Copenhagen: Academsig Forlag, 1989). Interestingly even Jack Goody and David Olson have reconsidered their own somewhat rigid divide between orality and literacy. See Goody, *The Logic of Writing* and Olson et al., *Literacy, Language and Learning*.

26. See part 1 and 2 of Street, *Cross-cultural Approaches to Literacy*, pp. 25–219.

27. Tambiah too insists that participation and causality are 'contrasting and complementary and coexisting orientations to the world.' Thus, he realistically affirms 'the obvious and incontestable fact that elements of participation are not lacking in scientific discourses, and features of causality are not necessarily absent in participatory enactment.' *Magic, Science, Religion*, p. 110.

28. Clarence Walhout, 'Christianity, History, and Literacy Criticism: Walter Ong's Global Vision', in *Journal of the American Academy of Religion*, no. LXII/2 (Summer, 1994): 440.

29. Murray Jardine, 'Sight, Sound, and Epistemology: The Experiential Sources of Ethical Concepts', in *Journal of the American Academy of Religion*, no. LXIV/1 (Spring, 1996): 3.

30. Ibid., p. 6.

31. Much of what I am arguing in this section comes from the chapter entitled 'Word as Sound' of Walter J. Ong., S.J., *The Presence of the Word: Some Prolegomena for Culture and Religious History* (New York: Simon and Schuster, 1970), pp. 110–32. Ong, of course, delineates five points when analysing the nature of Sound: that which is 'related to present actuality' (p. 111); 'a special sensory key to interiority' (p. 117); 'an effective means to unite groups of living beings' (p. 122); something that 'situates man in the middle of actuality and in simultaneity' (p. 128); and that which 'fosters different personality structures and different characteristic anxieties' (p. 130). I have found that his points can be reduced meaningfully to three that I describe, without losing the comprehensiveness that he achieves. I am indebted to Walhout's article for bringing this to my attention.

32. Ong, *Presence of the Word*, p. 125.

33. Ibid., p. 122.

34. As summarized in Walhout, *Walter Ong's Global Vision*, pp. 441–42.

35. Ibid., p. 442.

36. Ong, *The Presence of the Word*, p. 117.

37. 'Since in primary oral culture conceptualized knowledge that is not repeated aloud soon vanishes, oral societies must invest great energy in saying over and over again what has been learned arduously over the ages.' Ibid., p. 41.

38. Jardine, *Sight, Sound, and Epistemology*, p. 7.

39. Ibid.

40. Goody, *The Logic of Writing*, pp. 1–44. Although Goody is primarily writing out of his research done in Africa, he consciously and continuously takes into consideration aspects of Indian religions.

41. Ibid., p. 8.

42. Ibid., p. 10.

43. See chapter three, section II.

44. For my discussion of this 'fluidity' in the composition of oral myths among the Paraiyar see chapter three, specially the section on 'Ellaiyamman as iconic symbol'.

45. For an excellent discussion of the oral and textual dimensions of the Vedas,

see Laurie L. Patton, *Authority, Anxiety, and Canon. Essays in Vedic Interpretation* (Albany, NY: State University of New York, 1994). The above quotations are from Patton's *Introduction*, pp. 3–4.

46. Walhout, *Walter Ong's Global Vision*, p. 442.
47. Ong, *Orality and Literacy*, p. 55. See Aleksandr Romanovich Luria, *Cognitive Development: Its Cultural and Social Foundations*, ed. Michael Coles (Cambridge, MA.: Harvard University Press, 1976).
48. This correlation between oral cultures and concrete or 'operative' thinking can be interpreted in the light of a parallel connection between the decisive formalization of the mechanics of writing and the possibility for abstract thinking. Havelock attributes the rise in Greek analytical and abstract thinking to the Greeks' introduction of vowels into the alphabets. See Eric A. Havelock, *Origins of Western Literacy* (Toronto: Ontario Institute for Studies in Education, 1976). Goody and Watt have further suggested that the 'kinds of analysis involved in the syllogism and in other forms of logical procedure are clearly dependent on writing'. Jack Goody and Ian Watt, 'The Consequences of Literacy', in Goody, ed., *Literacy in Traditional Society*, p. 68.
49. Patricia Greenfield makes a similar distinction between oral 'context-dependent' communication and written 'context-independent' communication. See P.M. Greenfield, 'Oral and Written language: The Consequences for Cognitive Development in Africa, The United States and England', in *Language and Speech*, 15: 169–78.
50. Ong, *Orality and Literacy*, p. 45.
51. Ibid., p. 46. Goody points out that

   it is not accidental that major steps in the development of what we now call 'science' followed the introduction of major changes in the channels of communication in Babylonia (writing), in Ancient Greece (the alphabets), and in Western Europe (printing).

   Goody, *The Domestication of the Savage Mind*, p. 51.
52. Goody, *The Logic of Writing*, pp. 12–13.
53. See my discussion of drumming among the Paraiyar in chapter three, section III.
54. The directions of this argument were stimulated by a lecture delivered by Kancha Ilaiah on March 6, 1997 at the United Theological College (Bangalore) entitled 'Dalit Religion as a Resource for Human Emancipation'. I am also thankful to him for the extended discussions that we had after the lecture.
55. Walhout, *Walter Ong's Global Vision*, p. 442–3.
56. Jardine, *Sound, Sight and Epistemology*, p. 6.
57. Goody, *The Logic of Writing*.
58. See my discussion in chapter two, section III.
59. Goody, *The Logic of Writing*, pp. 16–17.
60. Ibid.

61. Recent interpretations of Derrida's notion of 'logocentricism' (privileging of the spoken word over and against the written) points to the fact

    that in the western philosophical tradition, the affirmation of the civilizational role of writing has usually gone hand in hand with the denigration of concrete writing or the actual written text. [Thus,] the spoken word has been considered primary and natural, while writing was seen as secondary, representational and supplementary.

    Ajay Skaria, 'Writing, Orality and Power in the Dangs, Western India, 1800s–1920s', in *Subaltern Studies IX*, p. 16.
62. See my discussion of this in chapter one, section II.
63. James Massey, 'Ingredients for a Dalit Theology', in *A Reader in Dalit Theology*, p. 146.
64. Ibid.
65. Ibid., pp. 146–50.
66. K. Wilson, 'Towards A Humane Culture', in *A Reader in Dalit Theology*, p. 158.
67. Antony Mookenthottam, MSFS, *Towards a Theology in the Indian Context* (Bangalore: Asian Trading Corporation, 1980). For a systematic study of the history of Indian Christian theology and its dependence on the textual tradition, see Antony Mookenthottam, MSFS, *Indian Theological Tendencies* (Berne: Peter Lang, 1978). For a brief overview of early missionary approaches of correlation between Hindu texts and the Christian gospel, see Wilhelm Halbfass, *Indian and Europe: An Essay in Understanding* (Albany: State University of New York, 1988), pp. 36–53. It may be relevant to quote Halbfass's assessment of the approach of one early missionary who lived and worked in Tamil Nadu, South India, since our study concerns the Paraiyar who mostly live in this region. In pointing to Robert Nobili's (1577–1656) approach he writes,

    Nobili's Tamil writings ... demonstrate the practices of one who wrestles with the '*word*' and the attempt to be understood; they also illustrate the basic problems involved in the transmission or transplantation of Christian ideas and concepts into the complex context of Indian religious-philosophical terminology, with its rich associations.

    Emphasis mine. Ibid., p. 39.
68. S.J. Samartha, *One Christ-Many Religions: Towards a Revised Christology* (Maryknoll, NY.: Orbis Books, 1991), p. 65. Samartha draws the readers' attention to the 'spoken' and the 'aural' importance given to scripture in Hinduism and Buddhism. See pp. 64–75. For a detailed exposition of the import and prominence given to sound in the religious tradition of Classical Hinduism, see Guy Beck, *Sonic Theology: Hinduism and Sacred Sound* (Columbia, SC: University of South Carolina Press, 1993). For a study of the oral aspects of the written word in the history of religions, see William Graham,

Beyond the Written Word: Oral Aspects of Scripture in the History of Religions (Cambridge, UK: Cambridge University Press, 1987).

69. Robert C. Neville, *Behind the Masks of God: An Essay in Comparative Theology* (Albany, NY: State University of New York Press, 1991), p. 47.

70. Ibid.

71. Ibid., pp. 1–50.

72. Ibid., p. 49.

73. For a discussion of the benefits of presenting an abstract theological concept as an interpretant, see ibid., pp. 48–9. Later I will show that a concrete interpretant is not without its own potential for generating a level of abstraction.

74. Lawrence E. Sullivan, 'Seeking an End to the Primary Text' or 'Putting an End to the Text as Primary', in *Beyond the Classics? Essays in Religious Studies and Liberal Education*, Frank E. Reynolds & Sheryl L. Burkhalter, eds (Missoula, MO: Scholars Press, 1990), p. 42.

75. Ibid.

76. A convincing argument to accept drumming as a surrogate language has been advanced by Sebeok and Umiker-Sebeok. See the two volume work edited by Thomas A. Sebeok and Jean Umiker-Sebeok, *Speech Surrogates: Drum and Whistle Systems* (The Hague: Mouton, 1976). In the Introduction they write,

> Drum ... surrogates are of interest, then, as specimens of one species of transmutation, one which is (a) a true substitutive system, (b) a first-order rather than a second-order system, and (c) in the acoustic modality, with the attendant potential for the utilization of iconicity as the dominant semiotic principle. (p. xix (1)).

77. James George Frazer, *The Golden Bough: A Study in Magic and Religion* (New York: Macmillan Company, 1940), p. 335. Also for interpretations of music as a reflector and a generator of culture and religion, see John Blacking, *How Musical is Man?* (Seattle: University of Washington Press, 1973) and *A Commonsense View of All Music* (Cambridge, UK: Cambridge University Press, 1987); John E. Kaemmer, *Music in Human Life: Anthropological Perspectives on Music* (Austin: University of Texas Press, 1993); Joseph Kerman, *Contemplating Music: Challenges to Musicology* (Cambridge, MA: Harvard University Press, 1985); Henry Kingsbury, *Music, Talent, and Performance: A Conservatory Cultural System* (Philadelphia: Temple University Press, 1988); Alan P. Merriam, *The Anthropology of Music* (Evanston, Ill.: Northwestern University Press, 1964); Leonard B. Meyer, *Music, the Arts, and Ideas* (Chicago: Chicago University Press, 1967) and *Explaining Music* (Berkeley: University of California Press, 1973); and Gilbert Rouget, *Music and Trance: A Theory of the Relations between Music and Possession* (Chicago: University of Chicago Press, 1985).

78. The important role of the drum in Native American and African religious traditions is well known and better documented. For an introduction to the uses of the drum in Native American religions, see Joseph H. Howard, *Drums*

in Americas (New York: Oak Publications, 1967); Sullivan, *Icanchu's Drum*, pp. 180–85, 220–3, 266–88, 639–40. For an introduction to the drumming in African religious traditions, see John Carrington, *Talking Drums of Africa* (London, 1949); J.H. Kwabena Nketia, *Our Drums and Drummers* (Acra: Ghana Publishing House, 1968); John S. Mbiti, *African Religions and Philosophy* (Garden City, NY: Anchor Books, 1970); Francis Bebey, *African Music: A Peoples Art* (New York: Lawrence Hill, 1975); John M. Chernoff, *African Rhythm and African Sensibility* (Chicago: Chicago University Press, 1979). For an introduction to the utilization of drumming in the cultural and religious life of African-Americans, see Sterling Stuckey, *Slave Culture: Nationalist Theory and the Foundations of Black America* (New York: Oxford University Press, 1987). For introductory information on the significance of religious drumming in Korea and Japan, see Edward R. Canda, 'Gripped by the Drum: The Korean tradition of Nongak', in *Shaman's Drum: A Journal of Experimental Shamanism*, 33, (Fall-Winter, 1993): 18–23 and Marilyn Green, 'Voices of the Drum', in *Sky*, 22, no. 11 (1993): 32–7. It is indeed interesting that this is something that manifests itself in oral and non-Eurocentric traditions. Although an extensive study of the role of the drum in all such religious traditions will bolster my claim that the drum is an organizing symbol that is representative of a distinct mode of thought, i.e. orality, this lies way beyond the scope of this book.

79. Sebeok & Umiker-Sebeok, *Speech Surrogates*, p. xix.
80. This opens up for theology the possibility of transforming itself as a discipline that critically and constructively reflects on human dialogical symbolic intercourse in its multimedia expression.
81. David Tracy, *Plurality and Ambiguity: Hermeneutics, Religion, Hope* (San Francisco: Harper and Row, 1987), p. 83. Although within a very different context, I am struck by Carter's call for a realistic assessment of the impact of communal religious devotion in the realm of American law and politics. More specifically he reminds us of the resistive power of religion:

> A religion, in this picture, is not simply a means for understanding one's self, or even contemplating the nature of the universe, or existence, or anything else. A religion is, at its heart, a way of denying the authority of the rest of the world; it is a way of saying to fellow human beings.... 'No, I will not accede to your will.'

Stephen L. Carter, *The Culture of Disbelief: How American Law and Politics Trivialize Religious Devotion* (New York: Basic Books, 1993), p. 41.
82. See my discussion under these subtitles in chapter three, section III.
83. For a fuller explanation of the drum as a pollution-imbued and pollution-transmitting object which is generalized to represent the whole community of the Paraiyar see chapter two, specially the section on 'the History of the Paraiyar'.

5

Christ as Drum: Faith Imaginatively and Daringly Seeking Resonance

The affirmation that Jesus is the Christ is an act of faith and consequently of daring courage. It is not an arbitrary leap into darkness but a decision in which elements of immediate participation and therefore certitude are mixed with elements of strangeness and therefore incertitude and doubt. But doubt is not the opposite of faith; it is an element of faith. Therefore, there is no faith without risk.

(Paul Tillich)

Their inhuman atrocities have carved caves
in the rock of my heart
I must tread this forest with wary steps
eyes fixed on the changing times
The tables have turned now
Protests spark
now here
now there.
I have been silent all these days
listening to the voice of right and wrong
But now I will fan the flames
for human rights.
How did we ever get to this place
this land which was never mother to us?
Which never gave us even
the life of cats and dogs?

I hold their unpardonable sins as witness
and turn, here and now,
a rebel.
('Caves' by Jyoti Lanjewar)

In this concluding chapter I venture to test out the conceptual reflections
that have been developed in the preceding chapters. This will help
demonstrate the concrete directions and contextual potentialities of
doing theology in India if some of the proposals that have been advanced
are put to work. Having chosen to work within the area of christology
I start with further conceptual clarifications. In the first part of this
chapter I shall elucidate my christological method by focussing on the
relationship between the conception of Christ and the enterprise of
Indian-Christian theology. In the second part of this chapter I explicate
the substantive meaning of the term Christ in consonance with the
religious themes that were expounded in our study of the drum. In
the final part I present an experimental rendition of Jesus. The interpretive tack that determines the features of the emergent figure of
Jesus is largely influenced by the proposed conception of Christ as
drum. Through the working out of this christology, I continually correlate the central themes that were drawn from the symbol of the
drum in the previous chapters with themes that can be exacted from
the conceptions of Christ and Jesus.

Before proceeding further, however, two qualifications are in order.
First, the tentativeness of this constructive proposal must be registered
again. Apart from the general built-in assumption that all theological
proposals are provisional and tentative, my own theological constructions
are bound by the dictates of its own definition. I suggested that theology
aspires to make sense of, find meaning in and determine order for
living collectively under the Divine. An important dimension of theology, thus, has to do with facilitating collective living under the Divine.
If this indeed is the case, then, the proposals that I initiate cannot be
proved to be relevant and fruitful until the Indian-Christian community,
through a process of reconnecting with and reclaiming its Dalit identity,
attests to the sensibility, meaningfulness and collective livability of this
theological construction. The question concerning the effectiveness of
the theological construction suggested in this chapter will, therefore,
have to await the verdict of the Dalit and Dalit-identified Christian
communities of India.

Second, the interpretations presented in this constructive experiment arise from perceptions that are distinctly my own. It is informed by a complex of commitments and interests which I have explicitly laid bare in the Introduction. In a sense through this resymbolization of Indian Christology I purport to represent an imaginary community. This imaginary community is constituted by the Dalits as exemplified by one chief representative population in South India, i.e. the Paraiyar; the academy (theologians, anthropologists and religionists), which is significantly influenced by Western scholarship, but, which also attempts to take seriously Dalit intellectuals and Indian-Christian theologians who write from the Dalit perspective; and my personal life experience in all its complexity. The unfolding of the reflections of this imaginary community mirrors my explicit commitment to 'advocacy scholarship' from the standpoint of the silenced Dalits.

I.   Indian-Christian Theology and the Conception of Christ

In chapter one, I suggested that the key to any Christian theology involves the category of Jesus Christ. Consequently, a fitting definition of Christian theology was propounded: critical and constructive reflection on human dialogical symbolic interaction in its attempt to make sense of, find meaning in, and determine order for living collectively under God through the paradigm of Jesus Christ.[1] In accordance with this definition, Christian theology is both distinguished by and dependent on the category of Christ in a methodologically significant way. The words of Galvin are relevant:

> While no theology can confine itself exclusively to christology, no Christian theology would be complete without serious reflection on Jesus Christ.[2]

First, within the context of the various theologies of world religion, '[i]t is this category in particular ... that distinguishes and defines a perspective as "Christian".'[3] Thus, the central symbol of Christ distinguishes Christian theology from other religious frameworks, providing Christian theology with its distinctiveness and uniqueness. Confronting the 'raw fact of Christ' thus becomes an overt priority for Indian-Christian theology.[4] In the words of Chenchiah, 'we [Indian-Christian theologians] accept nothing as obligatory save Christ.'[5] A second point dovetails with the first. Because of the Christian claim that a normative understanding of human collective living under God is appropriated through the paradigm of Jesus Christ, this symbol takes on a peculiarly pivotal methodological posture.[6] It functions as a symbol through which Christian theology 'qualifies' and 'modifies' its understanding of God and humanity.[7] The theological rationale for this stems from the Christian affirmation that Jesus as Christ represents the complete image of both God and human being. For Christians, Christ mirrors abundantly all that needs to be said about God ('He is the image of the invisible God... For in Him all the fullness of God was pleased to dwell.')[8] even as Christ reflects sufficiently all that needs to be said about the human being ('[H]aving been made perfect, he became the source of eternal salvation').[9] The symbol of Christ, thus, is the lens through which all aspects of the symbols of God and humanity are viewed. In this sense, the symbol of Christ is normative in Christian theology; all other symbols are fleshed out in relation to it and evaluated in reference to it. But principally, the conception of God and humanity are continuously defined and modified according to the symbol of Christ.

As noted in the first chapter, Indian-Christian theology in seeking to construct this symbol of Christ concerns itself with at least two factors. On the one hand, there is an ongoing interpretive retelling of the Christian story, i.e. the good news of God's decisive act in Jesus who is affirmed to be the Christ. On the other hand, there is a dynamic and creative remembering of the historical situation of the Indian people as they testify to the traces of this christic presence operant among them. The main drawback with Indian-Christian theology was that it predominantly used the religion of dominant-based literacy (caste Hindu textual tradition) to retell the Christian story of Jesus and to remember the Indian heritage that testified to the christic presence among them. This resulted in two problems. First, Indian-Christian theology became exclusionary: it tended to be non-dialogical and non-representative of the symbolic intercourse of the whole community. Specifically, it silenced the voices of the Dalits; not only did they not share in this orientation of literacy but, more importantly, they were marginalized by it. Second, Indian-Christian theology became an instrument of ideological co-option rather than human liberation for a majority of its members, i.e. the Dalits. It sustained a process of hegemony by which the interests of the caste community were espoused and advanced as normative for the whole community.

As mentioned earlier, this book seeks to correct this trend. The previous three chapters accomplished the objective of recollecting and remembering the discursive and non-discursive religious resources of one typical Dalit community (the Paraiyar) as representative of subaltern religion and examined their import for Indian-Christian theology. In this chapter I attempt to present a comprehensive conception of Christ by retelling the story of Jesus through a process of remembering the historical traces of the christic presence as appropriated by this subaltern community.[10]

The term Christ, as I see it, embraces two dimensions. On the expansive side, it is both trans-historical and pan-geographic. While being situated within the confines of Christian discourse, it seeks to capture and name a Divine motif that is relevant to all time and space. On the constrictive side, it is bound up with the life and praxis of Jesus of Nazareth and the impact this had on the early Christian community which proclaimed him as the Christ.

Although we are dealing with two poles, this book opts to interpret Jesus and his impact on the early Christian community (the constrictive pole) in terms of the trajectories of the Christ dynamic as expressed by a Dalit community (the expansive pole) through the symbol of the drum. This does not make Jesus any less historical. It merely opts to explicate the historical dimensions of Jesus in a manner that would accent its continuity with the christic presence as experienced by the Paraiyar through the symbol of the drum.[11] In taking this methodological option, this book finds itself in continuity with the overall direction of the liberation method: the starting point of christology is the context of marginalized people's experience to which reflections on Jesus Christ become accountable. In the words of Clodovis Boff, 'In current liberation theology ... the starting point is the oppressed and not abstract topics or general ideas like "justice", "politics", "praxis", or even "liberation".'[12]

Implicit in the terminology concerning two poles is the general structure of the method of correlation. However, there are many digressions from and addendums to Tillich's basic proposal.[13] Basically, the christology worked out in this chapter starts from the presupposition that the 'human situation' (Tillich would also want to use the term 'form') as represented by the religion and culture of the Dalits cannot be utterly distinguished from the 'Christian message' (Tillich would also want to use the term 'content'). The inextricability of the questioning-dimension and the answering-dimension of theology lies in the fact that Dalit culture and religion are a symbolic manifestation of the actualization of the Christ dynamic. Thus, the so-called 'form' is, in fact, also the 'content' of theology. A.P. Aleaz, through his book, *The Gospel of Indian Culture*, does valuable theological service by systematically working out aspects of 'a double gospel emerging from Indian culture.'[14] Explicating further on this two-foldness of the gospel of Indian culture, he says,

> One is the gospel of integral relation between religion and culture, resulting in cultural symbiosis and a composite culture through an ongoing interaction between religions. The second meaning of the gospel of culture points to an understanding of God in Jesus emerging from the Indian culture.[15]

From the standpoint of the Paraiyar, the religious appropriation of the drum does not merely raise relevant, in-depth and leading questions that Jesus as the Christ answers; rather it already provides the basis for an 'answering theology' through which the christic mystery is apprehended. The gospel of the drum is revealed through the culture of the Dalits. In other words, if the immanental presence of the Christ is affirmed as embracing all human beings from the beginning of creation, the christic presence as manifest among the Paraiyar through the symbol of the drum cannot be viewed merely as the context since it also represents the particular content of God's relational and mediating activity among God's people. This aspect of Dalit experience as the womb of the revelation of God has already been convincingly set forth by A.P. Nirmal. The context of suffering and pathos of the Dalits in India is indeed the substantive content of Christian theology. Thus, for Nirmal, 'What we need is to interpret the indigenous God in our indigenous history in its religious, cultural, philosophical and socio-political aspects.'[16]

The correlative stance of this theological effort rests in a willingness to accept a distinction between the expansive pole, which testifies to the presence of Christ in creation, even if quite apart from Jesus, and the constrictive pole, which affirms that the human gestalt of the Christ is wholly instantiated in Jesus.[17] The choice of starting with the expansive pole is deliberate. First, I want to correct the misapprehension and misconception that the Paraiyar's religious tradition, apart from its western Christian expression, is either primitive or demonic. Instead of starting with Jesus and then pointing to the redeeming features of the Paraiyar religious tradition, I start with exposing the christic presence in this tradition which can be affirmed independent of the figure of Jesus. Second, my discussion of Christ in its general signification is in continuation with the discussion in chapter four which dealt with the Divine as appropriated by the Paraiyar. The themes of Christ in the expansive pole of christology are intimately connected with the themes that were explicated in the study of the Divine in the previous chapter. Third, by starting with the expansive pole I set into motion the particular tack with which the figure of Jesus is exegeted. The constrictive pole is no doubt determinedly biased. But, this time it is directed by the dictates of those that have been silenced in theological discourse. By opting to begin with the expansive pole I also opt to valorize a particularly slighted and scorned perspective of interpreting Jesus.

However, even though I begin with the blatantly overlooked collective experience of the christic mystery within a Dalit community, the dialectical relationship between the Christ-now-and-then and the Jesus-then-and-now is maintained. On the one hand, although I start with the expansive pole of Christology and then extrapolate elements of the constrictive pole through the lens of the former, there is a sense in which both these poles can be understood as correlates that mutually throw light upon each other: they are dialectical. On the other hand, within Christian theology it is through a critical and constructive conjoining of both these elements that the Christian community is able to lift up the paradigmatic conception of Jesus Christ, which functions to qualify God under whom living collectively makes sense, provides meaning and gives order.

II. Drum as Christ: The Expansive Pole of Christology

In this book Christ is conceived of from within the Christian context. Thus, it is one component in a triune configuration of the Christian understanding of God, which has conventionally insisted on belief in monotheism through the axiom 'Three in One and One in Three'. Traditionally, this Trinity (one Triune God) has been captured by the metaphors Father, Son and Holy Ghost, or, in its more inclusive and less anthropomorphic appellations, Creator, Redeemer and Sustainer. Christ is consistently identified with the second motif of this trifiguration.

The challenge in dealing with the expansive dimension of christology lies in developing the widest or broadest portraiture of Christ, while also keeping this representation distinct from the other two motifs of the Christian understanding of God. Let me briefly outline my position concerning the triune figuration of God.[18] God as Creator represents

God as independent from creation: that which is both its source and originator. God as Christ symbolizes God as redemptively embracive of the world by becoming immanent. Redemption in this context signifies a movement towards living within the vector of 'the human and the humane'. God as Holy Spirit represents God as the immediate and sustaining presence within all of creation in its return towards God the creator. Christ in this framework is differentiated from the first Divine motif by being immanent in the world in order to mediate God's redemptive purposes and distinguished from the third Divine motif by being primarily circumscribed within the realm of the human and the humane. It must be admitted that the line between Christ and the Holy Spirit is blurred. For me, the spirit of Christ cannot be completely distinguished from the Holy Spirit. While Jesus fully epitomizes the spirit of Christ that is immanent in the world from the inception of creation, it is this same Spirit that is sent into the world after Jesus's resurrection to continue the purposes of drawing and directing human beings to live within the redemptive purposes of God. Two clarifications are in order. On the one hand, in this christological discussion I develop the term Christ to fit into the sphere of human life. Solely because of this can Jesus be affirmed as the Christ. Jesus mediates the redemptive design of God by fully concretizing the 'human and the humane'. On the other hand, this obscurity with regards to the boundaries between Christ and the Holy Spirit reminds us that we are not talking about different gods but one God who is represented in three motifs. Gunton, I believe, expresses in a concise manner the characteristics of Christ within the framework of the Christian trinity:

> God comes into relation with that which is not himself through his Son, the mediator between himself and the creation, and the Son is rightly conceived as the Logos, not only the Word spoken to time from eternity, but the immanent dynamic of meaning which holds time and space together.[19]

Starting from the general trinitarian framework as succinctly, even if sketchily, recounted above, let me paint in broad strokes the manner in which I wish to describe the term Christ in its expansive dimension. In my exposition I shall be drawing from the christological work of Hodgson, Kaufman and Taylor.[20] Hodgson's basic categorization presents Christ as the figure that encompasses the world as different from Godself by becoming immanent in the world; Kaufman enables us to configure the general directionality of Christ by identifying its vectors of 'the human and the humane'; Hodgson further makes us aware of the tragic and the praxiological dimensions of the trajectories of Christ; and Taylor offers us specific socio-political and religio-historical concretions of the trajectories of Christ by examining the practice of 'reconciliatory emancipation'. It will be noticed through this discussion that the dynamic of the presence of Christ shares similar strains with the power of the Divine that was extrapolated in relation to the drum in the previous chapter: the drum is a vehicle of Divine-human mediation that energizes and steers subaltern resistive and emancipatory communal potentialities towards living in freedom in the midst of colossal human suffering.

Christ as the immanental presence of God in creation

Christ refers to the immanental presence of God in creation.[21] Within the Christian trinitarian framework, the possibility and tangibility of the presence and working of Christ as knowable outside of God's own internal relationality exists from the inception of creation. Christ inhabits all of creation from the instance that the world was created as different from God. Cobb encapsulates this idea well: 'Christ as an image does not focus on deity in abstraction from the world but as incarnate in the world.'[22] In other words, the distinctive aspect of the word Christ has to do with its immanence in all of the created order.[23] There was no time or place in creation where Christ was and is not present because there is nothing in all of creation that is outside of the dynamics of mediation between God and God's own creation.

It may be recalled that the drum in the communal experience of the Paraiyar is intimately tied up with the forces of the Divine that operate among them. In an historical context in which the sacred Word (both in its written form as embodied in the Hindu scriptures and in its oral form as passed on in Sanskrit prayers and mantras) was kept away from the Paraiyar for centuries, the drum took its place as the means of communicating the mediating presence of the Divine. In this sense, the drum represents the immanental presence of the Divine that was specifically and concretely experienced in their communal history. It is because of this central communal affirmation that the drum represents the immanental motif of the Divine at the heart of this community (even while they are deliberately severed from the sacred Word as conceived by caste Hindus) that one can dare to suggest that Christ is manifested in the drum. A similar motif was identified when discussing subaltern-based oral communities. The drum as representing the many facets of subaltern-based communication is projected as the medium of Divine sound which reaches out to the interiority of subaltern communities, connecting them together through being immediately present to them, even as it makes them present to each other. Further, the immanental presence of the Divine is experienced as 'present actuality' in the midst of the productive real-world of subaltern creation, which is why the Divine mediation of the drum holds together spiritual and material blessedness.

The assertion that the drum represents the christic presence among the Dalits can be further amplified. The drum, which mediates this christic presence to the Dalits, assures them that there was and is no time in which they were or are without the presence of the immanental God. In this situation there needs to be a refocussing of the medium in order to capture traces of this immanental presence that we are referring to as the Christ — a shift from an engrossment with the Word in its written and conventionalized form to the drum and drumming in its oral and contextualized form. The drum also provides a clue to appropriate the pan-geographic dimensions of the christic presence. In this particular example, the drum immanentalizes the presence of God in realms that are closed to the sacred Word because of the oppressive structural mechanisms of human beings. In other words, it is through the medium of the drum that the immanental presence of God (the Christ) penetrates all realms of human living space; even those geographical, social, cultural, and religious realms that are impenetrable by the sacred Word. In the context of South India, where the Paraiyar and other Dalit communities have been forced to maintain some sort of boundary between their living space and the living space of caste communities for many centuries, the drum through its soundings and, at times, through its physical presence is able to transgress these borders assuring them that God is with them.

Conceptually, this interpretation offers us a way to reject a dualistic theological position that is simplistic and misdirected. On the one hand, it counters the theological school that propounds that the religion of the Dalits represents a primitive stage of religious reflection, which must be aided in its predictable evolvement into a religious system, which in turn is equated with the culture of literacy. On the other hand, it refutes the theological faction which fears that the religious field of the Dalits is a breeding ground for the forces of the demonic that ought to be challenged and overcome by the presence of a 'Christian

God'. Rather, in this christological construction it is suggested that 'Christ is the primordial sacrament (*Ursakrament*), unique and necessary, of human beings' encounter with God.'[24] Therefore, the aspects of the Paraiyar's collective religious experience as represented in the drum, which, as consistently argued, symbolizes their particular ongoing encounter with the Divine, cannot but be symptomatic of the transhistorical and pan-geographic christic presence embracive of all creation.

Christ as the immanental presence of God that directs and draws creation towards the human and humane

Christ is the preexistent relational countenance of the immanent God that functions to consistently and continually direct and draw creation towards 'the human and the humane'.[25] On this issue Hodgson provides us with the flesh for Kaufman's skeleton. While Kaufman furnishes the general trajectories that concern the christic presence, Hodgson further scrutinizes and clarifies its historical unfolding. On the one hand, Hodgson is better able to substantively incorporate the 'tragic' realities into the trajectories that direct creation towards the human and the humane. This tragic mode is foundational to the communal history of the Dalits and its conscious assimilation into the process of creativity is crucial to our constructive task. On the other hand, Hodgson is more willing to explicitly stress the relationship between human emancipatory praxis and the immanental working of God. His focus, thus, as different from Kaufman's, is less on the cosmic and metaphysical aspects of 'the world' and more on its cultural, political and economic dimensions. In Hodgson's words, 'God and history are conjoined at the point of praxis... Such praxis is the concrete universal — God and history together in the shapes of Freedom.'[26] On the whole both these theologians help us comprehend that the working of Christ is intimately coupled with the 'tragicomic' forces operant in creation that direct and draw created beings towards the human and humane.

In the analysis of the functioning of the drum among the Paraiyar we noted that, in spite of it being a symbol that was denigrated, defamed and vilified by caste communities, the Paraiyar judiciously preserved and pervasively utilized it. In other words, the drum effectively served as a paradigmatic symbol of the social, economic, cultural and religious human identity of the Paraiyar. The import and relevance of the drum is substantial when viewed against the backdrop of the discussion regarding Christ as the Divine motif of directing and drawing creation towards the human and the humane. Let me suggest why I contend that the christic presence can be associated with the functioning of the drum among the Paraiyar.

The drum as sketched out in chapter two and three is a dominant symbol that is at the very heart of the communal religious world of the Paraiyar. It is through centuries of communal experience that it has emerged as a central vehicle that mediates the Divine power, functioning powerfully and effectively among and on behalf of the Paraiyar. The drum thus becomes the dominant symbol that has given the Paraiyar an identity of being a human community in relation to the Divine within a historical context in which they were regarded either as non-human or less-than-human by the majority of people that lived around them. The drum then is a representative vehicle through which the Paraiyar both appropriated their human identity before God and actualized their human capacities of self-reflexivity. While the former can be demonstrated in their claim of being the 'people and priests of the drum', the latter can be supported by the complex process of human reflection in the areas of ritual and theology revolving around the drum.

The drum thus functions to steer and draw the Paraiyar towards asserting and validating their own human and humane identity within an overall context in which this was not recognized and sanctioned. To put it differently, this process of appropriating and actualizing the human and humane among the Paraiyar is linked to finding their human communal identity within the context of the presence of the Divine as symbolized and actualized by the drum. In Christian parlance we can speak of this as a christic presence in and through the drum, empowering the Paraiyar both (a) to ascertain their humanness and humaneness in a social and historical situation in which this is systematically denied and (b) to actualize this human identity in their relationship with other human beings despite many odds. Christ enables them to assert their own communal identity before God and in the face of other human beings. It is because of the experiencing and appropriating of their own human identity before God, as mediated and sustained by the drum, that the Paraiyar are able to ascertain and assert their collective humanity in the midst of the devaluative and derogatory judgements of caste communities.

In this interpretation, on the one hand, the conception of 'the human and humane' is itself defined through the christic presence working among the Paraiyar through the drum.[27] The drum mediates the Divine presence which empowers them to appropriate their human and humane valuation as communicated to them within the nexus of this Divine-human relationship. On the other hand, the christic presence represented by the drum enables them to assert this human self-affirmation acquired before the Divine in the face of a concerted religious, social, economic and cultural scheme devised and perpetuated by caste communities to valuate the Dalits as either non-human or less-than-human.[28]

Christ as the emancipatory immanental presence of God that draws creation towards the human and humane through the dynamics of resistance and reconciliation

The search for a more concrete expression of the directionality towards 'the human and the humane' leads us to the third characterization of Christ. Christ is (a) the Pre-existent countenance of the immanent God that (b) consistently and continuously draws creation towards 'the human and the humane' in (c) the gestalt of emancipatory resistance and reconciliation. Here Mark Kline Taylor supplies the blood to the flesh and skeleton of Hodgson and Kaufman respectively. As noted earlier, Kaufman enables us to figure out the general directionality of Christ; Hodgson makes us aware of the tragic and the praxiological dimensions of the trajectories of Christ; and Taylor offers us specific socio-political and religio-historical concretions of the trajectories of Christ by examining the practice of 'reconciliatory emancipation'. For Taylor, Christ is associated with 'an intersubjective, sociohistorical force', whose special character is 'reconciliatory emancipation'.[29]

In chapter three I argued that for the Paraiyar, the drum functioned as a dominant symbol of both resistance and emancipatory theography. In that discussion of the religion of the Paraiyar, as exemplified by the drum, I stressed its two-fold dimensionality — resistance and emancipation. In chapter four this discussion was expanded to encompass subaltern-based communities of orality. Again, through the symbol of the drum, I explicated the manner in which subaltern religion dexterously and subtly weaves together elements of creative resistance and calculating compliance with a view to attaining realistic aspects of emancipation. The primary object of this resistance–emancipation process was to retain and actualize Dalit communal subjectivity. In line with Taylor, we may want to contend that the drum represents the subaltern dynamic activity of emancipation through resistance and reconciliation. Notably, the christic presence, as exemplified by the drum, can be said to be active in the realm of resistance in order to counter the colonizing proclivities of caste communities and operative in the venture of tactful reconciliation so as to live in realistic consonance with these same communities.

As discussed earlier, the drum depicts the 'NO' of the Paraiyar to the colonizing and demonizing tendencies of the valuation system of caste communities. The resistive activity of the drum is preserved by the various ways in which it functions as a counter and as a complement to the sacred Word; as also in the manner in which it symbolically resists the valuations of the communal identity that is carved out for the Paraiyar by the caste communities. It is in this setting that the Christ dynamic through the drum participates in the activity of emancipatory resistance for and with the Paraiyar. This very symbol of resistance also functions as an instrument of emancipatory reconciliation. On the one hand, the emancipatory activity of the drum is integral to the process whereby the Paraiyar are able to assert and reiterate their own human identity. As discussed earlier, while it is in and through the drum that the Paraiyar resist and declare a symbolic 'NO' to the identity or, more accurately, non-identity that is being crafted for them by the caste community, it is also in and through the drum that they pronounce a symbolic 'YES' to their own communal identity. This communal identity, as set forth in their religious and cultural practices is accepted as being different from the caste communities; and this difference is embraced through the Paraiyar's retention of the drum as an auspicious and empowering religious symbol despite its inauspicious characterization by the caste community. On the other hand, it is by means of the drum that the Paraiyar gain a foothold into the cultural and religious world of the caste community. Although the Paraiyar drummers are required to perform ritual tasks that will not be done by caste persons because it is considered degrading and inauspicious, they continue to render this religious service. Drumming during the funeral of a caste person and through certain stages of the caste communities' annual festival are examples of this.

Easy and simple interpretations stemming from an analysis of the systemic dynamics of caste and class have been advanced. From such a vantage point it has been assumed that the Paraiyar drummers' amenability to perform such specialized ritual services is driven either by dire economic necessity or oppressive social pressure or a combination of both. While these cannot but be influential factors that are relevant to any explication of the actions of Dalit communities, I have consistently emphasized the need to accept the fact that the Paraiyar in particular and the Dalits in general are primarily actors rather than participants in the drama of communal life. Religion is an important means of meaning-making that enhances their own corporate self-actualization. Thus, the participation of the drummers in the ritual life of the caste community is a considered decision by the Paraiyar. It exemplifies the activity of 'reconciliatory' positioned within the primary dynamic of resistance with an eye towards emancipation.[30]

The Christ dynamic of emancipatory reconciliation is thus concretized in the drum. It allows the Paraiyar to gain acceptance into the human, religious and social world of the caste community. The human identity of the Paraiyar, even if explicitly denied by the caste communities, is implicitly conceded to by their utilizing the ritualistic service of the Paraiyar drummers in certain religious rites. In this setting the Paraiyar, in being 'people and priests of the drum', become invaluable to the correct and fitting human arrangements necessary for certain communal rituals of the caste community. Markedly, the drum that is the resistive symbol of the difference denoted in the collective identity of the Paraiyar also functions as a means of reconciliation with the caste community. Even if it is not fully validated as an honourable and auspicious ritual component, the Paraiyar by means of the drum both (a) establish their human identity (despite it being rooted in difference) in interrelationship with other caste groups through their common participation in the ritual community and (b) reiterate their particular authority as human mediators and controllers of sacred powers with which the caste communities need to be reconciled.

In this reflection of the Christ dynamic in terms of emancipatory resistance and reconciliation, I reformulate Taylor's original proposal. He works within a two-fold category of emancipation and reconciliation. I agree with him about emancipation being the primary category. He states:

> Reconciliatory emancipation, though a phrase insisting on an inextricable relation between the two elements of the Christ dynamic, does not entail the claim that they are equal in importance. To the contrary, I give primacy to the emancipative or liberative element. The primacy is signaled in my casting this element as the substantive noun when naming the Christ dynamic's special character... The adjectival status that I have given to the reconciliatory element, which signals its secondary significance, in no way denies that it is essential to the special character of the Christ dynamic.[31]

However, the Christ dynamic, as determined from this study of the drum in the life of the Paraiyar and other Dalit-identified subaltern communities, is associated with the elements of resistance and reconciliation within the overall vector of emancipation. From the Paraiyar's collective experience of the Divine it is important that the Christ dynamic be grounded in the process of resistance without overlooking the tendencies of reconciliation and be established in the process of reconciliation within the overall context of resistance. In this interpretation, the cost of this process involves a history of immense and multifaceted communal suffering and the pay off in terms of emancipation is always in the future and, even if actualized in some measure, is only fragmentary and provisional.

This feature of the drum representing communal suffering cannot be left unaddressed when interpreting the Christ dynamic. Christ as the immanental presence of God that directs creation towards the human and the humane through the dynamic of emancipatory resistance and emancipatory reconciliation is predisposed to suffering. The way of the suffering and the path of the Christ are intimately bound up in the drum. Suffering in a way becomes the meeting place of the working of Christ and the striving of subaltern collective subjectivity; and the drum symbolizes this collusion within the framework of colossal corporate suffering. Here one must pause to notice that the manifestation of the Christ presence is far from the promise of an always prosperous, triumphant, enchanting, successful and jubilant religion. In fact, both notions of the 'God as guarantor of worldly success and prosperity' and 'Religion as the assurance of a Pie in the sky by and by' are repudiated by the subaltern representation of Christ. Instead the activity of Christ and the striving of the subaltern people take place within the locus of suffering for which the drum is an apt symbol.

In the above discussion on the expansive pole of christology, I have suggested that from the Paraiyar's religious tradition and from the traditions of subaltern-based orality, it makes sense to interpret Christ in relation with and in reference to the drum. In western theology this immanental Christ's mediatory function is generally conceptualized by the term Logos. The Logos as explicating Christ was supposed to hold together two cardinal dimensions: the personal energy of God (the pre-existent countenance of the immanent God that consistently and continuously draws creation towards 'the human and the humane' in the gestalt of emancipatory resistance and reconciliation) and the cosmic reason of God ['The Divine clue to the structure of reality (metaphysics) and, within metaphysics, to the riddle of being (ontology).[32]] In the words of Pelikan, who draws upon Alfred North Whitehead,

> The epitome of that insistence and of that combination of beliefs — the 'personal energy of Jehovah' plus the 'rationality of a Greek philosopher' — was the medieval and Christian doctrine of Jesus Christ as the incarnate Logos.[33]

However, the western emphasis on rationality coupled with its advocacy of the culture of literacy has almost irreversibly construed the Logos along the lines of reason, rationality and literacy of the Word. Thus, through this reflection it is suggested that christology need not depend on the same concept (Logos) to faithfully represent both these function. Because of the history of interpreting the Logos as almost synonymous with the Word which has gradually and successfully been identified with underlying rationality (primarily western constructions of rationality), on the one hand, and the sacred written Word (culture of literacy), on the other, I find it judicious and fruitful to introduce another symbol to complement the Logos. I have valorized the concept of the drum to represent the complementary function of the Logos as Word. In this section I have demonstrated that the drum is able, more appropriately and approximately, to gather up, and hold together the immanent dynamic/energy of Christ ('the personal energy of Yahweh') in the culture of the Paraiyar, even as the Logos has been made to stress the metaphysical and ontological dimension of Christ ('the Rationality of a Greek philosopher'). Instead of depending on the concept of the Logos to represent both dimensions of the Christ, I utilize the conception of the drum to designate one of the functions while the Logos can be associated with the dimensions of the Word. Thus, Christ as Logos and Christ as Drum are complementary ways of talking about the functions of the 'son' or 'Redeemer' within the Christian trinity.

Before moving on to the constrictive pole of christology we must pause to answer a couple of queries about the use of the drum as a Christian symbol. First, it may be objected that the drum is not a legitimate religious symbol because it is not authenticated either by Christian scripture or tradition. There is no doubt that the drum is alien to scripture and western Christian tradition. In fact, membranophones (timbrels and tambourines in particular, which are closest to drum types) were not permitted in the temple even though they were quite popular. 'Its function in the Bible was restricted to secular or religious frolicking, cultic dancing or possessions.'[34] None-theless, the fact that the drum does not receive favourable endorsement in scripture and Christian tradition bespeaks more of the latter's cultural limitations than of the former's unsuitability. Moreover, there is ample evidence to suggest that many of the theological symbols, which are now established as productive and orthodox, are indeed rooted in 'pagan' religious and philosophical traditions. Tillich points to this process operating in the Early Church Fathers:

> On the level of theological thought they [the Church Fathers] took into Christianity some of the highest conceptualizations of the Hellenistic and, more indirectly, of the classical Greek feeling toward life-terms like physis (natura), hypostasis (substance), ousia (power of being), prosopon (persona, not person in our sense), and above all logos (word and rational structure in the later stoic sense). They were not afraid to call the God to whom they prayed as the Father of Jesus, the Christ, the unchangeable One.[35]

The protest, thus, that the drum does not have sanction from scripture and Christian tradition does not in and of itself rule this out as a possibly productive Christian symbol.

Second, it may be asked whether the Paraiyar converts to Christianity utilize the drum in any of their rituals? The answer to this question is both a no and a yes. No, because, as mentioned earlier, Indian Christian leaders overtly and covertly discouraged the Paraiyar from bringing even traces of their religion and culture with them into Christianity. This also suited the Paraiyar since they may have used conversion as a means of sanskritization. Yes, because as Christian minister to the Dalit Christian community in South India (1984-87), I noticed that before marriages and during funerals I would often hear the sonorous beating of the drums, which strangely ceased well before the marriage parties or mourners came in contact with the Christian minister. This demonstrated that the Paraiyar continued to use the drum despite pressure to sever all ties with their cultural and religious past. However, it was concealed from the purview of their Christian ministers so as not to offend the official theological tenets of the Church.

III. Christ as Drum: The Constrictive Pole of Christology

The constrictive pole of Christology focusses on Jesus of Nazareth and his impact on the early Christian community. Of course there is no possibility for an immaculate conceptualization of the historical Jesus for constructive theology.[36] The influences of our culture, religious framework and communal experience of the Divine cannot be adequately dispensed with in any interpretation of Jesus. Biblical scholars such as Crossan, who have spent years researching the historical Jesus, are aware of this:

> The New Testament itself contains a spectrum of divergent theological interpretations, each of which concentrates on different aspects of clusters of aspects concerning the historical Jesus, or better, different historical Jesuses... I think, therefore, that different visions of the historical Jesus present a certain dialectic with different theological interpretations and that the New Testament is itself an obvious expression of that plurality's inevitability.[37]

Witherington's pithy comment at the conclusion of a comprehensive evaluate study of 'the Jesus quest' in modern scholarship is a truism: 'As always the historical Jesus remains elusive.'[38] While accepting this limitation, I agree with him that 'some roads, even if less traveled, may provide the keys to fruitful further discussions of what Jesus [as the Christ] was actually like.'[39] Therefore, in this particular christological essay a reconstruction of Jesus is attempted through the traces of Christ as encountered by the Paraiyar of South India. More specifically, this reflection highlights elements of a constrictive christology (an extrapolation of the characteristics of Jesus) as viewed through Christ presence that was and is encountered by the Paraiyar through the drum. This collective experience of the Paraiyar of the christic mystery is an aid that allows us to hear the sonorous qualities of Jesus that are relevant and meaningful to the Dalits. This authorizes Dalits to consider Jesus as a progression of their experience of the Christ dynamic as manifested by the drum:

> The only perspective open to us [Dalits] is the one given to us by the historical situation in which we [as Dalits] find ourselves. If we cannot achieve an unobstructed view of Jesus from the vantage point of our present circumstances, then we cannot achieve an unobstructed view of him at all.[40]

As an Indian-Christian liberation theologian working with elements of the methodology of Constructive theology (as spelled out in chapter one) my task is two-fold. On the one hand, I am committed to excavating and circulating themes that make sense, give meaning and determine order for collective living under the Divine, particularly as expressed by communities that have been silenced or ejected from human dialogical social intercourse. In this chapter by designating christology as an experimental field, I have attempted to fulfil this objective by reinterpreting the christic presence as appropriated by the collective experience of the Paraiyar through the symbol of the drum. On the other hand, I am dedicated to utilizing these subjugated thematizations of the excluded communities of Dalits to transform the propensity of theology from ideological co-option to human liberation. In this chapter I attempt to do this concretely by interpreting Jesus through the elements of the Christ dynamic that is meaningful to the Paraiyar. With this approach the Dalits are able to appropriate their emancipatory collective experiences and integrate them into the liberative purposes of Christian theology. As pointed out earlier, both Christian theology and the Dalits are enriched: Indian-Christian theology is liberated from its exclusionary and hegemonic tendency while Dalits are liberated both from their situation of having to live in a conceptual house that is not their own, and towards an emancipation that is holistic (it uses their own religious collective experience in a striving for economic, social and cultural liberation). Specific to the task of christology, the Dalits are able to unveil distinctive and necessary dimensions of Jesus that can become a resource in the dialogical process of constructing a Christian paradigm for living under God.

General interpretive trends for an exposition of Jesus in harmony with the christic resoundings of the drum

On a general level, interpreting Jesus via the christic presence as operative within the Paraiyar tradition, specifically as appropriated by the symbol of the drum, has at least two implications. First, it entails a move away from preoccupations about the nature of Jesus to concerns about his praxis. Recent theologians working with subaltern people have consistently argued that christology would be better served if liberation theology moves from abstract and metaphysical curiosity with the historical Jesus to a focus on his praxis.

> The most historical element in the historical Jesus is his practice, that is, his activity brought to bear upon the reality around him in order to transform it in a determinate, select direction, the direction of the kingdom of God.[41]

This is closely related to the differences between 'logological' and 'pneumatic' christologies as conceived by Berkhof.[42] While 'logologic christologies, are 'principally concerned with correctly establishing the relationship between the Divine and human natures in the person of Jesus Christ,[43] the primary purpose of 'pneumatic' christologies is concerned with exposing the manner in which Jesus proved to be a faithful ally to 'the Spirit of Yahweh' (Spirit-in-action) in an effort to enact Yahweh's will on earth.[44] A similar distinction has been made by Schuurman between christological trends that either pursue an 'ontological' or a 'functional' approach:

> With ontology we are in a climate of Neoplatonism, and we realize that christological titles represent first of all an effort to solve the problem of being and individuation. 'Functional', on the other hand, refers rather to the historical, to the question of relevancy.[45]

The christic presence as interpreted through the drum may not be helpful in dealing with issues about the Divine-human ontology of Jesus. Conversely, the drum is intimately connected with the element of functional power. Thus, it would help throw light on the functional dimension of Jesus. On the one hand, on an elemental level we detected in chapter three that among the Paraiyar, the relationship of the drum to functional power may be differentiated from the relationship of the Word to the power of knowledge — a correlation between actualization and realization. On the other hand, in our recent explication of the christic presence we talked about ways in which the drum manifests (a) the preexistent countenance of the immanent God that (b) consistently and continuously draws creation towards 'the human and the humane' in (c) the gestalt of emancipatory resistance and reconciliation. In both these instances Christ as drum exemplifies the functional or performative dimension. When this is interpreted against the backdrop of our previous discussion of the Logos (as best capturing 'the rationality of a Greek philosopher') and the drum (as representing the 'personal energy of Yahweh') it becomes clear why the drum is much better equipped to deal with elements concerning the function of Jesus rather than his Divine-human nature.

Second, interpreting Jesus through the christic presence as symbolized by the drum involves a shift in focus from a correspondence model of affirming truth about Jesus to a pluralistic model that is also accepting of ambiguities. Again, a general distinction may be made between the Logos and the drum as complementary symbols through which Jesus is interpreted. The Logos's major influence on the theory of knowledge had to do with its ability to check a tendency towards ambiguity. In the words of Pelikan:

> [T]he identification of the Logos as the Reason and Mind of the cosmos acted to countervail the tendency, which had seemed endemic to the Christian movement from the very beginning, to revel in the paradox of faith in Christ to the point of glorifying the irrational.[46]

This may have been a necessary contextual shift that was needed at the time of the Early Church Fathers. However, from the viewpoint of the Dalits we have demonstrated in the previous chapter that the problem in this century is that the culture of literacy is in the process of displacing or colonizing the cultures of orality through the written word. Thus, what is needed for Dalit christology is to affirm and celebrate the features of plurality, ambiguity, and open-endedness that characterize subaltern-based communities of orality. Furthermore, our study of the manner in which Logos based christologies have led to the 'logological' emphasis of western theological scholarship forces us to admit that today's context calls for a revoicing of the dimensions of ambiguity that are being threatened.

The drum does just that. It enables the constrictive pole of christology to stress the ambiguity involved in interpreting Jesus. Thus, Jesus as constituted through the symbol of the drum may not appear as the perfectly crystalline representation of the object, i.e. Christ. Instead, Jesus is hermeneutically open-ended. Just as the drum implies a plurality of musical notations that cannot be deciphered by studying whether it does or does not correspond with what it is connoting so also Jesus expresses the christic mystery in its ambiguity and plurality. Let me hint at the implications of such a proposal within the discourse of Jesus in relationship to the question of religious pluralism.

What can be said for the absolute uniqueness and universality of Jesus as the manifestation of the Christ as interpreted through the symbol of the drum? Within the correspondence model of establishing validity the discussion is embroiled in a conceptual contestation involving the exclusivism, inclusivism, pluralism categories. However, when one raises the pluralism question from the realistic and pragmatic context of Dalit communities, such as the Paraiyar, the question undergoes a change in tune with the phenomena of plurality and ambiguity that characterize their living situation. It is no longer so much the task of *thinking through* the issue of religious pluralism, which is somewhat more of an abstract intellectual exercise. Rather, in India, from the standpoint of the Dalits, theologians are compelled to face the challenge of *living out* religious pluralism. The symbol of the drum more than the Logos can facilitate this living out dimension of religious pluralism. The questions asked in the realm of the drum are somewhat different and may inform the direction of our discussion on this issue: Is it appropriate to dance and/or sing or simply listen when the drum is beaten? Is one inside or outside of the auditory field of the drum or within its pulsating rhythm? When is it fitting for other drums to join in and to keep from joining in?

Let me conclude this section with a caveat. Within the framework of our definition of Christian theology ('Critical and constructive reflection of human dialogical symbolic intercourse....') it must be categorically asserted that the construal of Jesus through the reverberations of the drum is one conceptual model within the dialogical discourse of theology. On the one hand, I emphasize both (a) the functional and performative and (b) the ambiguous and pluralistic dimensions of Jesus through the soundings of the symbol of the drum. However, on the other hand, I am unwilling to undermine or invalidate the theological bid that pursues either (c) the ontological and individuational (issues of identity) or (d) the rational and transparent dimensions of Jesus. The conceptual basis of my christological position, even while open to a plurality of symbols to interpret Christ, proposes that Christ as Drum and Christ as Logos are complementary routes. The concrete basis of my christological labour is concerned with advocating that the neglected aspects of the drum as Christ be utilized heuristically in the interpretation of Jesus.[47] By the same logic of plurality, however, I am unable to allow the advocacy of the symbol of the drum to silence the reflexivity of the symbol of the Logos. The challenging task of harmonizing at least these two respective religious representations of Jesus, in a manner that allows for complementarity, within the framework of a theological community in dialogue, still awaits us.

Jesus as Deviant: A concrete improvisation by tapping into the repercussions of Christ as Drum

As stated earlier, all historical reconstruction of Jesus are also hermeneutically situated. In this final section I speculate briefly on a rendition of Jesus that will be consonant with our explication of the christic presence through the drum. This, I believe, will introduce features of a Dalit Jesus within an orchestrated theatre of western and caste-community funded christological renditions.[48] Thus, the symphony is enriched and the dialogue extended.

Malina and Neyrey through a meticulous and enlightening study of the social world of first century Palestine come up with various social labels for Jesus. Their scholarly contribution to the field of christology enables Jesus to emerge within the social and cultural context of his time. Jesus through this process, acquires many diverse names. 'Jesus the Deviant' is one such name that affords us significant insight into the praxis of Jesus.[49] This particular appellation is most relevant as we seek to unpack the praxis of Jesus through the symbol of the drum.

Jesus embodies the praxis of deviance which is prefigured in the christic presence as appropriated by the drum. In so doing, Jesus becomes the concrete echo of the ceaseless Divine vibrations, which summon human beings to live within the kingdom of God. The first characteristic of Jesus' deviance results from his deliberately 'being out of normal place'. Crossan's observation regarding the concreteness of Jesus's location is a good starting point. He remarks: 'Christians believe that Jesus is, according to John 1:14, the Word of God made flesh, but seldom ask to what social and economic class that flesh belonged to.'[50] Our reflections on the implications of the drum forces us to start with the actual social and economic situatedness of Jesus. His placement is deliberately with those that are displaced. A significant feature of Jesus results from his being immanent among those 'out of normal place'. The drum associates the christic presence particularly among those outside of the realm and space of the sacred word. Jesus's manifestation of glory outside the respectable space at the inn, and at the heart of the stable (which puts him among those associated with cattle from which comes the leather drum), is a graphic symbol of this deviant locatedness. Jesus life and ministry also unfolds within a similar position of deliberate displacement in solidarity with those 'outcasts': he represents the available and cognizant presence of God with the deviantalized of the world. He announces the 'good news of the kingdom' by pitching his tent outside the kingdom of human power and prestige. The kingdom call is in accord with the sonorous Divine drum beat that the Dalits have had hope in and have sought solace in; and here it appears in the concrete figure of Jesus the deviant.

One must be careful to further circumscribe that Jesus's deviance was a form of 'achieved deviance'. Again, this is consonant with the tack of this reflection which lays stress on the function rather than the ontology of Jesus:

> Jesus' alleged deviance was not an ascribed characteristic or quality, such as blindness, illegitimacy, gender or age, but his own achievement based on his public, overt action, which was or should have been banned.[51]

Moreover, this is also analogous to the process of displacement among the Dalits in South India that we examined in chapter two. The Dalits acquired their deviant status through a well-strategized and multi-dimensional mechanism of labelling by the caste community. Because the Dalits represented a culture and tradition (best represented by the symbol of the drum) that was at variance with the dominant caste Hindu communities they were made deviants by them. And one significant way by which this was (geo)graphically represented was the way in which Dalits were confined to living spaces that were outside of normal places. It was here that Jesus the deviant truly shares with the Dalits by being with them 'out of normal place'. This is why it is easier for the Dalits to be grasped by the good news of Jesus. They simply have to tune themselves into the vibrant sound of the drum that has always surrounded them. The proximity of Jesus to those outside the walls of the city or the ritual purity of the temple is what makes them blessed.

The second characteristic of Jesus' deviance is marked by his being out of line: on the one hand, he contemptuously 'violates lines' that are accepted as distinguishing the pure from the polluted;[52] on the other hand, his actions, especially those directed against the dominant communities, suggest that he was initiating and inspiring subaltern resistance against the deviance-producing forces. Deviance, thus, is a way by which Jesus embraces those who have been labelled as outside the contours of the 'human and the humane' and contests the socially engineered definitions of the same. In the Indian context, in the first instance, Jesus as deviant pervades the social, economic and cultural situatedness of the Dalits and authenticates their humanity before God even though they have been placed outside of the definitions of the human by the caste community. In the second instance, Jesus as deviant embodies the forces of Christ that resist the colonizing and demonizing interpretive trends of the hegemonic knowledge-producing human machinery through an affirmation of the particularity of the humaneness and humanness of the Dalits, which is realized in the context of the presence of God with them.

A correlation may be observed between the drum and the functioning of Jesus: they both manifest visages of deviance in its resistance to the logic of the status quo that promotes its own version of the human and the humane at the expense of other possibilities.[53] Deviance in this context 'refers to those behaviours and/or conditions perceived and assessed to jeopardize the interests and social standing of persons who negatively label the behaviour and/or conditions.'[54] In Jesus we perceive an agent of the Divine who says 'NO' to the valuation of the vested class/caste/gender. Furthermore, the deviant status is espoused as a means by which an authentic affirmation of the human and humane (one which is appropriated in the presence of and through the mediation of God) is asserted. Here the praxis of the kingdom of God is mediated through the working of Jesus the deviant. Jesus echoes the rhythm of the kingdom which both unites groups of human beings by linking 'interiority with interiority' and energizes these collectives towards actualizing their collective subjectivity, in spite of being vilified as deviant by the dominant communities.

This feature of Jesus as deviant contrasts with the Jesus who is pictured as merely meek, passive, gentle and kind. In fact, this provides a model for Christian Dalits who are seeking a way to move from a situation in which Jesus has been crafted to serve the interest of pacification to a position in which Jesus is transfigured into a gestalt that drums up support against the oppressive dictates of religion and for the resistive dimensions of the christic presence.[55] This restlessness of the Christian Dalits is best typified in the words of Antony Raj: 'I feel that it is better for us Dalit to die on our feet than live on our knees before insolent men.'[56]

A process of 'de-pacification of Jesus' is already set in motion when one delves into the significance of Christ as drum for constructing the constrictive dimension of christology. It depicts a Jesus who will not 'leave reality in peace'.[57] This 'undomesticated Jesus' is indeed the practitioner of deviance: this is his way of showing solidarity with the 'outcastes' and joining them in their resistance against their oppressive social, economic, religious and cultural systems. Borg captures this element of Jesus aptly:

> [T]he way which Jesus taught threatened to undermine both religious tradition and society... Thus the alternative consciousness of Jesus collided with the dominant consciousness of his culture — it was wrong from the standpoint of those who devoutly pursued holiness, and destabilizing to those with a stake in preserving the present order.[58]

Lest we get carried away with this feature of the resistive and destabilizing Palestinian leader, it must be remembered that Jesus was calculatingly enigmatic in his contestation.[59] Here again we may notice the affinity with the manner in which the drum functions in the religious tradition of the Paraiyar. It is utilized symbiotically both to contest the hegemonic valuation of the caste communities and to invite their acceptance of the human corporate identity of the Paraiyar. The art of resistance demonstrated by Jesus reflects a similar symbiosis. Crossan's judgment is relevant. He states:

> What Jesus was doing is located exactly between the covert and the overt arts of resistance. It was not, of course, as open as the acts of protesters, prophets, bandits, or messiahs. But it was more open than playing dumb, imagining revenge, or simply recalling Mosaic or Davidic ideals. His eating and healing were, in theory and practice, the precise borderline between the private and public, covert and overt, secret and open resistance.[60]

This brings us to the third characteristic of Jesus's deviance: Jesus affirms the deviants' full humanity before God and postures this within the possibility of reconciliation. The emancipatory resistance of the christic presence is conjoined with the emancipatory reconciliation in this depiction of Jesus. Analogous to the drum in the religion of the Paraiyar, which functions as a symbol of the text of resistance and emancipatory theography, Jesus deliberately continues the behaviour of deviance in order to alter society's system of valuation. In other words

> What was previously labelled 'deviant' came to be called normative for Jesus. The characteristic behaviour of Jesus, then, remained the same, but society had altered its view and redefined the deviant behaviour in positive terms of approval.[61]

Again, this reversal is the invitation of the echo of the ceaseless vibration of the kingdom of God. It is a drum beat that invites all human beings to dismantle the respective borders that characterize their kingdoms and celebrate the borderless kingdom of God. Just as sound is available to all irrespective of boundaries, the kingdom call goes out to all people — first to the Dalits and then to the caste communities.

This focus on Jesus's deviance as bringing together the aspects of emancipatory resistance and emancipatory reconciliation is grounded in recent biblical scholarship and corroborated by the christic experience of the Paraiyar as interpreted through the drum. The Jesus that emerges from Crossan's historical work exemplifies a figure who is centred around 'magic and meal' or 'miracle and table'. In his reconstruction Crossan contends that 'Jesus's theory and practice of eating' (open commensality) coupled with 'his theory and practice of healing... [e]ach separately, and especially both together challenged the Mediterranean hierarchies, distinctions and discriminations.'[62] Crossan explicitly presents both these dimensions of Jesus as being fundamentally a challenge to the moral values of the Mediterranean world which was rooted in a system of 'honor and shame as well as on patronage and clientage.'[63] Implicit in his reconstruction exists the invitation that is directed to both those who participate in the honour/patronage (dominant/caste communities) and those who are forced to participate in the shame/clientage (subaltern/Dalit communities) of society to live within the realm of the borderless kingdom of God. In Jesus's time, the dominant communities met this invitation of Jesus by simply labelling him 'deviant'.[64] However, the subaltern communities continued to draw solace and strength from Jesus's presence with them even if he was labelled deviant.

Jesus's practice of deviance becomes an occasion for calling all people to conversion. Both for the patrons who gained honour from the communal system (dominant caste communities) and equally for the clients who accepted shame from the social world (subaltern Dalit communities) it implies a call to live in 'unmediated physical and spiritual contact with God and unmediated spiritual and physical contact with one another.'[65] The rendition of the third characteristic of Jesus's deviance as sketched out above provides us with the resources by which this dialectic between the resistive and the reconciliatory dimensions of Jesus can be held together.

All features of Jesus as deviant are couched within an overall context of suffering. To characterize suffering as a fourth category does not do justice to the exhaustive and trenchant nature of this reality in the life, ministry and death of Jesus. Suffering becomes the price that this embracement of deviance demands. And Jesus is willing to pay the ultimate price through his life and, in the end, with his life. Ironically, it is through accepting death as the price for being a deviant that God is said to vindicate Jesus through the resurrection. Through this act of God 'Jesus was transformed from a deviant who was executed as dangerous charlatan to a prominent who was enthroned as Lord of all.'[66] This reality of being enveloped by suffering is also the collective experience of the Paraiyar. The drum represents the way of suffering that is the hallmark of the communal history of the Paraiyar.[67] Not only does it symbolize their deviance, it also empowers them to retain this deviance as an affirmation of themselves and as a resistance to the valuation of the patrons/prominents. The drum mediates the christic presence in and through this context of suffering. Jesus as deviant clues us in on the relevant truth that it is in and through this way of suffering that God works God's vindication.

To sum up, Christ is a methodologically vital concept in doing Indian-Christian theology. Christ enfleshes and qualifies the conception of God, giving it its Christian distinction and particularity. The score for a Dalit christology is produced through the harmonizing of its expansive and constrictive poles. On the one hand, Christ as drum is presented as a contextual, enriching and fruitful theological affirmation with which to integrate the collective religious experiences of the Dalits. On the other hand, a potentially serviceable Jesus as deviant is construed in consonance with the collective appropriation of the christic presence through the drum.

The expansive pole of christology posits a creative interpretation of the christic presence in consonance with the drum in the religious tradition of the Paraiyar. Accordingly, it was argued that Christ as drum may best be comprehended as the immanental presence of God that directs and draws creation towards the human and the humane through the dynamics of emancipatory resistance and emancipatory reconciliation. The constrictive pole of christology focusses on Jesus of Nazareth. On a formal level, interpreting Jesus through the christic presence as appropriated by the drum involves two things: a shift from concerns of Jesus's ontology to his functionality and from a correspondence notion of determining validity to an acceptance of ambiguity and plurality. On a material plane, it involved an experimental rendition of Jesus as deviant.

It was suggested that Jesus as deviant is deliberately 'out of place'. By being immanent among the people living within the space that is labelled 'polluted' Jesus manifests God's affirmation of their humanity in the face of society's concerted scheme to displace them. Moreover, Jesus as deviant sets into motion the resistive forces that seek to challenge the social, cultural, economic and religious structures that maintain the status quo: a small powerful group of patrons/prominents lording over a large mass of clients/deviants. By reiterating the status of deviance Jesus calls into question and subverts the hierarchies, distinctions and discriminations of the system. Finally, even in the midst of the dynamics of the affirmation of the deviant's human identity and the contestation of the valuation that discredits this identity, Jesus is postured in the inbetweenness of resistance and reconciliation. This borderline positionality, nonetheless, situates him at the heart of suffering. For Jesus the deviant, thus, the way of suffering at the borderline of resistance and reconciliation expectantly anticipates emancipation; on the one hand, both for the patrons/prominents and the clients/deviants of human society; and on the other hand, from a God who will vindicate all those who commit themselves to this reverberating echo to submit to the kingdom of God.

While it is hoped that this book will be liberative for the Christian Dalits, there is no doubt in my mind that I, a patron and prominent, have been convicted and converted by this process. Thus I am able to confess with Samuel Rayan:

> When we are converted and make the faith-commitment we shall discover that we are with the dalits, the people of God, God's beloved Christ, crucified and buried outside the gate. Their tombs God is breaking open in the night when the non-dalits are sleeping. With the break of day we shall see the wounds we have inflicted on crucified bodies and lives filled with light and life. We shall see them and touch them reverently and come to have faith in fresh depths, and come to express it in the cry, My Lord and my God. A cry in which all the crushed and crucified of history shall be affirmed as the body of Christ on whose unveiled face the glory of God shines and from whose heart streams the water of life in which non-dalits, if they change, may find cleansing and life.[68]

Notes

1. The procedure of qualifying the particularity of Christian theology by adding this supplementary clause ('through the paradigm of Jesus Christ') to the general definition of theology is influenced by the work of the Constructive theologian, Gordon D. Kaufman. From a Christian theologian's point of view, one of the salient, albeit overlooked, contributions of Kaufman's theological work has to do with the central and strategic methodological position delegated to the symbol of Christ. Perhaps this is overlooked mainly because Kaufman's most explicit and systematic statement with regard to the role of the symbol of Christ in Christian theology has only been published recently in his *In Face of Mystery* (1993). In my view, the category of Christ has taken on a progressively more pronounced place in Kaufman's work. Let me attempt to justify this observation by pointing to his major works after the mid 1970s. I take the cut off point between the early and later writings of Kaufman to be 1975 with the publication of his monograph *An Essay on*

Theological Method, which registered a unique and substantive contribution to the methodological options in theology.

Notably, this book is marked by its silence on the Christ symbol's role in theological construction. It is interesting that the only passage in this book that refers to Christ is quite unflattering:

> So far as the universality of God is modified by henotheistic impulses, it is no longer God about whom the theologians are speaking but only one of the idols of their particular tribe; and their work is open to the most serious sort of theological criticism. Christian theologians particularly, because of their intense fixation on Christ, have often been guilty of such distortions.

Ibid., p. 66. In his next book, *The Theological Imagination* (1982), Kaufman addresses the issue of the symbol of Christ and incorporates it as a fourth category that 'is just as fundamental and indispensable in defining and articulating the Christian world-view as are the other three.' The other three categories are God, the world and humanity. However, the methodological significance of the Christ symbol is left somewhat undetermined at this point. In Kaufman's own words:

> I am holding here that the Christian world-view is structured by four fundamental categories, each with its own intrinsic meaning and thus a certain independence from the others, yet dialectically interconnected and interdependent with each other. It is always an open and difficult question how far the concept of God is to be defined with reference to Christ, how far independently on the basis of other considerations; how far the human is to be defined by Christ, how much in terms of general human experience or Freudian insights or Marxist perspectives or Buddhist understandings. Our attempt to clarify the Christian categorical scheme does not foreclose any of these questions: it simply specifies the issues to which serious attention must be given and the points of reference in terms of which Christian theology works.

Ibid., p. 290 f. In a subsequent booklet, *Theology for a Nuclear Age* (1985), Kaufman appears to flesh out the significance of the category of Christ for Christian theology. In a methodologically deliberate move he suggests that God and Christ are 'the two central symbols in terms of which the Christian faith orients and understands itself.' Ibid., p. viii. Thus, 'the proper business of Christian theology is the analysis, criticism, and reconstruction of the two grounding symbols of Christian faith, God and Christ.' Ibid., p. 22.

Kaufman's most recent and systematic book, *In Face of Mystery* (1993), positions the symbol of Christ in such a manner that it both 'qualifies' and 'modifies' the other three categorical schemes of which Christ appears to be the key. The role of the symbol of Christ is at the heart of Christian theology as elucidated by Kaufman in this major work. Much of my own reflections in this chapter are based on this recent *magnum opus*.

2. John P. Galvin, 'Jesus Christ', in *Systematic Theology: Roman Catholic Perspectives*. vol. I, Francis Schussler Fiorenza and John P. Galvin, eds (Minneapolis: Fortress Press, 1991), p. 351. On the same theme Ruether says, 'No topic in Christian theology has been as exhaustively studied as that of christology. As the pivot of Christian theology, it is not only central to every theological reconstruction, but it is also subject to the constant revisions of historical scholarship.' Rosemary Radford Ruether, *To Change The World: Christology and Cultural Criticism* (New York: Crossroads, 1990), p. 1.
3. Kaufman *In Face of Mystery*, p. 84.
4. This phrase is attributed to the South Indian theologian, P. Chenchiah (1886-1959). See Robin Boyd, *Indian Christian Theology*, p. 145.
5. Ibid., p. 147.
6. The methodological configuration involved in this suggestion is sketched out by Kaufman in *In Face of Mystery*, p. 395. In this diagrammatic model the symbol of Christ is at the centre, signifying the functions of 'qualifying' and 'modifying' the other three categories. However, one must not gloss over Kaufman's insistence of the existence of 'a complex dialectical interdependence' among the three symbols of God, Christ and humanity:

    > it is not possible to understand what is meant by 'Christ' without bringing in the concepts of God and humanity; but it is also not possible properly to understand either 'God' or 'humanity' without reference to Christ.

    Ibid., p. 86.
7. For Kaufman, Christ is a category that 'qualifies' and 'modifies' the other three categories of God, world and humanity. However, even he will be the first to admit that in practice the symbol of Christ does not work 'directly' in reference to qualifying the category of the world, Ibid., p. 89.
8. Colossians 1: 15a & 19, *The Holy Bible*, (New Revised Standard Version).
9. Hebrews 5: 11a, *The Holy Bible* (New Revised Standard Version).
10. For a similar constructive christology from a South Indian context, see M. Thomas Thangaraj, *The Crucified Guru: An Experiment in Cross-Cultural Christology* (Nashville: Abingdon Press, 1994). Thangaraj draws heavily on the methodology of Gordon. D. Kaufman. He uses the Tamil philosophy of Saiva Siddhanta as the backdrop against which he exploits the image of the Guru as a contextual symbol for explicating the many dimensions of Christ.
11. I am aware that I have not touched upon the relation of Jesus to the christic presence within the context of the claims of other religious traditions. A speculative and sketchy attempt to ponder the directionality of this issue will be suggested in my discussion on the difference between the model of correspondence and plurality in determining validity concerning Jesus. Nonetheless, there is no doubt that this relationship will be commensurate with the general characteristics of ambiguity, flexibility, inbetweenness, fuzzy boundaries, incorporativeness, and pragmatism that were pointed to in my analysis of the religion of subaltern-based orality.

12. Clodovis Boff, 'Methodology of the Theology of Liberation', in *Systematic Theology: Perspectives from Liberation Theology*, eds Jon Sobrino & Ignacio Ellacria (Maryknoll, NY: Orbis Books, 1996), pp. 1–21.

13. For an overview of Paul Tillich's method see, *Systematic Theology: Three Volumes in One* (Chicago: The University of Chicago Press, 1967), vol. I, pp. 1–68 and vol. II, pp. 13–16 and 'The Problem of Theological Method', in *The Journal of Religion*, XVII, no. 1 (1947): 19-26. Also for a critical discussion of the method of correlation see, David Tracy, *Blessed Rage for Order: The New Pluralism in Theology* (New York: The Seabury Press, 1979), pp. 43–63; John P. Clayton, *The Concept of Correlation: Paul Tillich and the Possibility of a Mediating Theology* (New York: De Gruyters, 1980); and Langdon Gilkey, *Gilkey on Tillich* (New York: Crossroads, 1990).

14. K.P. Aleaz, *The Gospel of Indian Culture* (Calcutta: Punthi Pustak, 1994), p. 2. It must be added that though Aleaz does operate out of an advaitic framework, in this book, his study incorporates the many strands of Indian Christian thought, inclusive of Dalit theology. For a cogent and concise precursor to this argument, see the work of Christopher Duraisingh, 'Alternate Modes of Theologising now Prevalent in India', in *Religion and Society*, vol. XXVII, no. 2 (June, 1980): 81–101; 'Reflections on Theological Hermeneutics in the Indian Context', in *The Indian Journal of Theology*, vol. 31, nos. 3 and 4 (July-Dec., 1982): 259–78; and 'Reflections on Indian-Christian Theology in the Context of Indian Religious Reality', in *Bangalore Theological Forum*, vol. 14, no. 3 (Sept.-Dec., 1982): 176–87.

15. Ibid.

16. As summarized by Aleaz in ibid., p. 137. Also, see Arvind P. Nirmal, 'Theological Implications of the Term "Indigenous"', in *Dialogue in Community: Essays in Honour of S.J. Samartha*, ed. C.D. Jathanna (Mangalore: The Karnataka Theological Research Institute, 1982).

17. On the issue of Jesus being the human gestalt of the christic presence I find myself differing from recent feminist objections concerning the maleness of Jesus. Their argument maintains that since Jesus is male he cannot epitomize the wholeness of the human gestalt, particularly as represented by the female gender. I do not share this concern that the issue of maleness is essentially problematic to the christic gestalt being identified with Jesus. I believe this to be the case primarily because I advocate that the point of christology, when viewed through the drum, has everything to do with the praxis and functioning of Jesus rather than his metaphysical and biological identity. Accordingly, the christic gestalt is associated with the gestalt of resistive and reconciliatory emancipation that was practiced by Jesus.

18. Through this discussion I am indebted to Hodgson and Kaufman. Peter Hodgson's symbolization of the three-foldness of the Christian conception of God is compelling. This is not the appropriate setting to discuss Hodgson's proposal in detail. However, a synopsis of his general trinitarian design is in order. The nomenclature he employs to talk about the triune figuration is

as follows: 'God as the One' represents the ideal subjectivity of God; 'God as Love' encompasses the world as different from Godself by becoming immanent in the world; and 'God as Freedom' mediates and surmounts this difference by transfiguring it and returning God to Godself. See Peter C. Hodgson, *God in History: Shapes of Freedom*, (Nashville, Tenn.: Abingdon Press, 1989), pp. 60–5 and 84–90.

Like Hodgson, Kaufman's Christian theology is also construed within an overall trinitarian framework. In his work the 'three intentions' or 'motifs' are described along the following lines: the first motif has to do with that which grounds the 'originary source and foundation' of all creativity; the second motif, 'which expresses itself in the modes and patterns of order in the world', names the trajectories in this creativity that are pointed towards 'the authentically human or humane'; and the third motif refers to the 'immediate and continuing presence of the divine creative activity.' Kaufman, *In Face of Mystery*, p. 296f. Also see 'A Trinitarian God', in ibid., pp. 412–25.

19. Colin E. Gunton, *The One, The Three And The Many: God, Creation and the Culture of Modernity* (Cambridge, UK: Cambridge University Press, 1993), p. 178 f.

20. Mark Kline Taylor, *Remembering Esperanza: A Cultural-Political Theology for North American Praxis* (Maryknoll, NY: Orbis Books, 1990).

21. This notion of the preexistent Christ has its roots in the early Church Fathers' reinterpretation of the Greek philosophical notion of the Logos. The work of Justin, Irenaeus of Lyon and Clement of Alexandria may be cited as examples. For a succinct introduction to the relationship between these patristic writings and the preexistent Christ see, Jacques Dupuis, *Jesus and His Spirit* (Bangalore: Theological Publications in India, 1977), pp. 3–19; Jean Danielou, *Gospel Message and Hellenistic Culture*, vol. 2 (London: Darton, Longman and Todd, 1973); Jacques Dupuis, *Jesus Christ at the Encounter of World Religions* (Maryknoll, NY: Orbis Books, 1991), pp. 125–90; and Jaroslaw Pelikan *Jesus Through the Centuries: His Place in the History of Culture* (New York: Harper and Row Publishers, 1985), pp. 57–70.

Also, I am quite aware that Raimundo Panikkar deals at length with this notion of a cosmic Christ or a christic mystery. Within Indian theology Panikkar has done a great deal to inculcate expansive space into the symbol of Christ. Although I have been quite influenced by his work, I am deliberately refraining from utilizing it for the following two reasons: on the one hand, Panikkar's work is a system in itself and I do not feel I can do justice to the complexity and systematicity of his many decades of reflection in a conclusion; on the other hand, Panikkar has long been identified as a champion of the Hindu classical culture and religion, which would make Dalit interpreters somewhat resistant to his theological suggestions. For an adequate understanding of Panikkar's theological contribution, see *The Intra-Religious Dialogue* (New York: Paulist Press, 1978); *Myth, Faith and Hermeneutics: Cross Cultural Studies* (New York; Paulist Press, 1979); *The Unknown Christ of Hinduism: Towards an Ecumenical Christophany*, Revised and enlarged edition, (Maryknoll, NY: Orbis Books, 1981); *The Cosmotheandric Experience* (Maryknoll, NY: Orbis Books, 1993); 'The Jordon, the Tiber and the Ganges: Three Kairological Moments of Christic Self-Consciousness', in John Hick & Paul Knitter, eds, *The Myth of Christian Uniqueness* (Maryknoll, NY: Orbis Books, 1993); and *Invisible Harmony: Essays on Contemplation and Responsibility* (Minneapolis: Fortress Press, 1995).

22. John B. Cobb, *Christ in a Pluralistic Age* (Philadelphia: The Westminster Press, 1975), p. 76. While utilizing Cobb to stress my first point I want to distance myself from his effort in this book to identify Christ with 'creative transformation'. This is mainly because the notion of 'creative transformation' is too closely tied with an evolutionary and linear process that is universally applicable. It is by design thus that Cobb is easily ready to interpret the Christ in terms of the logos which is associated with creative transformation. The term logos is explained as 'the cosmic principle of order, the ground of meaning and the source of purpose' (ibid., p. 71), which does not sufficiently take seriously, for the purposes of this reflection, the resistive forces that are represented by the Dalit people both in their culture and religion. On a more general level the criticisms of Cobb's proposals can also be directed against the overall metaphysical tack of process philosophy: it does not do justice to the extant plurality of world views; it professes a metaphysics that is transcultural and transhistoric; and it does not take a sufficiently critical view of novelty. I also differ from Cobb in that I am consciously narrowing my discussion of Christ to the realm of human life.

23. Cobb is careful to suggest ways by which the transcendence of the conception of Christ is retained in spite of his stress on its essential immanent characterization. See ibid., pp. 70–7.

24. Dupuis, *Jesus Christ at the Encounter of World Religions*, p. 144. Dupuis argues for a much tighter bond between the Christ and Jesus of Nazareth than either Kaufman or Hodgson.

25. I am aware that M.M. Thomas has developed a 'Christ-centred humanism' which recognizes that the universal presence of Christ is operant in all contexts where religion provides the capital and energy for the realization of economic and social justice. Kaufman has been somewhat influenced by Thomas's work, specifically in the area of salvation being intimately wedded to humanization. See M.M. Thomas, *Salvation and Humanization*. For a detailed exposition of Thomas's christology also see, *The Christian Response to the Asian Revolution; The Acknowledged Christ of the Indian Renaissance*, pp. 241–319; *Man and the Universe of Faiths*; and *Risking Christ for Christ's Sake*.

26. Hodgson, *God in History*, p. 191.

27. We will see that this foreshadows the paradigmatic image of Jesus who epitomizes the 'human and humane'.

28. It is pertinent at this juncture to highlight the fact that the drum in being this sort of symbol is packed with the spirit of suffering (the tragic) and

creativity (the comic). See chapter 4 for a discussion of the drum as an instrument of managing suffering in relation to my explication of the relaxing dance-drum in chapter 3. These two dimensions of the dynamic of the presence of Christ that works in creation as it steers and draws human beings towards the human and the humane is analogous to the tragedy (suffering) and creativity that is manifest in the praxis of Jesus as Deviant.

29. Mark Kline Taylor, *Remembering Esperanza*, p. 192. In this book Taylor utilizes Hodgson's notion of God as Freedom, particularly as expressed within the realm of liberative praxis. See also, Peter C. Hodgson, *New Birth of Freedom: A Theology of Bondage and Liberation* (Philadelphia: Fortress Press, 1976). For a similar Christian theological proposal that puts freedom at the centre, see Daniel L. Migliore, *Called to Freedom: Liberation Theology and the Future of Christian Doctrine* (Philadelphia: Westminster Press, 1980).

30. It will be noticed that I have recast the terminology of Taylor. I shall explicate my divergence from his constructive revision of Christ as the dynamic of 'reconciliatory emancipation' at the end of this sub-section.

31. Taylor, *Remembering Esperanza*, p. 176.

32. Pelikan, *Jesus through the Centuries*, p. 58.

33. Ibid., p. 57.

34. E. Werner, 'Musical Instruments', in *The Interpreter's Dictionary of the Bible*, vol. 3 (New York: Abingdon Press, 1962), p. 474. Interestingly this prejudice against membranophones and '[i]ts possible absence in the temple ritual was possibly due to the strong female symbolism.' Werner illustrates the timbrel and the tambourine as a musical instrument with two membranes and 'a typical women's instrument.' Ibid.

35. Paul Tillich, *Christianity and the Encounter of the World Religions* (New York: Columbia University Press, 1963), p. 35.

36. The attempt to go back in time and retrieve a composite representation of the historical Jesus has a long and complex history. The first historical search began with the publication of David F. Strauss's work *Das Leben Jesu* (1835–1836). Using the much heralded historical-critical method there was an unprecedented confidence in the possibility of the 'unbiased' recovery of the Jesus from Nazareth. This search was however soon to conclude with the indictment of Albert Schweitzer's meticulous critical study of the scholarship of this quest in his book, *The Quest of the Historical Jesus: A Critical Study of Its Progress from Reimarus to Wrede* (1906). Schweitzer 'had come to the conclusion that most of these fresh attempts to say what we could really know about the historical Jesus actually told us more about their authors than about the person they sought to describe. The authors seem to have looked into the well of history and seen their own reflection.' [As summarized by Ben Witherington III, *The Jesus Quest: The Third Search for the Jew of Nazareth* (Downers Grove, Ill: Intervarsity Press, 1995), p. 9.] The second search for the historical Jesus came in the mid-twentieth century with the publication of Ernst Kasemann's lecture entitled 'The Problem of the Historical

Jesus' and Gunther Bornkamm's book *Jesus of Nazareth* (published in German
in 1956 and in English in 1960). The new tack of this quest concerns itself
with the relevance of Jesus's teachings for contemporaneous living. [see James
M. Robinson, *A New Quest for the Historical Jesus* (Naperville, Ill: A.R. Allenson,
1959)] However, it too ran its course and wrapped up by the early 1970s.
'It is fair to say that as the towering influence of Bultmann and the enthusiasm
for existentialism began to wane, so did the enthusiasm for the Second Quest,
leaving the movement dead in the early 1970s.' [Witherington, *The Jesus
Quest*, p. 11.] The Third search for the historical Jesus has been dominated
by the work of North American members belonging to 'the Jesus Seminar'
over the last couple of decades. This movement is well and alive and seems
to be growing in the present. However, it has essentially remained a western
phenomenon. For an influential introduction to the many facets of this Third
Quest, see Marcus J. Borge, ed., *Jesus at 2000* (Boulder, CO.: Westview
Press, 1997).

37. John Dominic Crossan, *The Historical Jesus: The Life of a Mediterranean
Jewish Peasant* (San·Francisco: HarperCollins Publishers, 1991), p. 423.
38. Witherington Ill, *The Jesus Quest*, p. 248.
39. Ibid.
40. Albert Nolan, *Jesus Before Christianity*, (Maryknoll, NY: Orbis Books, 1978),
p. 4.
41. Jon Sobrino, *Jesus in Latin America* (Maryknoll, NY: Orbis Book, 1987), p.
66. Also see his *Christology at the Crossroads: A Latin American Approach*
(Maryknoll, NY: Orbis Books, 1978). In the latter work Sobrino even interprets
the notion of the person of Jesus in operational terms: 'more in terms of
surrender or dedication to another', p. 74. From a feminist vantage point
Rosemary Radford Ruether has also argued for taking the praxis of Jesus as
a model rather than his identity which happens to be a specific gender. See
Rosemary Radford Ruether, *Sexism and God-Talk: Toward a Feminist Theology*
(Boston: Beacon Press, 1983).
42. See, Hendrikus Berkhof, *Christian Faith: An Introduction to the Study of Faith*
(Grand Rapids, Michigan: Eerdmans, 1979), pp. 280–93.
43. As interpreted by Lamberto Schuurman, 'Christology in Latin America', in
Faces of Jesus: Latin American Christologies, ed. Jose Miguez Bonino (Maryknoll,
NY: Orbis Press, 1984), p. 166.
44. Ibid.
45. Ibid., p. 167.
46. Pelikan, *Jesus Through the Centuries*, p. 63.
47. I am also aware of the argument that the Logos is riddled with masculine
overtones. Robinson states,

> Though the comparable christological hymn embedded in the prologue
> to the Gospel of John does not begin with the masculine relative pronoun
> but with an analogy to Genesis 1:1, the introduction of the masculine
> noun Logos provides the equivalent male orientation.

James M. Robinson, 'Very Goddess and Very Man: Jesus' Better Self', in *Encountering Jesus: A Debate on Christology*, ed. Stephen T. Davis (Atlanta: John Knox Press, 1988), p. 116. While I am empathetic and supportive of exploring various symbols by which theologians can contextually and fruitfully explicate Jesus, in this discussion I am not willing to claim that the drum is suited to galvanize the collective experience of a specific gender, i.e. the female in this case. Having said this, there can be no denying that the drum is closely associated with the power of the goddess in the Paraiyar religious tradition. As stated earlier, an attempt to exploit the drum as a feminist symbol to explicate veiled aspects of Jesus must be left to some other theologian.

48. For a recent, though very sketchy and unsystematic, example of such an effort, see M.R. Arulraja, *Jesus The Dalit: Liberation Theology by Victims of Untouchability, an Indian Version of Apartheid* (Hyderabad, Arulraja Volunteer Centre, 1996). This book provides relevant insight into the existing problems of the Dalits within the Roman Catholic Church in India.

49. Bruce J. Malina and Jerome H. Neyrey, *Calling Jesus Names: The Social Value of Labels in Matthew* (Sonoma, CA.: Polebridge Press, 1988).

50. John Dominic Crossan, *Jesus: A Revolutionary Biography* (San Francisco: Harper Collins Publisher, 1994), p. 23.

51. Malina and Neyrey, *Calling Jesus Names*, p. 62.

52. Arulraja attempts to demonstrate the numerous ways in which 'Jesus the Dalit' went about challenging the traditional Jewish lines that separated the pure from the polluted: 'It is a tremendous experience for Dalit Christians to reread the gospels and Jesus putting up a struggle against discrimination based on purity-pollution distinctions.' Arulraja, *Jesus the Dalit*, p. 118.

53. It is pertinent to note that the process of labelling someone a deviant is connected with their being labelled demon-possessed. See Malina and Neyrey, 'Jesus the Witch', in *Calling Jesus Names*, pp. 3–32. This ties into the whole social and religious dynamics that I have documented in this book whereby the Paraiyar were demonized whenever they could not be colonized by the caste communities.

54. Ibid., p. 40.

55. This is a major theme of Latin American Christology. A return to the historical Jesus is deliberate. On the one hand, it is meant to 'produce indignation at what is done in his name.' On the other hand, 'in returning to Jesus [what is sought] is that Christ not be able to be presented in connivance with idols.' In this case idols are defined as that which 'actually shapes reality' through the process of producing 'victims in order to subsist.' Sobrino, *Jesus in Latin America*, p. 59.

56. Antony Raj, 'Disobedience: A Legitimate Act for Dalit Liberation', in *Towards A Common Dalit Ideology*, p. 51. He goes on say that 'if the Dalit Christians were to break away from the hierarchical domination and create history, where they can celebrate their human dignity, they can do so only through disobedience.' p. 50.

57. Sobrino, *Jesus*, p. 59.
58. Marcus J. Borg, *Jesus, A New Vision: Spirit, Culture, and the Life of Discipleship* (San Francisco: Harper and Row Publishers, 1987), p. 183.
59. Here I want to somewhat distance myself from the radical and systematic nature that marks the political agenda of Jesus as a social revolutionary. As I have demonstrated in chapter three and four, this is quite incommensurate with the general character and dynamics of Dalit and subaltern religion. Thus such revolutionary structural changes may be much more a part of the wishful imaginings of the idealists from among the dominant communities. For one view of such a revolutionary Jesus, see Richard A. Horsley, *Jesus and the Spiral of Violence: Popular Jewish Resistance in Roman Palestine* (San Francisco: Harper and Row Publishers, 1987); *Sociology and the Jesus Movement* (New York: Crossroads, 1989); Richard A. Horsley and John S. Hanson, *Bandits, Prophets and Messiahs: Popular Movements of the Time of Jesus* (Minneapolis: Winston, 1985).
60. Crossan, *Jesus: A Revolutionary Biography*, p. 105.
61. Malina and Neyrey, *Calling Jesus Names*, p. 65.
62. Crossan, *Jesus: A Revolutionary Biography*, p. 103.
63. Ibid.
64. More specific to his 'open commensality', they designated Jesus as 'glutton and drunkard'. In the words of Kee, 'For those who continued to define God's people in terms of ethnic and ritual requirements, Jesus could be perceived only as a threat to their tradition and their expectations. He is to be denounced and dispatched, as were the historical gluttons and drunkards.' Howard Clark Kee, 'Jesus: A Glutton and a Drunkard', in *New Testament Studies*, vol. 42, no. 3 (July, 1996): 393.
65. Crossan, *The Historical Jesus*, p. 422. I am still not convinced about the notions of the 'brokerless kingdom' and 'the unmediated' role of Jesus that Crossan advocates. On the one hand, it fails to take into consideration the Jewish expectations of a Messiah (a kind of broker) and, on the other hand, it ignores the yearnings of people for a subaltern-biased broker. The ideal of a radically egalitarian Jesus may in itself be more a commitment of Crossan to the egalitarian and democratic ethos of the United States of America than a pronouncement on the Jesus of Nazareth. As Leander E. Keck says of Crossan, 'Ironically, the brokerless Jesus is himself thoroughly brokered by this biographer.' [As quoted in Witherington, *The Jesus Quest*, p. 92.]
66. Malina and Neyrey, *Calling Jesus Names*, p. 91.
67. See my discussion in chapter four under the heading 'Drum as means of exemplifying and managing communal suffering.'
68. Samuel Rayan, 'The Challenge of the Dalit Issue', in *Dalits and Women: Quest for Humanity*, ed. V. Devasahayam (Madras: Gurukul, 1992), p. 136.

Bibliography

Adamson, Walter L., *Hegemony and Revolution: A Study of Antonio Gramsci's Political and Cultural Theory* (Berkeley: University of California Press, 1980).

Aiyangar, Srinivasa M., *Tamil Studies: Essays on the History of the Tamil People, Language, Religion and Culture* (New Delhi: Asian Educational Services, 1982).

Aleaz, K.P., *The Gospel of Indian Culture* (Calcutta: Punthi Pustak, 1994).

Ambedkar, B.R., *Annihilation of Caste* (Bangalore: Dalit Sahitya Akademi, 1987).

Appadurai, Arjun, 'Is Homo Hierarchicus?', *American Ethnologist*, 13:4 (November, 1986): 745–61.

Arulraja, M.R., *Jesus the Dalit: Liberation Theology by Victims of Untouchability, An Indian Version of Apartheid* (Hyderabad, Arulraja Volunteer Center, 1996).

Ashcroft, Bill, Griffiths, Gareth & Tiffin, Helen, eds, *The Post Colonial Studies Reader* (London: Routledge Press, 1995).

Ayrookuzhiel, A.M. Abraham, *Swami Anand Thirth – Untouchability: Gandhian Solution on Trial* (Delhi: ISPCK, 1987).

———, 'Dalit Theology: A Movement of Counter-Culture', in *Towards A Dalit Theology*, ed. M.E. Prabhakar (New Delhi: ISPCK, 1988).

———, Dalits Move Toward the Ideology of Nationality', in *A Reader In Dalit Theology*, ed. Arvind P. Nirmal (Madras: Gurukul, 1992).

Azariah, M., *The Un-Christian Side of the Indian Church* (Bangalore: Dalit Sahitya Academy, 1985).

Baago, Kaj, *Pioneers of Indigenous Christianity* (Madras: CLS, 1969).

Bailey, F.G., *Caste and the Economic Frontier* (Bombay: Oxford University Press, 1957).

Balley, L.R., 'India Needs a Cultural Revolution', in *Untouchable: Voices of the Dalit Liberation Movement*, ed. Barbara R. Joshi (Zen Books: London, 1986).

Bebey, Francis, *African Music: A Peoples Art* (New York: Lawrence Hill, 1975).

Beck, Brenda E.F., *Peasant Society in Konku: A Study of Right and Left*

Subcastes in South India (Vancouver: University of British Columbia Press, 1972).

Beck, Guy, *Sonic Theology: Hinduism and Sacred Sound* (Columbia,
SC: University of South Carolina Press, 1993).

Berkhof, Hendrikus, *Christian Faith: An Introduction to the Study of
Faith* (Grand Rapids, Michigan: Eerdmans, 1979).

Beteille, Andre, *Caste, Class, and Power: Changing Patterns of Stratification in a Tanjore Village* (Berkeley: University of California Press,
1965).

————, *Inequality and Social Change* (Delhi: Oxford University Press,
1972).

Bhabba, Homi K., *The Location of Culture* (London: Routledge, 1994).

Bhadra, Gautam, 'The Mentality of Subalternity: Kantanama or
Rajdharma', in *Subaltern Studies VI: Writings on South Asian His-
tory and Society*, ed. Ranajit Guha, (New Delhi: Oxford University
Press, 1989).

Blacking, John, *How Musical is Man?* (Seattle: University of Washington
Press, 1973).

————, *A Commonsense View of All Music* (Cambridge, UK: Cambridge
University Press, 1987).

Boff, Clodovis, 'Methodology of the Theology of Liberation', in *Systematic Theology: Perspectives from Liberation Theology*, eds Jon
Sobrino & Ignacio Ellacria (Maryknoll, NY: Orbis Books).

Boggs, Carl, *Gramsci's Marxism* (London: Pluto Press, 1976).

Borg, Marcus, J., *Jesus, A New Vision: Spirit, Culture, and the Life of
Discipleship* (San Francisco: Harper and Row Publishers, 1987).

————, *Jesus at 2000* (Boulder, CO.: Westview Press, 1997).

Boyd, Robin, *An Introduction to Indian Christian Theology* (Madras:
CLS, 1969).

Brubaker, Richard L., 'Barbers, Washermen, and Other Priests: Servants
of the South Indian Village and its Goddess', *History of Religions*
19:2 (November, 1979): 128-53.

Buchanan, Francis, *A Journey from Madras through the Countries of
Mysore, Canaras, and Malabar in Three Volumes*, vol. II, Reprint,
(New Delhi: Asian Educational Services, 1988).

Buchler, Justus, ed., *Philosophical Writings of Peirce* (New York: Dover
Publications, 1995).

Bynum, Caroline W., 'The Complexity of Symbols', in *Experience of
the Sacred: Readings in the Phenomenology of Religion*, ed. Sumner
Twiss & Walter Conser (Hanover: Brown University Press, 1992).

Canda, Edward R., 'Gripped by the Drum: The Korean tradition of Nongak', *Shaman's Drum: A Journal of Experimental Shamanism*, 33, (Fall-Winter, 1993): 18–23.

Caplan, Lionel, *Class and Culture in Urban India: Fundamentalism in a Christian Community* (Oxford: Clarendon Press, 1987).

Carman, John B., *The Theology of Ramanuja: An Essay in Interreligious Understanding* (New Haven: Yale University Press, 1975).

Carman, John B. & Vasudha Narayanan, *The Tamil Veda: Pillan's Interpretation of the Tiruvaymoli* (Chicago: Chicago University Press, 1989).

Carmody, Denise, *Christian Feminist Theology: A Constructive Interpretation* (Oxford, UK: Blackwell Publishers, 1995).

Carrington, John, *Talking Drums of Africa* (London: Carey Kingsgate, 1949).

Carter, Stephen L., *The Culture of Disbelief: How American Law and Politics Trivialize Religious Devotion* (New York: Basic Books, 1993).

Census of India 1991, volume II (New Delhi: Registrar General and Census Commission of India, 1992).

Census of India 1981, Series 20, Tamil Nadu, Part XII.

Chandran, J. Russell, 'A.P. Nirmal: A Tribute', in *Bangalore Theological Forum*, vol. XXIX, no. 1 & 2 (March & June, 1997): 19–35.

Chatterjee, Partha, 'Caste and Subaltern Consciousness', in *Subaltern Studies VI: Writings on South Asian History and Society*, ed. Ranajit Guha (New Delhi: Oxford University Press, 1989).

Chatterji, Saral K., 'Why Dalit Theology?', in *A Reader in Dalit Theology* (Madras: Gurukul, 1992).

Chernoff, John M., *African Rhythm and African Sensibility* (Chicago: Chicago University Press, 1979).

Chitty, Simon Casie, *The Castes, Customs, Manners and Literature of the Tamils* (New Delhi: Asian Educational Services, 1988). First published in 1934.

Chopp, Rebecca S., *The Power to Speak: Feminism, Language, God* (New York: Crossroads, 1991).

Chopp, Rebecca & Mark Taylor, eds, *Reconstructing Christian Theology* (Minneapolis: Fortress Press, 1994).

Clayton, John P., *The Concept of Correlation: Paul Tillich and the Possibility of a Mediating Theology* (New York: De Gruyters, 1980).

Clifford, James, 'Introduction: Partial Truths', in *Writing Culture: The Poetics and Politics of Ethnography*, James E. Clifford & George E. Marcus, eds (Berkeley: University of California, 1986).

Clough, E.R., *While Sewing Sandals* (New York: Hodder and Stroughton, 1899).

Cobb, John B., *Christ in a Pluralistic Age* (Philadelphia: The Westminister Press, 1975).

Cobb, Kelton, 'Reconsidering the Status of Popular Culture in Tillich's Theology of Culture', in *Journal of the American Academy of Religion*, vol. LXIII/i (Spring, 1995): 53–84.

Compact Edition of the Oxford English Dictionary, vol. II, (P-Z) (Oxford, UK: Oxford University Press, 1971).

Cone, James H., *God of the Oppressed* (San Francisco: Harper and Row, 1975).

———, *Black Theology and Black Power* (San Francisco: Harper and Row, 1989).

Cook-Gumperz, J., ed., *The Social Construction of Literacy* (Cambridge, UK: Cambridge University Press, 1986).

Cox, Oliver C., *Caste, Class, and Race: A Study in Social Dynamics* (New York: Monthly Review Press, 1959).

Crossan, John Dominic, *The Historical Jesus: The Life of a Mediterranean Jewish Peasant* (San Francisco: Harper Collins, 1991).

———, *Jesus: A Revolutionary Biography* (San Fransisco: Harper Collins Publisher, 1994).

Cutler, Norman, *Consider Our Vow: An English Translation of Tiruppavai and Tiruvempavai* (Madurai: Muthu Patippakam, 1978).

———, *Songs of Experiences: The Poetics of Tamil Devotion* (Bloomingdale: Indiana University Press, 1987).

Daniel, Valentine, *Fluid Signs: Being a Person the Tamil Way* (Berkeley: University of California Press, 1984).

Danielou, Jean, *Gospel Message and Hellenistic Culture*, vol. 2 (London: Darton, Longman and Todd, 1973).

Das, Veena, *Structure and Cognition: Aspects of Hindu Caste and Ritual* 2nd ed. (Delhi: Oxford University Press, 1982).

Dehejia, Vidya, *Slaves of the Lord: The Path of the Tamil Saints* (Delhi: Munshiram Manoharlal Publishers, 1988).

———, *Antal and Her Path of Love: Poems of a Women Saint from South India* (Albany, NY: SUNY Press, 1990).

Deliege, Robert, 'Patriarchal Cross-cousin Marriage among the Paraiyars of South India', *Journal of the Anthropological Society of Oxford*, no. 18 (1987): 223–36.

————, 'Les mythes d'origine chez Paraiyar', *L'Homme* 109 (1989): 107–16.

————, 'A Comparison between Christian and Hindu Paraiyars of South India', *Indian Missiological Review* (April, 1990): 53–64.

Deliege, Robert, 'Replication and Consensus: Untouchability, Caste and Ideology in India', *Man*, vol. 27 (March, 1992): 155–73.

Detels, Claire, 'Soft Boundaries and Relatedness: Paradigm for a Postmodern Feminist Musical Aesthetics', *Boundaries 2*, vol. 19:2 (Summer, 1992): 184–204.

Dube, Saurabh, 'Myths, Symbols and Community: Satnampanth of Chhattisgarh', in *Subaltern Studies VII: Writings on South Asian History and Society*, Partha Chatterjee and Gyanendra Pandey, eds (New Delhi: Oxford University Press, 1993).

Dubois, Abbe J.A., *Hindu Manners, Customs and Ceremonies*, 3rd ed., trans. Henry K. Beauchamp (Oxford: Clarendon Press, 1906).

Dumont, Louis, *Homo Hierarchicus: An Essay on the Caste System*, Trans. Mark Sainsubury (Chicago: The University of Chicago Press, 1970).

————, *A South Indian Subcaste: Social Organization and Religion of the Pramalai Kallar* (Delhi: Oxford University Press, 1986).

Dupuis, Jacques, *Jesus and His Spirit* (Bangalore: Theological Publications in India, 1977).

————, *Jesus Christ at the Encounter of World Religions* (Maryknoll, NY: Orbis Books, 1991).

Duraisingh, Christopher, 'Indian Hyphenated Christians and Theological Reflections: A New Expression of Identity', in *Religion and Society*, vol. XXVI, no. 4 (December, 1979): 95–101.

————, 'Alternate Modes of Theologising now Prevalent in India', in *Religion and Society*, vol. XXVIII, no. 2 (June, 1980): 81–101.

————, 'Reflections on Theological Hermeneutics in the Indian Context', in *The Indian Journal of Theology*, vol. 31, nos. 3 & 4 (July–Dec., 1982): 259–78.

————, 'Reflections on Indian-Christian Theology in the Context of Indian Religious Reality', in *Bangalore Theological Forum*, vol. 14, no. 3 (Sept–Dec., 1982): 176–87.

Eck, Diana L., *Darsan: Seeing the Divine Images in India* (Chambersburg, PA: Anima Books, 1985).

Eliade, Mircea, *Patterns in Comparative Religion*, Trans. Rosemary Sheed (Cleveland: The Word Publishing Company, 1963).

Ellingson, Ter, 'Ancient Indian Drum Syllables and Bu Stone's *Sham Pa Ta* Ritual', *Ethnomusicology: Journal for the Society of Ethnomusicology*, vol. XXIV: 1 (January, 1980): 431–52.

Elmore, W.T., *Dravidian Gods in Modern Hinduism* (New Delhi: Asian Educational Services, 1984).

Fentress, James & Chris Wickham, *Social Memory: New Perspectives on the Past* (Oxford, UK: Blackwell Publishers, 1992).

Fernandez, James W., 'Persuasions and Performances: Of the Beast in Every Body and the Metaphors of Everyman', *Daedalus*, 101:1 (1972): 39–80.

———, 'The Mission of Metaphor in Expressive Culture', *Current Anthropology*, 15:2 (1974):119–45.

———, *Persuasions and Performances: The Play of Tropes in Cultures* (Bloomington: Indiana University Press, 1986).

Fiorenza, Elizabeth Schussler, *In Memory of Her:A Feminist Reconstruction of Christian Origins* (New York: Crossroads, 1983).

———, *Bread Not Stone: The Challenge of Feminist Biblical Interpretation* (Boston, MA: Beacon Press, 1984).

Fishman, A.T., *Culture Change and the Underprivileged* (Madras: The Christian Literature Society, 1941).

———, *For This Purpose* (Madras: American Foreign Mission Society in India, 1958).

Forgacs, David, ed., *An Antonio Gramsci Reader* (New York: Schocken Books, 1988).

Foucault, Michel, *Discipline and Punish: The Birth of The Prison*, Trans. Alan Sheridan (New York: Vintage Books, 1979).

———, *Power/Knowledge: Selected Interviews and Other Writings, 1972–1977*, ed. Colin Gordon (New York: Pantheon Books, 1980).

Frawley, W., ed., *Linguistics and Literacy* (New York: Plenum Press, 1982).

Frazer, James G., *The Golden Bough: A Study in Magic and Religion* (New York: Macmillan Company, 1940).

Freire, Paulo, *Pedagogy of the Oppressed* (New York: Continuum, 1990).

Friske, John, *Reading the Popular* (Boston: Unwin Hyman, 1989).

———, *Understanding Popular Culture* (Boston: Unwin, Hyman, 1989).

Frykenberg, Robert & Pauline Kolenda, eds, *Studies in South India: An Anthology of Recent Research and Scholarship* (Madras: New Era Publications, 1985).

Fuchs, Stephen, *At the Bottom of Indian Society: The Harijans and the Other Low Castes* (New Delhi: Munshiram Manoharlal Publishers, 1981).

Fuller, C.J., *The Camphor Flame: Popular Hinduism and Society in India* (New Delhi: Viking, 1992).

Galvin, John P., 'Jesus Christ', in *Systematic Theology: Roman Catholic Perspectives*, vol. I, eds Francis S. Fiorenza & John P. Galvin (Minneapolis: Fortress Press, 1991).

Gardner, Howard, *Frames of Mind: The Theory of Multiple Intelligences* (New York: Basic Books, 1983).

Gatwood, Lynn E., *Devi and the Souse Goddess: Women, Sexuality, and Marriages in India* (Riverdale, MD: Riverdale Company Inc., 1985).

Geertz, Clifford, *Interpretation of Culture* (New York: Basic Books, 1973).

————, *Local Knowledge: Further Essays in Interpretive Anthropology* (New York: Basic Books, 1993).

Ghurye, G.S., *Caste and Race in India* (Bombay: Popular Prakashan, 1969).

Gilkey, Langdon, *Gilkey on Tillich* (New York: Crossroads, 1990).

Giroux, Henry A., *Ideology, Culture, and the Process of Schooling* (Philadelphia: Temple University Press, 1981).

Glucklich, Ariel, 'Karma and Pollution in Hindu Dharma: Distinguishing Law from Nature', *Contributions to Indian Sociology*, (n.s.) 18:1 (1984): 25–43.

Godzich, Wlad, *The Culture of Literacy* (Cambridge, MA: Harvard University Press, 1994).

Goodman, Nelson, *Ways of Worldmaking* (Indianapolis: Hackett Publishing Company, 1978).

————, *Of Mind and Other Matters* (Cambridge, MA: Harvard University Press, 1984).

Goodman, Nelson, & Catherine Z. Elgin, *Reconceptions in Philosophy* (Indianapolis: Hackett Publishing Company, 1988).

Goody, Jack, ed., *Literacy in Traditional Societies* (Cambridge, UK: Cambridge University Press, 1968).

————, *The Domestication of the Savage Mind* (Cambridge, UK: Cambridge University Press, 1977).

————, *The Logic of Writing and the Organisation of Society* (Cambridge. UK: Cambridge University Press, 1986).

————, *The Interface between the Written and the Oral* (Cambridge, UK: Cambridge University press, 1987).

Goody, Jack, & Ian Watt, 'The Consequences of Literacy', Jack Goody, ed., *Literacy in Traditional Societies* (Cambridge, UK: Cambridge University Press, 1968).

Graham, William, *Beyond the Written Word: Oral Aspects of Scripture in the History of Religions* (Cambridge, UK: Cambridge University Press, 1987).

Green, Marilyn, 'Voices of the Drum', *Sky* 22:11 (1993): 32–7.

Greenfield, P.M., 'Oral and Written Language: The Consequences for Cognitive Development in Africa, The United States and England', *Language and Speech*, 15: 169–78.

Guha, Ranajit, 'Preface', *Subaltern Studies I: Writings on South Asian History and Society*, ed. Ranajit Guha (New Delhi: Oxford University Press, 1982).

————, 'The Small Voice of History', *Subaltern Studies IX: Writings on South Asian History and Society*, ed. Ranajit Guha (New Delhi: Oxford University Press, 1996): 1–12.

Gunton, Colin E., *The One, The Three And The Many: God, Creation and the Culture of Modernity* (Cambridge, UK: Cambridge University Press, 1993).

Gupta, Dipankar, ed., *Social Stratification* (New Delhi: Oxford University Press, 1991).

Guru, Nataraja, *Life and Teachings of Narayana Guru* (Fernhill, India: An East-West University Publication, 1990).

Gutierrez, Gustavo, *The Power of the Poor in History* (Maryknoll, NY: Orbis Books, 1983).

Halbfass, Wilhelm, *India and Europe: An Essay in Understanding* (Albany: SUNY, 1988).

Hanumanthan, K.R., *Untouchability: A Historical Study upto 1500 A.D. (with special reference to Tamil Nadu)* (Madurai: Koodal Publishers, 1979).

Hart, George L. III., *The Poems of Ancient Tamil* (Berkeley: University of California Press, 1975).

Havelock, Eric A., *Origins of Western Literacy* (Toronto: Ontario Institute for Studies in Education, 1976).

Hiltebeitel, Alf, *The Cult of Draupadi: Mythologies From Gingee to Kuruksetra* (Chicago: The University of Chicago, 1988).

Hodgson, Peter C., *New Birth of Freedom: A Theology of Bondage and Liberation* (Philadelphia: Fortress Press, 1976).

————, *God in History: The Shapes of Freedom* (Nashville, TN: Abingdon Press, 1989).

Horsley, Richard A., *Jesus and the Spiral of Violence: Popular Jewish Resistance in Roman Palestine* (San Francisco: Harper and Row Publisher, 1987).

————, *Sociology and the Jesus Movement* (New York: Crossroads, 1989).

Horsley, Richard A., and John S. Hanson, *Bandits, Prophets and Messiahs: Popular Movements of the Time of Jesus* (Minneapolis: Winston, 1985).

Howard, Joseph H., *Drums in Americas* (New York: Oak Publications, 1967).

Hutton, J.F., *Caste in India: Its Nature, Function, and Origins,* (Bombay: Oxford University Press, 1951).

Ilaiah, Kancha, *Why I am not a Hindu: A Sudra Critique of Hindutva Philosophy, Culture and Political Economy* (Calcutta: Samya, 1996).

————, 'Productive Labour, Consciousness and History: The Dalit-bahujan Alternative', in *Subaltern Studies IX: Writings on South Asian History and Society,* Shahid Amin and Dipesh Chakrabarty eds (New Delhi: Oxford University Press, 1996).

Inden, Ronald, 'Orientalist Constructions of India', *Modern Asian Studies,* 20:3 (1986): 401–46.

Ingole, Shiva, 'Ancient Mother Mine', *Poisoned Bread: Translations from Modern Marathi Dalit Literature,* ed. Arjun Dangle (Bombay: Oriental Longman, 1992).

Isaacs, Harold R., *Idols of the Tribe: Group Identity and Political Change* (Cambridge, MA: Harvard University Press, 1989).

Jagannathachariar, C., *The Tiruppavai of Sri Andal: Textual, Literary and Critical study* (Madras: Parthasarathy Swami Devasthanam, 1982).

James, William, *Pragmatism and the Meaning of Truth,* (Cambridge, MA: Harvard University Press, 1978).

Jardine, Murray, 'Sight, Sound and Epistemology: the Experiential Sources of Ethical Concepts', in *Journal of the American Academy of Religion,* no. LXIV/1 (Spring, 1996): 1–25.

Jayakar, Pupul, *Earth Mother: Legends, Ritual Arts, and Goddesses of India* (San Francisco: Harper and Row Publishers, 1990).

Johns, Roger Dick, *Man in The World: The Theology of Johannes Baptist Metz,* (Missoula, Montana: Scholars Press, 1976).

Joshi, Barbara R., ed., *Untouchable: Voices of the Dalit Liberation Movement* (London: Zed Books, 1986).

Kaemmer, John E., *Music in Human Life: Anthropological Perspectives on Music* (Austin: University of Texas Press, 1993).

Kamble, N.D., *The Scheduled Castes* (New Delhi: Ashish Publishing House, 1982).

Kaufman, Gordon D., *An Essay on Theological Method*, Revised Edition (Missoula: Scholars Press, 1979).

———, *The Theological Imagination: Constructing the Concept of God* (Philadelphia: The Westminster Press, 1981).

———, *Theology for a Nuclear Age* (Philadelphia: The Westminster Press, 1985).

———, *In the Face of Mystery: A Constructive Theology* (Cambridge, MA: Harvard University Press, 1993).

Kee, Howard Clark, 'Jesus: A Glutton and a Drunkard', *New Testament Studies*, vol. 42, no. 3 (July, 1996): 374–93.

Kerman, Joseph, *Contemplating Music: Challenges to Musicology* (Cambridge, MA: Harvard University Press, 1985).

Khare, R.S., *The Untouchable as Himself: Ideology, Identity and Pragmatism among the Lucknow Chamars* (Cambridge, UK: Cambridge University Press, 1984).

Kolenda, Pauline, 'Caste in South India', in *Studies of South India: An Anthology of Recent Scholarship*, Robert E. Frykenburg & Pauline Kolanda, eds (Madras: New Era Publications, 1985).

———, 'The Ideology of Purity and Pollution', in *Caste and Contemporary India: Beyond Organic Solidarity* (Prospect Heights, Ill.: Waveland Press, 1985).

Kingsbury, Henry, *Music, Talent, and Performance: A Conservatory Cultural System* (Philadelphia: Temple University Press, 1988).

Kinsley, David, *Hindu Goddesses: Visions of the Divine Feminine in the Hindu Religious Tradition* (Berkeley: University of California Press, 1986).

Kumar, Dharma, *Land and Caste in South India: Agricultural Labour in the Madras Presidency during the Nineteenth Century* (Cambridge: Cambridge University Press, 1965).

Lash, Nicholas, *Theology on the Way to Emmaus* (London: SCM Press, 1986).

Levine, K., *The Social Context of Literacy* (London: Routledge and Kegal Paul, 1986).

Levi-Strauss, Claude, *The Savage Mind* (Chicago: University of Chicago, 1966).

Lints, Richard, 'The Postpositive Choice', *Journal of the American Academy of Religion*, vol. LXI/no. 4 (Winter, 1993).

Lindbeck, George, *The Nature of Doctrine: Religion and Theology in a Postliberal Age* (Philadelphia: The Westminster Press, 1984).

Lott, Eric J., 'The Divine Drum: Interpreting a Primal Symbol', in *Sri Andal: Her Contribution to Literature, Philosophy, Religion and Art*, ed. M.N. Parthasarathi (Madras: Ramanuja Vedanta Centre, 1986).

Luke P.Y. & John B. Carman, *Village Christians and Hindu Culture: Study of Rural Churches in Andhra Pradesh, South India* (London: Lutterworth Press, 1968).

Luria, Aleksandr R., *Cognitive Development: Its Cultural and Social Foundations*, ed. Michael Coles (Cambridge, MA.: Harvard University Press, 1976).

Malina, Bruce J. & Jerome H. Neyrey, *Calling Jesus Names: The Social Value of Labels in Matthew* (Sonoma, CA.: Polebridge Press, 1988).

Manickam, S., *Slavery in the Tamil Country: A Historical Overview* (Madras: The Christian Literature Society, 1982).

Mann, Thomas, *The Transposed Head: A Legend of India*, Trans. H.T. Loew-Porter (New York, 1941).

Marcus, George E. & Michael M.J. Fischer, *Anthropology as Cultural Critique: An Experimental Moment in the Human Sciences* (Chicago: The University of Chicago, 1986).

Marriot, Mckim & Ronald Inden, 'Towards and Ethnosociology of South Asian Caste System', in Kenneth David, ed., *The New Wind: Changing Identities in South Asia* (Chicago: Aldine Publishers, 1977).

Marx, Karl & F. Engels, *The German Ideology* (London: Lawrence Wishart Publishers, 1965).

Massey, James, *Indigenous People: Dalits, Dalit Issues in Today's Theological Debate* (New Delhi: ISPCK, 1994).

———, *Towards Dalit Hermeneutics: Re-reading the Text, the History and the Literature* (New Delhi: ISPCK, 1994).

———, *Roots: A Concise History of the Dalits* (New Delhi: ISPCK, 1994).

Mendelsohn, Oliver & Marika Vicziany, 'The Untouchables', in *The Rights of Subordinated Peoples*, eds Oliver Mendelsohn and Upendra Baxi (New Delhi: Oxford University Press, 1994).

Mbiti, John S., *African Religions and Philosophy* (Garden City, NY: Anchor Books, 1970).

Mcgilvray, Dennis B., 'Paraiyar Drummers of Sri Lanka: Consensus and Constraint in an Untouchable Caste', 10:1 (February, 1983): 97–115.

Mencher, Joan P., 'On Being an Untouchable in India: A Materialist Perspective', in *Beyond the Myths of Culture: Essays in Cultural Materialism*, ed. Eric Ross (New York: Academic Press, 1980).

———, 'The Caste System Upside Down, or The Not-So-Mysterious East', *Current Anthropology*, 15:4 (December, 1974): 469–93.

Merriam, Alan P., *The Anthropology of Music* (Evanston, Ill.: Northwestern University Press, 1964).

Metz, Johann Baptist, *Faith in History and Society: Toward a Practical Fundamental Theology* (New York: The Seabury Press, 1980).

Meyer, Leonard B., *Music, the Arts, and Ideas* (Chicago: Chicago University Press, 1967).

———, *Explaining Music* (Berkeley: University of California Press, 1973).

Migliore, Daniel L., *Called to Freedom: Liberation Theology and the Future of Christian Doctrine* (Philadelphia: Westminster Press, 1980).

Minz, Nirmal, 'Dalit-Tribal: A Search for a Common Ideology', in *Towards A Common Dalit Ideology* (New Delhi: ISPCK, 1988).

Moffatt, Michael., *An Untouchable Community in South India: Structure and Consensus* (Princeton: Princeton University Press, 1979).

Mookenthottam, Antony, MSFS, *Indian Theological Tendencies* (Berne: Peter Lang, 1978).

———, *Towards a Theology in the Indian Context* (Bangalore: Asian Trading Corporation, 1980).

Morris, Brian, *Anthropological Studies of Religion: An Introductory Text* (Cambridge, UK: Cambridge University Press, 1987).

Nandy, Ashis, *The Intimate Enemy: Loss and Recovery of Self Under Colonialism*, (Delhi: Oxford University Press, 1983).

Neville, Robert, C., *Behind the Masks of God: An Essay in Comparative Theology* (Albany, NY: SUNY, 1991).

Nirmal, Arvind, P., 'Theological Implications of the Term "Indigenous"', in *Dialogue in Community: Essays in Honour of S.J. Samartha*, ed. C.D. Jathanna (Mangalore: The Karnataka Theological Research Institute, 1982).

———, *Heuristic Explorations* (Madras: The Christian Literature Society, 1990).

————, 'Doing Theology from A Dalit Perspective', in *A Reader in Dalit Theology* (Madras: Gurukul, 1992).

Nirmal, Arvind P. and V. Devasahayam, eds, *Dr. B.R. Ambedkar: A Centenary Tribute*, (Madras: Gurukul, 1991).

Nketia, J.H. Kwabena, *Our Drums and Drummers* (Acra: Ghana Publishing House, 1968).

Nyystrand, M., ed., *What Writers Know; The Language, Process and Structure of Written Discourse* (New York: Academic Press, 1982).

O'Flaherty, Wendy D., *The Origins of Evil in Hindu Mythology* (Berkeley, CA: University of California Press, 1976).

Olson, David R., 'From Utterance to Text: The Bias of Language in Speech and Writing', *Harvard Educational Review*, 47:3 (August, 1977): 257–81.

Olson, David R., ed., *Social Foundations of Language and Thought* (New York: Norton Publishing House, 1980).

Olson, David R., 'Mind and Media: the Epistemic Functions of Literacy', *Journal of Communications*, 38:3 (Summer, 1988): 27–36.

————, *The World on Paper: The Conceptual and Cognitive Implications of Writing and Reading* (Cambridge, UK: Cambridge University Press, 1994).

Olson, Torrance N. & A. Hildyard, eds, *Literacy, Language and Learning* (Cambridge, UK: Cambridge University Press, 1985).

O'Malley, L.S.S., *Modern India and the West: General Survey* (London: Oxford University Press, 1941).

Omvedt, Gail, *Dalits and the Democratic Revolution: Dr. Ambedkar and the Dalit Movement in Colonial India*, (New Delhi: Sage Publishers, 1994).

Ong, Walter, J., *The Presence of the Word* (New Haven: Yale University Press, 1967).

————, *The Presence of the Word: Some Prolegomena for Culture and Religious History* (New York: Simon and Schuster, 1970).

————, *Interfaces of the Word* (Ithaca: Cornell University Press, 1977).

————, *Orality and Literacy: The Technologizing of the Word* (London: Routledge, 1988).

Oommen, T.K., 'Sources of Deprivation and Styles of Protest: The Case of the Dalits in India', *Contributions to Indian Sociology* (n.s.) 18:1 (1984): 45–61.

Oppert, Gustav, *The Original Inhabitants of India* (Delhi: Oriental Publishers, 1972).

Organ, Troy Wilson, *Third Eye Philosophy: Essays in East-West Thought* (Athens, OH: Ohio University Press, 1987).

Ortner, Sherry, 'On Key Symbols', *American Anthropologist*, 75:6 (1973): 138–46.

Panikkar, Raimundo, *The Intra-Religious Dialogue* (New York: Paulist Press, 1978).

———, *Myth, Faith and Hermeneutics: Cross Cultural Studies* (New York; Paulist Press, 1979).

———, *The Unknown Christ of Hinduism: Towards an Ecumenical Christophany* (Maryknoll, NY: Orbis Books, 1981).

———, 'The Jordon, the Tiber and the Ganges: Three Kairological Moments of Christic Self-Consciousness', in John Hick & Paul Knitter, eds, *The Myth of Christian Uniqueness* (Maryknoll, NY: Orbis Books, 1993).

———, *The Cosmotheandric Experience* (Maryknoll, NY: Orbis Books, 1993).

———, *Invisible Harmony: Essays on Contemplation and Responsibility* (Minneapolis: Fortress Press, 1995).

Parry, Benita, 'Current Theories of Colonial Discourse', in Bill Ashcroft, Gareth Griffiths & Helen Tiffin, eds, *The Post Colonial Studies Reader* (London: Routledge Press, 1995): 36–44.

Patton, Laurie, L., *Authority, Anxiety and Canonn: Essays in Vedic Interpretation* (Albany, NY: SUNY, 1994).

Pawde, Kumud, 'The Story of My "Sanskrit"', in *Poisoned Bread: Translations from Modern Marathi Dalit Literature*, ed. Arjun Dangle (Bombay: Oriental Longman, 1992).

Pelikan, Jaroslaw, *Jesus through the Centuries: His Place in the History of Culture* (New York: Harper and Row Publishers, 1985).

Pepper, Stephen, *World Hypotheses* (Berkeley: University of California Press, 1942).

Picket, J.N., *Christian Mass Movements in India* (New York: Abingdon Press, 1933).

Pocock, David F., *Mind, Body and Wealth: A Study of Belief and Practice in an Indian Village* (Oxford: Blackwell, 1973).

Prabhakar, M.E., ed., *Towards A Common Dalit Theology* (New Delhi: ISPCK, 1988).

Prakash, Gyan, 'Writing Post-Orientalist Histories of the Third World: Indian Historiography is Good to Think', in *Colonialism and Culture*, ed. Nicholas B. Dirks (Ann Arbor: The University of Michigan Press, 1992).

Raj, Antony, 'Disobedience: A Legitimate Act for Dalit Liberation', in *Towards A Common Dalit Ideology* (New Delhi: ISPCK, 1988).

———, 'The Dalit Christian Reality in Tamilnadu', *Jeevadhara* xxii/128 (March, 1992): 78-89.

Rajayyam, K., *History of Tamil Nadu: 1565–1982* (Madurai: Raj Publishers, 1982).

Rajshekar, V.T., *Hinduism vs Movement of Untouchables in India* (Bangalore: Dalit Sahitya Academy, 1983).

———, *Christians and Dalit Liberation* (Bangalore: Dalit Sahitya Academy, 1987).

Ramanujan A.K. & Vinay Dharwadker, 'Sixteen Modern Indian Poems', *Daedalus* 118:4 (Fall 1989): 325–26.

Random Unabridged Dictionary, 2nd ed. (New York: Random House, 1993).

Rayan, Samuel, 'The Challenge of the Dalit Issue', in *Dalits and Women: Quest for Humanity*, ed. V. Devasahayam (Madras: Gurukul, 1992).

Ricoeur, Paul, *Interpretation Theory: Discourse and the Surplus of Meaning* (Fort Worth, Texas: The Texas Christian University Press, 1976).

Robinson, James, M., 'Very Goddess and Very Man: Jesus' Better Self', in *Encountering Jesus: A Debate on Christology*, ed. Stephen T. Davis (Atlanta: John Knox Press, 1988).

Robinson, James M., *A New Quest for the Historical Jesus* (Naperville, Ill.: A.R. Allenson, 1959).

Rouget, Gilbert, *Music and Trance: A Theory of the Relations between Music and Possession* (Chicago: The University of Chicago Press, 1985).

Ruether, Rosemary R., *Sexism and God-Talk: Toward a Feminist Theology* (Boston: Beacon Press, 1983).

———, *To Change the World: Christology and Cultural Criticism* (New York: Crossroads, 1990).

Sahi Jyoti, 'Dance in the Wilderness', in *Doing Theology with Asian Resources: Theology and Culture*, vol. II, ed. Yeow Choo Lak (Singapore: ATESEA, 1995).

Samartha, S.J., *One Christ–Many Religions: Toward a Revised Christology* (Maryknoll, NY.: Orbis Books, 1991).

Schreiter, Robert J., *Constructing Local Theologies* (Maryknoll, NY: Orbis Books, 1986).

Schuuman, Lamberto, 'Christology in Latin America', in *Faces of Jesus:*

Latin American Christologies, ed. Jose Miguez Bonino (Maryknoll, NY: Orbis Press, 1984).

Scot, James C., *Weapons of the Weak* (New Haven: Yale University Press, 1985).

Scousboe, K. & M.T. Larsen, eds, *Literacy and Society* (Copenhagen: Academsig Forlag, 1989).

Scott, David, 'Theological Reflection in Multiform Community: A Response to the Contextual Indian Proposal for Constructive Christian Theology', in *Bangalore Theological Forum*, vol. XXIX, nos. 1 & 2 (March & June, 1997): 112–17.

Scribner, Sylvia, & Micheal Cole, *The Psychology of Literacy* (Cambridge, MA.: Harvard University Press, 1981).

Sebeok, Thomas A, and Jean U. Sebeok, eds, *Speech Surrogates: Drum and Whistle Systems* (The Hague: Mouton, 1976).

Segundo, Juan Luis, *The Liberation of Theology* (Maryknoll, NY: Orbis Books, 1976).

Sharma, K.L., *Rural Society in India* (New Delhi: Rawat Publishers, 1997).

Shulman, David, *The King and the Clown in South Indian Myth and Poetry* (Princeton: Princeton University Press, 1985).

Singer, Milton, *When a Great Tradition Modernizes* (New York: Praeger Publishers, 1972).

Skaria, Ajay, 'Writing and Orality and Power in the Dangs of Western India, 1800s–1920s', in *Subaltern Studies IX*, 13–58.

Smith, Brian K., *Reflections on Resemblance, Ritual, and Religion* (New York: Oxford University Press, 1989).

Smith, Wilfred Cantwell, 'Comparative Religion: Wither-and Why?', in *The History of Religious: Essays in Methodology*, eds, Mircea Eliade & Joseph M. Kitagawa (Chicago: The University of Chicago, 1959).

Sobrino, Jon, *Jesus in Latin America* (Maryknoll, NY: Orbis Books, 1987).

Sobrino, Jon, *Christology at the Crossroads: A Latin American Approach* (Maryknoll, NY: Orbis Books, 1978).

Spivak, Gayatri C. 'Subaltern Studies: Deconstructing Historiography', in *Subaltern Studies IV: Writings on South Asian History and Society* (New Delhi: Oxford University Press, 1985), 330–63.

Srinivas, M.N., *Religion and Society Among the Coorgs of South India*, (London: Oxford University Press, 1952).

————, *Caste in Modern India and Other Essays* (Bombay: Asia Publishing House, 1962).

————, *Social Change in Modern India* (Hyderabad: Orient Longman, 1972).

————, *The Village Remembered* (Berkeley: University of California Press, 1976).

————, 'Some Reflections on the Nature of Caste Hierarchy', *Contributions to Indian Sociology*, (n.s.) 18:2 (1984): 151-67.

Stein, Burton., *Peasant State and Society in Medieval South India* (Delhi: Oxford University Press, 1980).

Stell, Stephen, 'Hermeneutics in Theology and the Theology of Hermeneutics: Beyond Lindbeck and Tracy', *Journal of the American Academy of Religion*, vol. LXI/no. 4 (Winter, 1993).

Sternberg, Robert J., *The Triarchic Mind: A New Theory of Human Intelligence* (New York: Viking Press, 1988).

————, *Metaphors of the Mind: Conceptions of the Nature of Intelligence* (Cambridge, UK: Cambridge University Press, 1990).

Street, Brian V., ed., *Cross-cultural Approaches to Literacy* (Cambridge, UK: Cambridge University Press, 1993).

Stuckey, Sterling, *Slave Culture: Nationalist Theory and the Foundations of Black America* (New York: Oxford University Press, 1987).

Subrahmanian, N., *Sangam Polity: The Administrative and Social Life of the Sangam Tamils* (Madurai: Ennes Publications, 1980).

Sullivan, Lawrence E., *Icanchu's Drum: An Orientation to Meaning in South American Religions* (New York: Macmillan Publishing Company, 1988).

————, '"Seeking an end to the primary text" or "Putting an end to the text as Primary"', in *Beyond the Classics? Essays in Religious Studies and Liberal Education*, eds. Frank E. Reynolds & Sheryl L. Burkhalter (Missoula, MO: Scholars press, 1990).

Talal Asad, Talal, 'Anthropological Conceptions of Religion: Reflections on Geertz', *Man*, 18 (1983): 237–59.

Tambiah, Stanley J., *Magic, Science, Religion, and the Scope of Rationality* (Cambridge, UK: Cambridge University Press, 1990).

Tannen, D., ed., *Spoken and Written Language: Exploring Orality and Literacy* (Norwood, NJ: Ablex Press, 1982).

Taylor, Mark K., *Remembering Esperanza: A Cultural-Political Theology for North American Praxis* (Maryknoll, NY: Orbis Books, 1990).

Thangaraj, Thomas, M., *The Crucified Guru: An Experiment in Cross-cultural Christology* (Nashville: Abingdon Press, 1994).

The Compact Edition of the Oxford English Dictionary, vol. II (P-Z) (Oxford, UK: Oxford University Press, 1971).

The Holy Bible: Containing the Old and New Testament, New Revised Standard Version (Nashville, TN: Holman Bible Publishers, 1989).

Thiemann, Ronald, 'Response to George Lindbeck', *Theology Today*, no. 43 (1986).

Thomas, M.M. & P.T. Thomas, *Towards an Indian Christian Theology: Life and Thought of Some Pioneers* (Tiruvalla: New Day Publications, 1992).

Thomas, M.M., *The Christian Response to the Asian Revolution* (London: SCM Press, 1964).

————, *The Acknowledged Christ of the Indian Renaissance* (Madras: Christian Literature Society, 1970).

————, *Salvation and Humanization* (Madras: Christian Literature Society, 1971).

————, *Man and the Universe of Faiths* (Madras: Christian Literature Society, 1975).

————, *The Secular Ideologies of India and the Secular Meaning of Christ* (Madras: Christian Literature Society, 1976).

————, *Religion and Revolt of the Oppressed* (Delhi: ISPCK 1981).

————, *Risking Christ for Christ's Sake: Towards an Ecumenical Theology of Pluralism* (Geneva: WCC Publications, 1987).

Thompson, P., *Customs in Common* (New York: Panteon Books, 1967).

————, *The Making of the English Working Class* (London: Merlin Press, 1991).

Thurston, Edgar, *Castes and Tribes of South India*, 7 volumes (Delhi: Cosmo Publications, 1975).

Tillich, Paul, 'The Problem of Theological Method', *The Journal of Religion*, XVII, no. 1 (1947): 19–26.

————, *Systematic Theology: Three Volumes in One* (Chicago: The University of Chicago Press, 1967).

Tracy, David, *Blessed Rage for Order: The New Pluralism in Theology* (New York: The Seabury Press, 1979).

————, *Plurality and Ambiguity: Hermeneutics, Religion, Hope* (San Francisco: Harper and Row, 1987).

Trautman, Thomas, 'The Study of South Indian Inscriptions', in Robert Frykenberg, & Pauline Kolenda, eds, *Studies in South India: An Anthology of Recent Research and Scholarship* (Madras: New Era Publications, 1985).

Trawick, Margaret E., 'Internal Iconicity in Paraiyar Crying Songs', in *Another Harmony: New Essays on the Folklore of India*, eds Stuart Blackburn & A.K. Ramanujan (Berkeley: University of California Press, 1986).

————, 'On the Meaning of Sakti to the Women in Tamil Nadu', in *The Powers of Tamil Women*, ed. Susan Wadley (Syracuse: Syracuse University, 1980).

————, 'Spirits and Voices in Tamil Song', *American Ethnologist*, 15:2 (May, 1988): 193–215.

Turner, Victor, *The Forest of Symbols: Aspects of Ndembu Rituals* (Ithaca: Cornell University Press, 1967).

Walhout, Clarence, 'Christianity, History, and Literacy Criticism: Walter Ong's Global Vision', in *Journal of the American Academy of Religion*, no. LXII/2 (Summer, 1994): 435–59.

Webster, John C.B., *The Dalit Christians: A History* (Delhi: ISPCK, 1992).

————, 'From Indian Church to Indian Theology: An Attempt at Theological Construction', in *A Reader in Dalit Theology* (Madras: Gurukul, 1992).

Wietzke, Joachim, ed., *Paul D. Devanandan: Selected Writing with Introduction*, vol. I & II (Madras: CLS, 1983 & 1986).

Welch, Sharon D., *A Feminist Ethic of Risk* (Minneapolis: Fortress Press, 1990).

Welch; Sharon D., *Communities of Resistance and Solidarity: A Feminist Theology of Liberation* (Maryknoll, NY: Orbis Press, 1985).

West, Cornel, *Prophesy Deliverance! An Afro-American Revolutionary Christianity* (Philadelphia: The Westminster Press, 1982).

Whitehead, Henry, *The Village Gods of South India*, 2nd. ed. (New Delhi: Asian Educational Services, 1988).

Wiener, Philip P., ed., *Charles S. Peirce: Selected Writings* (New York: Dover Publications, 1958).

Williams, Raymond, 'Base and Superstructure in Marxist Cultural Theory', in *Schooling and Capitalism: A Sociological Reader*, eds Roger Dale et al. (London: Routledge & Kegan Paul, 1976).

Wilson, K., *The Twice Alienated* (Hyderabad: Booklinks Cooperation, 1982).

Wilson, Sule Greg, *The Drummers Path: Moving the Spirit with Ritual and Traditional Drumming* (Rochester, VT.: Destiny Books, 1992).

Witherington III, Ben, *The Jesus Quest: The Third Search for the Jew of Nazareth* (Downers Grove, Ill.: Intervarsity Press, 1995).

Zaehner, R.C., ed., *Hindu Scriptures* (London: J.M. Dent & Sons, 1966).

Ziegenbalg, Bartholomaeus, *Genealogy of the South Indian Gods*, Reprinted Version (New Delhi: Unity Book Service, 1984).

Name Index

Subject Index

act of faith 179

actuality, context-dependent 4

advocacy affirming discourse 10

agricultural, assets 69; labourers 69, 101; rest day 79

Alvars 142; poetic devotion (*Bhakti*) of 143

Ambedkar, B.R. 44, 55

Andal, *Tiruppavai* 143

aniconic forms of religiosity 137, n. 56

anthropos 23

Appasamy, A.J. 39

Bhakti movement 143

Bible 30; and resistive drum 152–3

Black theology 51 n. 20

border, Dalit habitation 3

Brahmins 32; Indian-Christian theology and 37, 42, 68; –king relations, *see* tradition

Brahmo Samaj 37; demand for National Christianity 37

caste 45; breaching laws of 66; (and) control of resources 69; groups relation to totemic object 122; mindset (internalization) 56 n. 67; oppression 43; sanctions against Dalits commensality) 69, (sanskrit learning) 123, 137 n. 60, 164

caste Hinduism, colonizing/ coopting tendencies of 3, 102–3, 122, 152, 192; Dalit contestation/ transformation of religions symbolism of 109, 134 n. 28, 126; degradation of drum as inauspicious by 165; disinterest in foreign culture 37; four-fold hierarchy in 35; hegemonic mythology of 3, 104; (and) Dalit inter-relatedness by rituals 193; male gods in 125; text-based theology of 156

ceeri (Paraiyar colony) 71

Census, Dalit population in 64–5

Chinglepet district 67

Chirographic culture 155

Christ/(Jesus), -centred humanism 189, 213 n. 25, 190; as deviant 6, 201–7; dominant community and 206; as drum 196–207; functionality of 5, 199; historical 31, 197, 214–15 n. 36; and Holy spirit 186; as immanental presence (God) in creation 187–9; Logos/drum (complementary) in interpreting 199–201; meaning of 180; mediation

of redemptive design of God 186; of Nazareth 196; as normative in Christian theology 34, 182; ontology of 5, 199; open commensality of 217; paradigm of (in theology) 181; praxis of 6, 198; and reconciliatory emancipation 191–4; tragic/praxiological dimension of 187
Christian Church 192; imperialistic attitude of 62
Christian Dalits 204; aspirations in conversion 36, 44; disassociation from native tradition 12, 196; dual identity of 62, 138 n 66; sacred geography of 61
Christian Feminist theology 52, 141
Christianity, culturally at home (India) 39; drum not legitimate symbol for 195–6; expansionism in western 38; high caste converts to 40; mass conversion, *see* sanskritization, 43–4, 92 n. 11, 12; three-fold conception of God in 185, 211
Christic presence 183; in Paraiyar (independent of Jesus) 184; feminist objection to human gestalt of 211 n. 17
christology 5; constrictive pole of 5, 183, 184–5; 196–207; constructive 183, 210 n. 10, 196; Dalit 5; expansive pole of 183, 184–5
collectives, categories in 7; of orality 13
colony *devata*, contractual relationship of 74; Ellaiyamman as 100
colloquial word (myths) 104
Communist Party (Italy) 41
community, *see* subaltern, 3, 4; discontinuty in Dalit/Hindu 48 n. 1; in Indian theological context 20
cultural–linguistic school 26; text-centredness and God in 27
culture of literacy, *see* literacy, 5

Dalit, *see* Paraiyar; religion; subaltern; alienation of 27, 55–6 n. 64; advocating liberation of 11, 47, 63, 208; as beef-eating community 118; christian interaction 53 n. 34; experience of 46–7; human communal identity and drum 46, 47, 67, 152, 190–1, 192; historiography 59–64; Jesus 30, 201; marginalization by Hindu human community 18, 67, 70, 101–3; non-textual religious reflectivity 22, 84; oppression of 67, 70, 94 n. 49, 101; passivity stereotype of 99, 109, 133 n. 18; subordination 7, 99
Dasu 18
dialectic between salvation/humanization 39
dialogue as activity 19
discourse of leaders/people 25, 51 n. 19
'dividual-particle' theory 66
Divine (The) 19, 34; energetic drumming vs. still wisdom as worship of 125; human communication, dialectics of mystery/materiality 165; association of drum with 142,